THE MIST-FILLED PATH

THE MIST-FILLED PATH

Celtic Wisdom for Exiles, Wanderers, and Seekers

FRANK MACEOWEN

FOREWORD BY Tom Cowan

NEW WORLD LIBRARY
NOVATO, CALIFORNIA

New World Library
14 Pamaron Way
Novato, California 94949

Front cover design by Mary Ann Casler
Text design and typography by Tona Pearce Myers

Grateful acknowledgment is given to the following authors for permission to reprint excerpts from the following:

The Essential Rumi translated by Coleman Barks © 1995 by Coleman Barks. Used by permission of HarperSanFrancisco.

"My Father's God Beneath the Waves: A Poem to Heal All Men" by Jathan Gurr © 2002 Jathan Gurr, published for the first time in *The Mist-Filled Path.*

The Underworld Initiation, by R. J. Stewart © 1990 by R. J. Stewart, published by Mercury Publishing; used with permission.

"The Old Traditions" in *Where Many Rivers Meet* by David Whyte © 1990 by David Whyte. Reprinted with permission of Many Rivers Press, Langley, Wash..

Library of Congress Cataloging-in-Publication Data
MacEowen, Frank Henderson,
The mist-filled path : Celtic wisdom for exiles, wanderers, and seekers / by Frank Henderson MacEowen ; foreword by Tom Cowan.
p. cm.
Includes index.
ISBN 1-57731-211-2 (pbk. : alk. paper)
1. Celts—Religion—Miscellanea. 2. Spiritual life—Miscellanea. I. Title.
BL900 .M444 2002
299'.16—dc21 2001008242

First Printing April 2002
ISBN 1-57731-211-2
Printed in Canada on acid-free, partially recycled paper
Distributed to the trade by Publishers Group West

10 9 8 7 6 5 4 3 2

This book is lovingly dedicated to:

the memory
of my maternal grandmother, Nonnie (1916–1999),

the keening women, poets, and Celtic seers
who walked the mist-filled paths before us,

and the future generations who will inherit
this earth from us.

May we come to know all people as the Chosen Ones,
all the Earth as our Holy Land.

Contents

Foreword
by Tom Cowan
ix

Acknowledgments
xv

Introduction
Waking Up in the Land of Sleepwalkers
xix

Chapter 1
The Threshold of the Mist
3

Chapter 2
People of the Shapes, Children of the Mist
25

Chapter 3
The Spirit of Longing
49

Chapter 4
Riding the Wind
67

Chapter 5
Dancing the Sun
89

Chapter 6
The Shape of the Sacred World
113

Chapter 7
The Great Song
131

Chapter 8
The Mothering Heart of God
155

Chapter 9
The Body as Holy
175

Chapter 10
The Hearth Way
187

Chapter 11
The Way of the Heart
205

Chapter 12
The Way of Earth
229

Conclusion
Working with the Great Mirror
239

Glossary
253

Resources
259

Index
261

About the Author
269

FOREWORD

BY TOM COWAN

Druids, poets, and storytellers shared a major responsibility in traditional Celtic communities: they reminded the Celtic people who they were. In former ages when wisdom stories and sacred histories were not written on the fragile page, where, it was feared, the tales would fade with the ink or be torn to pieces and lost forever, these keepers of memory orally passed on the wisdom of their people from generation to generation. Every people needs teachers who can tell them where they came from and what they are doing here. Or what they should be doing here if they hope to preserve the spiritual values and traditions of their culture and pass them on to their children. Without such teachers a people dies.

The Mist-Filled Path is a book by and about such a teacher, a modern Celt, the initiatory crises that led him to discover who he is, and his impassioned call to the rest of us to find the old paths once again, walk them, and discover the mystic beauties of the many worlds we live in. Frank MacEowen reminds us who we are. Or who we could be.

Frank really does love the mist. One summer he was a guest at my home in New York's Hudson River Valley, a damp, forested region, especially compared to the arid high plains of Colorado where he was living. One morning I found him sprawled on my porch at dawn, a walking stick across his lap, beads of perspiration running down his face, his boots and pant legs soaked in the morning dew and covered with burrs and sticktights. I asked where he had been. "With the apples and the deer," he answered. And I knew he had risen early to watch the sunrise from the orchard on top of the hill behind my house. The burrs and sticktights were a kind of red badge of courage, his wet boots and cuffs a fleeting keepsake from hillwalking in the morning mist. He looked weirdly contented.

There are reasons to love the mist. As you will discover in the pages that follow, the mist is a threshold state in Celtic spirituality. It is sacred. We might even think of mist as a sacrament in the old Catholic sense of that term: an outward sign of an interior state of grace. As Frank explains it, mist consciousness is druid consciousness, saint consciousness, shaman consciousness, and Christ consciousness. It is the awareness and perspective of a person standing at the threshold of sacred experience, even as you are now poised on that same threshold, with this beautifully written guide to accompany you in your wayfaring.

My own travels with Frank have opened doors and gateways into those invisible realms of our longing where we catch grail-like glimpses of the goodness for which we yearn. Longing too is a holy state for those not afraid, as Frank puts it, to surrender themselves to the great pull that lures us into life, to places we have not yet dreamed of, places where the Great Shaper of Life longs to shape us. Frank MacEowen has felt this lure and followed it and now invites us to lean into that Divine Power so that we might discover its presence and then honor and celebrate it in the simple events of our day.

Once hiking through the Catskill Mountains we paused at an old stone well, an ancient spring lined with Catskill bluestone by settlers in the nineteenth century. It was the kind of "thin place" where the mysteries of the Otherworld call out to be recognized and honored. So we made some prayers to whatever salmon, trout, or skull might dwell in the invisible depths of the waters. As we left, Frank reverently placed a reddish oak leaf on the bluestone at the head of the well, then a smaller yellow leaf on that; last, and meticulously, he set a green, gemlike pebble from the trail on top of the two leaves — a tender, heartfelt, and gentle offering to the Mother of the Waters who is the lifeblood of these mountains. Frank does things like that.

The Celtic spirit, like the Celtic mind, does not want to get locked into a rigid framework with no way of escape. Like the mist, the spirit wants to shift, rise, disappear, and return. Frank knows this. The rich treasure of Celtic mysticism presented in this book — pagan, Christian, and postmodern — is not a hoard for dragons to guard, but more like a sail to hoist into the wind to let the elements of God decide direction and destination. With an exciting boldness Frank pulls the old ways out of our many pasts and into the present but always with a sensitivity to what is authentic and appropriate for these new times and places. Nor is he blind to parallel teachings from other cultures and centuries that support, enhance, and make sense of the older Celtic ways. You will find in this book the indigenous wisdom of Africa, Asia, and Native America, Sufi and Buddhist teachings, some renegade Catholic ideas, a touch of modern depth psychology, and ideas about social and environmental activism, all seen through a Celtic lens. You can trust this guide as his eye wanders over the vast mystic landscape, and he points out the next stop on our pilgrimage. We are, to use his phrase, "people of the wandering fire," and we need to know the geography of the modern world we wander through if we hope to interact intelligently with others of different beliefs and values.

If you take this book to heart, it will not make you look like a strange remnant of a lost civilization caught in a modern time warp, trying to find your way back into a mythic past. As presented here, Celtic spirituality is not a romanticized artifact or an atavistic throwback to earlier times but a modern ethos for dealing with environmental crises, the poor and homeless, the uncertainties of a hostile and dangerous world, and the mind-numbing, spirit-numbing boredom that our consumer culture generates in so many people.

Confucius said, "The person who can reanimate the old and in so doing gain knowledge of the new is fit to be a teacher." Frank MacEowen is fit to be a teacher. *The Mist-Filled Path* is an engaging, lyrically written account of old Celtic ways and a challenging manifesto to live them in the twenty-first century. You may not be Celtic or even Western, but to study with such a teacher who can reanimate the wisdom of the past so that it sings in your modern heart is a wonderful experience.

Late one night on the Scottish island of Iona, after one of many long entangled discussions about the nature of the Otherworld, Frank invited me to light a votive candle with him in the chapel of St. Oran, a member of Columcille's settlers, who founded the first Christian hermitage on that island, which had once been a powerful druid sanctuary. Legend has it that Oran is buried in a grave beneath this chapel where he was placed, alive, by Columcille as a sacrificial offering for their new spiritual venture. After three days they dug up the grave to see how he was doing. He was still alive and kicking, and announced, "The Otherworld is nothing like you imagine." Whereupon he was reburied and, by all accounts, still lies there. Beneath our candle flames. Beneath our prayers and vigils. Beneath our own imaginings of what those other worlds are like.

This book helps us imagine and see those worlds. It helps us prepare for whatever surprises we might eventually discover. In it you will tromp through burrs and sticktights, make offerings by sacred springs, light candles late in the night. You will realize, I hope, as I did in reading these pages, the great joy that comes from mistwalking.

TOM COWAN
HIGHLAND, NEW YORK
AUTHOR OF *FIRE IN THE HEAD, SHAMANISM,*
AND *THE WAY OF THE SAINTS*

ACKNOWLEDGMENTS

First I would like to thank my editor, Georgia Hughes, of New World Library for her patience, guidance, and respectful presence as editor in this process. Your attentiveness and grace have felt akin to a midwife, gently bringing to the light of day the newborn face of this book, and another step on the road in my life as a writer. Thank you.

Thanks also to Mimi Kusch, whose insightful questions about the content assisted me in clarifying and refining the writing into its final shape.

Thanks to my mother, Dale, a.k.a., *Mathair Mathan,* Mama Bear, for being my teacher, my friend, and one of my dearest co-walkers in this life. Thank you, also, for making so many experiences available to me in the formative years of my life. Without you this book would not have happened.

To my Da, LaRue, a.k.a. Papa Rowdy and Hawkeye, for making sure that my childhood and young adulthood were saturated with the presence of the natural world. Your balanced perspective on the road of life — of being equally open to the mystery of life and nature while also seeking to ground the divine in the practical — has been a great teaching for me.

Deep gratitude to my lovely wife and "walking partner," Jan: for teaching me, daily, about the "Beauty Way," for loving me so deeply and tenderly on our path together in life, for holding me in all my complexity and, at times, confusion, and for gracing me with the opportunity to bear witness to your own evolving pathway in this life. You were pivotal in helping me to open the initial creative gates behind which I was storing much of the material in this work. Thank you. You are a healer, and your Ojibway, German, and African ancestors are deeply proud of you. May you know both of these truths.

Thank you to my grandparents, Paw Paw and Mimi. Your patience, love, and support of me means more to me than you can ever possibly know. Thank you for the simple things: teaching me to fly-fish, always having a Guinness in the fridge when I come to Mississippi, taking me out in the boat as a child, and telling me the stories.

Many thanks to Tom Cowan, a much-cherished fellow mistwalker, a true foster uncle in the old Highland style, and an ever-present wisdom source to me and so many others. I thank you deeply for the dynamic, creative, and visionary crucible that has always formed our dialogue and our bond.

Thanks to my friend, Lillie Burnett, who knows the power of the healing waters and the healing power of human touch. I pay homage to the wise-woman tradition of healing that has undoubtedly come down to the present day in who you are as massage therapist and Watsu practitioner.

Thank you to "Smom," my stepmother Ree, who must be given the "Patience of Job Award" for putting up with me during my pre-adolescent years, years in which I struggled to make sense of the terrain of the spirit world while simultaneously standing in the uncertainty of being a teenager in the modern world. I am deeply grateful to you for your presence in my life and your ever-present creative vision.

Thanks to Fatu Judy Henderson, master drummer and medicine woman of many forms and expressions of both Africa and Native America. Thanks to Joseph Conan Cassidy and Tatiana Sifri-Cassidy, for your ancient and abiding friendship. I still marvel at the way all of us have met, and I look forward to the adventures that lie ahead.

Much gratitude to Pieter Oosthaizen and Charlotte Rotterdam for being such wonderful co-walkers on a number of roads. Thank you Charlotte, for believing in this work and supporting its evolution and fine-tuning through the years at the Naropa School of Continuing Education. Thanks too, Pieter, for "shaking me awake" that day and offering such simple words to my soul as I faced some of the troublesome ancestors. Many thanks to Kat Kowalski and Erick Meyer for your love.

Deep thanks go to my dear brother, Jathan Gurr, author of the poem "My Father's God Beneath the Waves," which appears for the first time in print in the pages of this book. Your ever-present "somatic druidism" and process-oriented approach to life have been like a deep well from which I have been healed, quenched, and soothed. Blessings on your path as healer, sound-weaver, and musician.

In addition to these people who have known my struggle to give voice to the ineffable, there are so many other people whom I have had important moments with on the Mist-Filled Path. Some of these people do not even know the depth of meaning they hold in my heart. May you know it now.

Victor Zinn, who assisted me greatly in the work of "finding my voice"; Elisa Lodge, who taught me to move; Ken Thunderbear Trogdon, who first taught me to pray with the earth; Oscar Miro-Quesada, Edie Stone, Reilly Murphy-Evans, and Nancy Hansen-Zuschlag, ever the support for this road of "Celtic curandisimo"; Malidoma and Sobonfu Somé, for your preciousness in the world; the late Buzzy Boswell, for telling me stories of "the little people"; Robert Moss, for unabashedly putting the dreams out there; R. J. Stewart, for articulating as no one else has the living streams of fey wisdom; Geo Cameron, kinswoman of Cowal, for remembering; Luisah Tiesh, for your love; Philip Carr-Gomm, for believing; Mara Freeman, for your own rekindling of the need-fires; and Spider and Lisa at Enchanted Ink, for the sacred markings of the old tradition. Thanks to David Womack, Brian Johnson, Kitty Dennis, Larry McFall, Sherrill Berger, Sopan Greene, Awad and Rhoda Sifri, and Owen Lombardi.

The late Two Trees, the late Elichagaray, Joe Rose, Patricia

Firehorse Downs, Leslie Gray, Lorrain Fox-Davis, Eagle Cruz, Richard and Lora Dart, Diane DeFoe, Wallace Black Elk, John Tarwater of the Hawkwind Community, Buck Ghosthorse, the late Vernal Cross, and the many other First Nations people who have befriended me, welcomed me to their hearth, and taught me the graciousness of "being a good guest," not only in Native America but as a citizen of the earth.

Thanks to Lorraine MacDonald, Isle of Arran, Scotland, and the staff of Dalriada, for your tireless efforts at the Dalriada Celtic Heritage Trust and Taigh Arrain. The work you are doing is of such great importance and it is so refreshing to see a group of people in the arena of Celtic scholarship who live these ways as much as they write about them.

Thanks to John Davis, Jed Swift, and Elizabeth Roberts of the Naropa University for planting the seeds of ecopsychology there; David LaChapelle, keeper of stories, songs, and Alaskan sunsets; David Abrams of Whidby Island for his "delicious words" and "shamanic magic"; Julia Butterfly Hill, for reminding us that sometimes the flowing of tree sap is a tree crying; Jack Macguire, for his friendship, for apple seeds, for Zen blossoms, and for his magical tales of the old country and this one.

Thanks to my teachers and mentors at Naropa, masters of process, teachers of following the heart: Claudia Helade, Roland Evans, Darion Gracen, Dee Coulter, John Davis, Clyde Reid, Dale Asrael, Reggie Ray, Mary Schlesinger, Deb Bowman, Christina Kauffman, Bill Scheffel, Daphne Chellos, and Frank Berliner. Thanks also to those souls I grew to know while creating magic at Naropa: Phil Jacobson, Diane Butler, John Cobb, Max Regan, Steve Glazer, Peter Chipmann, Saul Kotzubei, Karen Brown, and Nancy Levin.

Thanks to Bob Wing Sensei, for teaching me that even my Scottish ancestors knew something of a form of bushidō, budō, and aikidō, and for aiding me in remembering this in my own body.

Thanks to Michael Piechowski, Kent Shifferd, Michelle Small, and Thomas P. Kasulis — who taught me to listen before speaking; and thanks to two dear brothers who walked the woodland paths with me in the north country, Dave Braun and Jon Berthel.

For those in name or in spirit whom I have not had room to list here: each of you is precious to me.

Introduction

Waking Up in the Land of Sleepwalkers

The breeze at dawn has secrets to tell you.
Don't go back to sleep.
You must ask for what you really want.
Don't go back to sleep.
People are going back and forth across the doorsill
where two worlds touch.
The door is round and open.
Don't go back to sleep.

— Jalal-ud-din Rumi[1]

Our world invites us to become what I call sleepwalkers. Many people, some without even knowing it, have accepted the invitation. When we're not truly alive within our senses, days bleed into days, night after night passes. Too many of us squander our lives, spending them in front of televisions, filling our minds with a crazed habitual raciness that is

1 Coleman Barks, trans., *The Essential Rumi* (San Francisco: HarperSanFrancisco, 1995), p. 36.

hard to throw off. I use the word *spend* on purpose, because the numbered days of our lives are a precious commodity. Where and how we choose to invest our energy and time is of great importance to the soul. Where we choose to place our awareness matters.

So many of us have unquestioningly bought the unspoken story that if we plop ourselves down in front of the blinking strobe box we will be magically transformed by its quicksilver images. Allow me to state the obvious. The "good life" portrayed there is not good, nor is it truly life. It is not the kind of living that deepens our relationship to authenticity. It is not the kind of life that brings us into contact with wakeful purpose or wonderment, which are our divine birthright.

The rumbling of this subliminal world of thirty-second sound bite commercials, fueled by the promise of instant gratification, sends millions of us on unconscious, often unscrupulous, journeys to the store to obtain more and more things that eventually serve no greater purpose than to clutter our living spaces. This gesture and ritual of accumulation is anchored in an illness within the modern zeitgeist. This illness is one of illusion, thinking that material objects will provide us with the inner satisfaction that, ultimately, can only be gained from valuable, wakeful life experiences.

I am not talking about objects that truly help our lives or provide for a deepening and richer experience of our earth walk. Put the right book in the hands of a person at the right time in his or her life, for example, and a transformation occurs. A candle, a framed photograph, a beautiful plant, a rustic desk, a journal — things like these can often provide for an aesthetic and spiritual doorway to an experience of our lives as a thing of beauty. In effect, they can support us in waking up and staying awake. Nonetheless, even these items are not the same as the actual experience of a deepened and awakened life. Owning a meditation cushion, a yoga mat, or a Scottish walking stick does not automatically grant the achievement of wakefulness. They are only tools.

Our homes, packed with all the latest gadgetry and accumulations from our travels, combined with the developed landscapes in which we live, begin to mirror quite succinctly the cluttered quality of the interior life of the modern person. As within, so without. Our living spaces, our city spaces, reflect our minds and souls.

Eventually we get claustrophobic with all the clutter, all the prized possessions crammed into closets. Suddenly, we cannot wait to travel as quickly as possible away from our homes, away from our cities and towns, to some other region. We grow tired of our possessions because they do not fill the void. They do not make us happy. They did not provide us with the sustained and sustainable *experience* of the inspirited life we were longing for in our bones. We see these objects differently from how we saw them when they were bought. We realize they do not, in the end, soothe the deep ache.

In time our possessions will go the way of the dinosaur, end up in landfills or yard sales, or get passed on to those less fortunate, granting us the brief feeling that we have been charitable. We then start the cycle again. We go for more objects. But a home filled with clutter is no home at all. In the words of Anthony Lawlor, author of *A Home for the Soul,* "We want our houses and apartments to be warm, nurturing, and beautiful, but they are sometimes areas of chaos and territories of conflict, isolation and confusion. The very places that hold the promise of harmony and revitalization can, instead, be abodes of disorder, friction and loneliness."

We are not at home in our homes, because we are not at home in ourselves. We are not at home among the living things of the earth. We are not satisfied or content. We are not at home in our minds. We are not at peace. If we look at our habits in the land of the sleepwalkers we see that, for some, the substance of true intimacy in relationships has been stripped from our vocabulary. The experience of personal human contact has been replaced by the less tangible, less complicated, less challenging and, therefore, less honest world of virtual chat rooms. We come and go from our homes and apartments, often with no real sense of who our neighbors are. Slowly but surely this reality begins to set itself up within our families and marriages, and our relatives and spouses become strangers to us, emotionally and spiritually.

A true association or fluency with the inner face of the soul is missing. Intimacy can be read as "into-me-see." It must start with our being willing to look deeply within, into the realm of both our untapped creativity and our shadows that hide in the corners. Intimacy is the human heart opened up to the world declaring fearlessly, "I invite you to see into me."

In the world of the sleepwalkers intimacy is all too often replaced by anonymity. Many people let years pass without letting others know them deeply. They are just as homeless in their inner lives as people living in cardboard boxes on the street. We have become exiles from one another, exiles from the lives we yearn to live; we have become disenfranchised from our dreams, strangers to our own inner faces, wandering like hungry ghosts for some sense of belonging.

Ultimately this is an exile that we all share. It is a common wound, for it is a collective exile from an enlightened society that we all know is possible. We all share the hope of this potential, this endowment of peace and ease, but for now we simply keep going, some of us half asleep. The seeds of a society rooted in illumination and wakefulness rest deep inside us. These seeds sleep beneath our own sleeping. They are the seeds of longing shared by all our ancestors.

Like the quickening seeds that tremble at the time of *Imbolg* (pronounced em-olk), the tremor of spring in Celtic tradition, we ourselves stir. These seeds twitch just beneath a frosty layer of earth and slowly move in their casings. In time they set their root and begin an upward pilgrimage to the gleaming sun. It is our time to set our root and wake up.

RETURN

My wish for you
is a homecoming in this life.
A coming in out of the cold;
a drying off the icy rain's touch.
In the holy reliquary
of childhood memory
may you find there the unshakable truth
of your preciousness.
May you remember the cool and padded graces
of your wet feet against stone.
In the middle of a long night,
a single burning light
serving as your peace,
may you fold back the pocket
holding your slights,
your jilted times,
your feelings of betrayal,
and discover small diamonds there,
created from the crushed coal
of your hates and rage.
May you taste resurrection
without the need of dying for it.

— FROM *BUILDING FENCES IN HIGH WIND: POEMS OF LONGING,*
FRANK MACEOWEN

SETTING OUR ROOT

Something begins to happen to us when we accept an invitation other than that offered in the land of sleepwalking described above. We take a deep and life-affirming breath. We slowly move from a life of exile and wandering to the life of seeking. In this holy seeking the ordinary becomes holy again, magical. Sleepwalkers begin to wake up. People in pain begin to find solutions. People racked with stress find ways to return to solace. People who feel outside life suddenly experience the blessing of homecoming, punctuated by the realization that there is no such thing as loneliness when one has the powers of the universe flowing through him or her.

Equally as powerful is when people who have set their root and have begun to wake up begin to extend their energy and presence into the world as a means of fostering wakefulness in others. Suddenly a person who felt cut off from others and from the beauty of life becomes an ambassador of this beauty, a shaper of it. Within this beauty lies a deep peace that is, we might say, a central hearthstone of the Celtic tradition.

The Celtic spiritual traditions are rooted in peace. Prayers, rituals, daily acts, and orientations focus on fostering peace. In essence, the Celtic spiritual path aims to facilitate three conditions: an opening within the human heart, a sheltering sense of solace in the world for those who struggle, and an ongoing sensual celebration of the beauty of life. These guideposts lie at the heart of the many soul-maintenance practices that are performed in these very old traditions.

Living a life that fosters these conditions of soul maintenance is what I mean here by setting our root. It is about changing our reality from one of discord to one of harmony. As trembling seeds of a hopeful future we choose to set our root in what some Celtic theologians called "goodness, love, and yearning." This process becomes the path. It becomes a way of changing self and the world.

This kind of waking up is noticeable, visceral. People begin dedicating their lives to transforming themselves and the world. People living in city apartments suddenly start saying "hello," extending themselves and the range of possibilities for human connection and the human condition. They join one another in instant communities on front porches, and suddenly the air becomes pierced with astonishing questions such as, "How is it with your soul?"

Individuals step out onto the streets and reach out to those living a life of struggle — the hungry, the displaced, the grieving — and ask, "What can I do to help?" People who have felt displaced from the holy landscape of the natural world enter back into the Green World and find themselves embraced. People in relationships who have fallen asleep, who have forgotten each other, suddenly remember with immense clarity the preciousness of the person with whom they share a home. They embrace and ask, "Where have you been? Where have I been?"

Being willing to entertain such questions as, "How is it with my soul?" requires us to slow down a bit. The willingness to *orient our lives* to such questions demands that we slow down a *lot.* If we are to truly set our roots in such soil we must aspire to create sanctuaries of stillness in our lives. We must find our places of resurrection, as it is spoken of in the Celtic-Christian tradition. We must rediscover our ancient "house of memory."

Imagine giving yourself a potent gift. I will describe it to you as a practice.

Practice: Setting Your Root

✣ Clear out a room in your home. Put some things in storage. Better yet, sell or donate them. Set aside a space specifically for consecrating a brief retreat that will focus on setting your root. Make this space a place to honor the ancient rhythms. Make it a place where you can be without distraction.

- Now choose a day over the course of a weekend. In our busy lives finding such time has become difficult, yet it is possible and merely requires a commitment. Plan in advance. Set aside a Saturday, perhaps, with the full knowledge that this day is *your* day. Ask friends or family to support you in this endeavor.
- Upon entering the room for what will be an entire day, dawn to dusk, watch what happens to your mind. There will be no e-mail, no World Wide Web, no television, no telephone, no dinner dates, no ritualized habits. There will be no movies, no coffee, no cigarettes, no alcohol — just the quiet edges of your soul being still, the tremor of your mind engaged in reclaiming your place in a more ancient rhythm. When we remove ourselves from the unnatural rhythms of the world, the more ancient rhythm of our earth selves returns. This is nature's healing power on us and within us. For we are part of nature.

Once you've made room, the questions come. For some people so do the fears, doubts, and worries.

- Stay with the questions that arise. Stay with the fears. Stay with the boredom, for undoubtedly your mind will continue to spin. Your mind will say, "But I could have taken a trip this weekend. I should have done some yard work. I should really do my taxes." Think of these things as a cold wind and turn yourself, instead, toward the warm, sweet sheltering spirit of silence.
- Stay with your questions, and think of this act as "warming your earth." It is like the sun thawing the frosty ground. Chew on the questions, the doubts, and the fears. Feel them to be what they really are — the necessary magnetism of moistness and warmth to activate the seeds of wakefulness within you. Where a moist chill meets warmth the luminescence of mist is born. The mist is the threshold, the guardian of the in-between

where vision is received. Within the mist of liminal time and space we are able to plant the seeds of a new life.

- Remember that the seed is you, and me, and the soulful life we long for.
- Use this time for setting your root. Think about what soil you want your soul to take root in now. Open yourself to vision. Open your heart to feeling. Face the fear of not knowing. Welcome all your doubts, and know that they too are companions and guides in this process.
- When you are ready to set your root, stand and face the four directions, starting with the east, the direction of the new rising sun. Move in a clockwise fashion, what is called *deiseil,* or sunwise, in the old Gaelic tradition. Announce out loud what you are setting your root in.
- Perhaps you are setting your root in waking up, in remembering sacred world, in coming back to your senses. Perhaps you're setting it in healing, in cultivating gentleness with yourself, in fostering a sense of true self-respect. Perhaps you are throwing off the shackles of a self-absorbed, materialistic life and are now setting your root in a life of kindness and service to others. In any case, speak this commitment, the new root of your life. Speak it out loud. Speak it to everything: to your ancestors. To the earth and sky. To the unseen world.
- When you have set your root, know this. Everything in your life from the time of your stated commitment forward becomes like the seed sending its shoot toward the sun. Your root is set. The seed that is your heart is now committed to being open. It is time to begin. Having set your root you are now looking for the sun, which is the same as a wakeful life. Feel the sun on your brow. Let the solar power, the Great Wheel of Light, pull you.
- When you are ready, slowly enter back into connection with others dear to you. Like the young sapling that emerges from

the ground into the light of day, greet the world. But, also like a young sapling, you must take great care. In facing the world again remember that the world does not know or understand what kind of soil you have emerged from; people will not necessarily know that you have undergone a change. What do you notice in facing the world again?

- You have spent an entire day in this process. You have announced your new root, your commitment, to the powers of life, but now you must share it with your community, with your family of blood and spirit. Ask for their support in assisting you to live a life rooted in this new energy.
- The Mist-Filled Path awaits you.
- NOTE: Once you have performed this daylong practice, you can expand it into a full weekend. Or perhaps, if you are at a significant crossroads in your life, you would be served by doing this practice for a full week.

Reclaiming Our Holy Senses

Many of you, upon reading the suggestions above, will recoil at the notion of both the stark surroundings and the extended solitude. For we have been conditioned to fear both. Many of us have been conditioned to fear ourselves, including the deeper call of our life passions. Certain schools, churches, and even families create distrust of our primal knowing and intuition. In light of such an inheritance it is no wonder that most of us have grown up not trusting ourselves, not knowing who we really are, and not knowing how to create the life we want. We sense something more, but the chasm between here and there feels as wide as a galaxy.

In a culture that measures worth by how much we own or by what we "do," it is a radical act to investigate who we truly are beyond our property values or professional titles. Equally as radical is the act of inviting extended moments of silence to recover our more ancient senses. It is precisely from these recovered holy senses that we are granted potential methods and solutions for dealing with the undeniable pains that grip our souls today.

Senses, much like muscles, can become atrophied over time without exercise and use. This is especially true of our ancestral, primal, and spiritual senses. According to Basque mystic and anthropologist Angeles Arrien, the Basque people have mapped out 137 senses, far above and beyond the more well-known 5 senses of sight, hearing, smell, taste, and touch — 137 senses that are possible for us to use and access, nearly all of which can only be cultivated by giving ourselves over to a slower, more ancient earth rhythm.

The modern pace does not allow for such slowness and silence. Meditation or contemplation is often perceived as lifeless inactivity. Many people fear that slowing down will cause them to miss something, and yet it is our society's velocity that is causing us to miss something very important. Besides the attrition of what I call our otherworldly senses, we have also lost the ability to have a moment-to-moment awareness of our passage through life.

On many occasions I have heard people remark that they feel "out of place," "out of sorts," "depressed," or "bored" when a true moment of quiet descends on them. This is how fundamentally exiled we are from the natural texture of our own silence. As modern people we don't know what to do with this great teacher of teachers. She can be an uncomfortable teacher and guide. Yet great power and healing wait in the folds of silence and solitude.

Mirroring the creation of the universe, all great things have come forth from the ancient weave of silence. It is a part of us we must welcome home, yet in the land of the sleepwalkers, silence is avoided at all costs. For many there is only collapse at the end of the day from all the effort expended to avoid looking, to avoid feeling, to avoid authentic contact, to avoid admitting our misery or suffering. All too often yet another day devoid of freedom and true awareness awaits on the other side of a stirring, dreamless night.

Another path exists, however. Oddly enough, it is already beneath our feet and is accessible in this very moment. It says:

> Don't go back to sleep.
> You must ask for what you really want.
> The breeze at dawn has secrets to tell you.
> People [many of them our own ancestors and the souls of great teachers,
> who wish for us a liberated existence] are going back and forth across the doorsill
> where two worlds touch.
> The door is round and open.
> Don't go back to sleep.

The Purpose of This Book

This book is not an anthropological thesis about the Celtic world. It is not an archaeological treatise on the Iron Age Celts, or even — specifically — a scholarly or historical exploration of Celtic religions and culture. Scholars and historians with far more ability than I have, have already given the world an immense gift in the form of their works. My intention here is not to reinvent the wheel but rather to articulate how we may truly live in the spirit of the wheel, an ancient symbol used in the druidic traditions of Ireland, the shamanic traditions worldwide, and even in the Celtic-Christian tradition of earth-honoring mysticism. This sacred wheel is the cycle of our days, the circle of our horizon, the Celtic wheel of living.

The central aim of this book is to articulate a way of seeing the world and a possible way for being in it that re-enlivens a relationship to that which is holy. I have come to call this the Mist-Filled

Path, mist being a teacher or tutelary spirit for me in my childhood. It is an invitation into a slower, more ancient earth rhythm as it has been worked with in the living streams of perennial Celtic spirituality, animism, druidic philosophy, shamanism, and mysticism. It is a particular kind of orientation, one that looks to restore the ancient dialogue between the human being and the sacred world.

A portion of this book involves descriptions and accounts of experiences I have had that fall within the domain of the transpersonal, the paranormal, and the shamanic. I share these experiences not only to illuminate the themes and principles we are working with but also to normalize the nonordinary, the otherworldly, and the transpersonal dimensions of human experience, all strands of human experience that our world has largely lost. Some of these experiences involve spirits, ancestors, nature, and other presences not so easily defined, but these are not supernatural; these things are simply natural. My personal experiences are rooted in my own journey of waking up to my life that occurred through a deep depression, a near-fatal illness, and a unique cellular initiation into the realms of Celtic mysticism. I have come to refer to this process as "ancestral transmission."

Other aspects of this book include visionary exercises, meditations, and other reflections. My only instructions regarding these practices, other than those contained in the actual description of them, is to open yourself to the spirit or concept that is being explored and see how it resonates with your life path. These small "stopping places" on the path are designed to foster a process of deepening with the themes of this book. These guiding themes are undoubtedly anchored in the life-affirming spirituality of my ancient Celtic ancestors, yet I have strived to discern ways to apply these themes to the here and now — the life each of us has and the world that each of us faces, whatever our ancestral background.

From a Celtic perspective, the sacred world is vast. It includes our ancestors, the spirit world, the world of nature, the human world, and the rich inner world of each person as expressed through dreams. The sacred world, as it is worked with in Celtic tradition, is replete with thresholds of opportunity, renewal, and healing. I have strived to design the flow of this book to mirror these thresholds, and yet as Esther de Waal has said of the Celtic spiritual path, it is not necessarily one that follows a "clear-cut pattern of having some end and goal in view so that the purpose can be clearly established and then followed. For the really significant journey is the interior journey."

Thus this book may feel to the reader a bit like the flowing cords of Celtic knot work one sees in both pre-Christian and post-Christian Celtic art. We will weave back in on themes at times in service of remembrance and deepening. At times it may feel as if we have doubled back onto familiar ground. This flowing weave represents the nature of holy dialogue in Celtic tradition, which encounters the sacred world once via the journey or quest and a second time via pilgrimage and remembrance.

The Mist-Filled Path as a spiritual vision is characterized by communion and holy contact with what we will call here the in-between, those thresholds of numinosity and liminality, or in Rumi's words, those luminous places "where two worlds touch." Opening ourselves to this kind of contact, encounter, and dialogue with life, as well as having a willingness to hang out with the unknown, are all characteristic of the Celtic spirit. These same qualities are ones I hope that you will feel supported in cultivating.

The Mist-Filled Path is not about sequined magical robes, long-lost priesthoods, or stereotyped media notions of Celts, druids, shamans, and mystics. Though undoubtedly influenced by the ancient legacy of the druidic tradition, with its love of nature and emphasis on merging with the sacred, this book is more generally about our collective human tradition of making life holy. It is about finding true magic in every moment by reclaiming a view and experience of the sacred world that is already around and within us. It is about welcoming the influence of this sacred world and orienting ourselves to the sacred questions in our hearts.

This book is a revisioning, from a Celtic perspective, of the invitation that all the contemplative and shamanic traditions have extended to us over time. It is an invitation to slow down and to ask important questions, such as: What uncharted roads in the landscape of your soul await you? How are you a conduit for healing energies that our world is in such dire need of? What is your calling?

The Compass of Our Questions

Our questions speak quite profoundly about the quest we are on. Whether or not we ever receive an answer, just posing certain questions about our lives is a process of soft illumination into the shaded domains of our inner world. The nature and quality of our inner worlds shape the malleable outer world in which we all live. As John Perkins, author of such books as *Psychonavigation* and *The Spirit of the Shuar,* has so often said, "The world is as we dream it."

Friends, this is such important work. We underestimate our power as shapers of the world. We also underestimate the power of the world to shape us in ways that are unholy. This book is about this holy path of shaping and being shaped. It is about aiming our consciousness at the right places and realizing that the questions we hold in our hearts are like hands on clay.

The haphazard and frenetic pace of our lives makes asking important questions like these difficult. Actively observing extended periods of silence to sit with these pivotal questions becomes almost an act of anarchy against the ego and our consumerist conditioning. In following this path we place ourselves firmly in the flow of an ancient legacy of people who have grappled with the "questing" questions, who have risen to challenge sleepwalking of any form.

The Mist-Filled Path is about stepping in among them. As Buddha said, "Make of yourselves a lamp."

The Celtic spiritual traditions originate in this same ancient legacy. From the druidic tradition of wise men and wise women to the followers of Christ in the Celtic world, the Celtic spiritual pathways are a multifaceted emerald that gleams with the light of an intelligent and sentient Creation. To make of ourselves a lamp in this sometimes-dark world we must ally ourselves with this holy light of Creation. The Celtic way is steeped in this process of alliance. It is a brightly woven cloak of wisdom and experience that is one of the precious antidotes to the spiritual pain of our era, what visionary Irish poet and mystic William Butler Yeats called "an outworn heart in a time outworn."

This book comes from my own heart, from one who has been a sleepwalker, who has struggled, who was "raked across the coals" of initiation, so to speak, and now walks a path of learning from the sacred world, endeavoring to listen deeply for the instructions from the sacred world and the many worlds in-between. These common-sense yet profound instructions are timeless. They are the perennial roots of the Celtic traditions, and they are about the heart that has announced, *I am not going back to sleep. I will feel, I will sense, I agree to shape and to be shaped by my life.*

This strand of primal Celtic wisdom is about coming by a fresh vision and looking out onto the landscape of the earth and of our lives and whispering, prayerfully, "Yes. I appreciate life and my place within it. I stand in the heart of my life." In this way, the Mist-Filled Path, when practiced authentically, is a path that bursts the heart open and causes us to truly remember our place "in the family of things," as poet Mary Oliver puts it. On such a path, as I say in one of my own poems, "all people are the Chosen Ones, all the earth our Holy Land."

THE Mist-Filled Path

Chapter 1

The Threshold of the Mist

The Celts believed that there was another dividing line that all people could straddle, if only they stretched themselves a bit. And that's the divide between the world and the otherworld.

— Steve Rabery, *In the House of Memory*

The mist called to me when I was a child. In the early mornings, and sometimes at dusk, I would look out the window into the thick woods behind our Georgia home, and a deep longing would fill my soul. The Cymru, the Celts of Wales, would say I had been consumed by the spirit of *hiraeth,* the longing for something my soul had known once upon a time.

Just beyond the mossy stone wall, just past the clusters of fern, I would often see the eerie gray-green mist swirling in the trees. It would hang there like a gull in the wind, as if searching for something. It seemed to capture something of my own quest, a deep childhood search for an experience of the mystery of the sacred world.

Some mornings I went outside to see the mist, up close and personal, and just as I would arrive at its edge, it would suddenly disappear from view, almost as if it had never been there. A strange shadowy afterimage would remain. At other times, I would look on with astonished eyes as the mist changed directions and moved away from me, visibly retreating from my presence. It would glide along the tree line, withdrawing itself from my overly analytical stare. In truth, my precocious and unrefined piercing gaze was exiling me from the teachings of the mist. I am reminded of the words of the beloved Irish mystic, Connemara poet, and nature-priest John O'Donohue, who states:

> There is an unprecedented spiritual hunger in our times. More and more people are awakening to the inner world. A thirst and hunger for the eternal is coming alive in their souls; this is a new form of consciousness. Yet one of the damaging aspects of this spiritual hunger is the way it sees everything in such a severe and insistent light. The light of modern consciousness is not gentle or reverent; it lacks graciousness in the presence of mystery.... When the spiritual search is too intense and hungry, the soul stays hidden. The soul was never meant to be seen completely.[1]

The soul possesses an ineffable intelligence that cannot be controlled. Like the mist, the soul, we might say, has a mind of its own. It cannot be forced, directed, or squeezed into a box where it does not belong. It cannot even be fully seen or perceived, for the soul is a timeless, feathered thing that flies in more worlds than one.

We can see, in tangible ways, the choices that the soul makes in service of itself. When a person is treated horribly, physically or emotionally assaulted, for instance, a fragment of his or her soul

---

1 John O'Donohue, Anam Cara: *A Book of Celtic Wisdom* (New York: Cliff Street Books, 1997), p. 80.

may slink off to a hidden unseen place where it cannot be harmed. In shamanist traditions this phenomenon is called soul loss. The soul knows what is needed for survival and returns, again, only when conditions are right or when someone engages in the work of inviting its fullness home. In this way the soul preserves itself. The soul's brilliance has allowed for this useful mechanism to ensure the continuity of the consciousness of the living person during his or her life, and sometimes even between lives.

All too often, however, when the soul elects to hide part of itself, it does not return very easily. When this happens we can say that although some external survival has been ensured, a condition of exile has also been created. It is an exile from the flowing awareness of peace that is our birthright. Our lives are meant to be steeped in peace, yet when we are living within a state of soul loss our destined unfoldment toward a life of peace is postponed until we have become whole again. We feel "beside ourselves" until we are reintegrated after a harsh experience or trauma. This is as true for whole groups that have survived a trauma as it is for individuals.

A Word about Exile

Exile is that undeniable sensation of being cordoned off from what is most essential to our souls. Perhaps we have become exiled from our childhood memories because of things that happened when we were young. We may be exiles from a basic sense of joy in our lives. Sometimes our exile is characterized by our sense of being a stranger in our own families, not able truly to share who and what we are without being criticized or judged. Family, in the Celtic sense, is meant to feel like a warm hearth fire, a downy nest of repose, and yet all too often our families contain the fiercest of blades that slash at the peace of our souls.

For many of us a kind of exile may lie at the very heart of our lives. It is an exile many people feel in the twenty-first century. It may express itself as an exile from nature, from ancestral traditions, from cultural homelands, or from spiritual lineages. Sometimes these lineages and traditions appear to be lost forever without the potential of reclamation, so the exile feels even more poignant.

In a very similar fashion, many people feel a dynamic sense of exile from an even closer domain than cultural homelands. They feel that they have been exiled from the interior lands and borderlands of their own spirit. No longer knowing the entrance to this realm or the routes of navigation once inside, they become exiled from the holy realm of the inner worlds. This is a profoundly sacred world in the Celtic tradition, one that those on Celtic spiritual paths actively seek to work with daily, because it is understood that our inner landscape is one entryway to the spiritscape of the Otherworld.

An old therapeutic axiom in Gestalt psychology, which also lies at the very heart of shamanism and contemplative mysticism worldwide, suggests that *the healing of a wound must come from the blood of the wound itself.* In other words, the healing of an emotional or psychospiritual wound is brought about precisely by entering into its terrain, not by avoiding it. In this way, healing our exile from our inner world comes from entering that inner world in search of the healing life force we need (the blood within the wound). The healing of our exile from the life-affirming expressions of our ancestral traditions comes from opening ourselves to these traditions of primacy in the same way that our ancestors did, whoever our particular ancestors were and whatever unique spiritual traditions may have shaped and sculpted them. And, last but not least, the healing of our exile from the natural world is linked with the practice of entering into a full and loving embrace of her and, once again, acknowledging the healing power of the primal land.

The healing of the soul of the earth and our relationship with her does not come about by closing ourselves off or by separating ourselves through our definitions, categorizations, and Latin nomenclature but rather by opening ourselves, dynamically, to the mysteries of the spiritscape of nature in a soulful and experiential way. To rediscover the sacred world we must reenter it, with wakeful physical and spiritual senses.

I sometimes think that when we experience soul loss or soul exile it is as if we have had our ancient citizenship revoked. We no longer have diplomatic status to travel freely into the inner sanctum of our own deeper senses or our deepest levels of knowing about the world around us. When we are in this condition, we sometimes need to do what friend and African shaman Malidoma Somé calls "setting up a squawk." We must set up a squawk and call the soul parts home.

MIST AS A TRICKSTER-TEACHER

Although we sometimes can call or sing exiled soul parts home, many times it is *we* who are living in a state of exile, not pieces of our souls. *We* are the ones who feel hidden from the soul of life, from the Soul of the World. We begin to have the sneaking suspicion that *we* are the part of our ancient soul's memory that has forgotten our place in the grand scheme of things.

In cases like these, sometimes the spirits, or sometimes the forces within nature (such as the faery folk, as perceived of in Celtic seership), will conspire to "trick" us through synchronicity, dreams, or outward events. Then it is almost as if we stumble into a process of learning a path that will lead us home. This path, at once illuminative yet seemingly hidden, is a road marked by a distinctive vibration. Its energy is of primal forces inhabiting a primal landscape that yearn for us to remember.

My initial experience of the mist was like this. It played tricks on me.

It attempted to reveal a deeper phenomenon that was all around me but to which I was, in effect, blind. I did not have the eyes with which to perceive the teachings of the mist when I first encountered them. Nonetheless, the mist got my attention in various ways, alerting me to the fact that to find the sacred within life I must cultivate the proper eyes with which to see the world. Cultivating sacred eyes is what Celtic spirituality holds as a silent wish for each of us.

My childhood tutelage with the mist began, in earnest, only after I loosened my soul and softened my piercing gaze. Until then my eyes did not allow me to see the magic of life around me. In time, however, I slowly came to understand that when approaching nature and spirit, one must enter these realms with a gentle openness of heart. We cannot make demands when encountering the sacred world. It is the overly analytical perception of reality, as well as the belief that we are somehow owed an experience, that immediately exiles us from the richness of the numinous power around us, within us, and within the earth. We have to be open. We must be, as the eloquent Zen tradition tells us, "empty cups," ready to be filled, without preconceived notions of what awaits us.

In time I experienced a gradual settling in my evolving childhood mysticism. It was a settling of my striving. This settling informed me that the sacred was all around me, and that, in addition to developing the proper eyes with which to see, I must also cultivate the proper feet with which to walk the path. One gains the proper eyes and proper feet, I have found, by slowing down. A verse from the rediscovered Gospel of Thomas comes to mind, which states: "His followers said to him, 'When will the kingdom come?' He replied, 'It will not come by watching for it. It will not be said, Look, here it is, or Look, there it is. Rather the Father's kingdom is spread out upon the earth, and people do not see it'" (verse 113).

As a little boy I came to associate the mist with special times that I would take for myself. Though at the time I was too young to have a working concept of spirituality or spiritual practice, at the mere age of six I was becoming aware of the delicious sensation of experiencing the Soul of Place. I would curl up for hours in one of my sitting places in the forest behind our house. A large oak tree behind me, an old holly tree beside me, I would be quiet, I would be still, and, with a soft gaze, I would watch the unfettered flow of a patch of ground that grew to love me. I was developing the soft eyes of my ancestors.

Several years later I would have a conversation with an Anishinabe (Ojibway) man from Canada, and I would hear him speak about the necessity of hunting or walking in nature with a soft gaze. He explained:

> The Four-Leggeds and the Winged Ones live to a different rhythm. Theirs is the rhythm of soft eyes and soft feet; Two-Leggeds have hard eyes and hard feet. When most humans go into the forest they enter with so much of the world on them that any possibility of feeling the sacred is removed. When we go into the forest we must become soft like the animal people and the tree people.

This rhythm of softness is something the mist taught me in the woods of Georgia. I sometimes think back on these childhood experiences and find myself laughing with delight at the name still held for the forested area where we lived: Druid Hills. Many of the trees are now gone, owing to the incessant influence of development. The old house is now gone. The landscape of this mysterious place of childhood awakening has now been taken over by ticky-tacky houses that seemed to go up over night. Nonetheless, the old oak still stands tall there, along with the holly and the stone I used to sit on, and those magical druid hills remain a reliquary of spiritual memory for me.

THE MIST AND THE SHIMMERING PEACE OF THINGS

We gave ourselves up in old times to mythology, and saw the Gods everywhere. We talked to them face to face. . . . Even today our country people speak with the dead and with some who perhaps have never died as we understand death; and even our educated people pass without great difficulty into the condition of quiet that is the condition of vision.[2]

— WILLIAM BUTLER YEATS

During my times of walking the Mist-Filled Path as a child, I was always filled with a blend of awe and the jitters. A sense of expectancy pulsed with each heartbeat, with each moving shadow in the shaded wood, as if at any moment a door might open up beside me. This amazing energy had an uncanny presence. When I look back on those times, with the eyes I have now, I see that the holiness of my childhood in nature was inseparably linked to the trees. I loved them, I love them now, and through them ancient unseen doors open.

We Celts are lovers of trees. In fact, the religion of our primal ancestors is one truly rooted in the mysticism of the trees. From old Celtic tales that speak of First Man being an alder tree, and First Woman being a rowan tree, to the ancient Roman accounts of the druids in the groves of old Gaul, trees play a central role in the ancient Celtic way of seeing. As world-renowned Celtic scholar and poet Jean Markale shares, "The yew is a sacred tree in Ireland. It is the druidic tree, the preeminent magic tree." As a descendant of the clan MacEwen, a Scottish clan with Irish roots, I contemplate the origins of our name in this light. In Gaelic the name MacEoghainn translates as "son of the yew tree." I discovered

---

2 William Butler Yeats, *The Celtic Twilight* (Dorset, U.K.: Unity Press, 1990), p. 70.

these threads of etymology later in life, but my relationship with the trees is one that hails from a mist-filled childhood.

On one day in particular when I was out in the trees, something happened. I had a sudden and shocking remembrance of the trees as guardians, allies, and as conduits for activating memory. Images flashed in my mind. The images were hauntingly familiar, achingly so. Like in Carl Jung's formative childhood mystical experience of merging with a stone he was sitting on, in that moment the trees suddenly told me that they were my ancient home, that I had known them intimately before, and that one day I would live among them again.

I was deeply stirred, and in the midst of this experience I realized that the spirit of the mist did not retreat from my presence that day. It moved in around me, encompassing me like a cool blanket. Slowly I began to feel at one with the forest, at one with the mist, and at one with myself in a way I never had before. I was suddenly self-aware, profoundly conscious that life is a path that we walk from the time of birth to the time of death. It was an old memory returned.

I wept with an emotion I can only describe as a feeling of being accepted by the sacred world. Woven within this moment of reawakening was a familiarity with something extremely old that stood just on the periphery of my awareness. Though it felt like a person, I saw no one. I imagined the face of an old man. I did not have words to put to this flow of experiences, but as a good Scots brother of mine says in one of his poems, "I felt watched and watching."

The mist is an ancient initiator and sacred reminder in the Celtic traditions. In the old tales of Britain, just beyond the mist lies the realm of Avalon. Likewise, in the primal Irish tradition we learn of the once-lost tale called the *Tain* and how this eclipsed strand of the tradition was rekindled, remembered, and bestowed on a single poet who sat, fasting, for three days and nights on the hillside grave of a great bard. This young poet, for these three days and nights, was completely enveloped within a mist.

A similar process stirred for me in my childhood, of having old things awakened within me. I was shown that the very fabric of reality shifts and changes in what the Celtic tradition thinks of as "thin places," or threshold places. Thin places are potent doorways within our sacred world, which includes the natural world (and aspects of the human world) and also domains that permeate and lie beneath our world. It is where the ordinary and non-ordinary come to rest in each other's arms. These places might be in-between places or particular in-between times, such as twilight. Celtic thin places are crossroads where the world of the spirits and the world of the embodied mingle. It is where the realms of human and faery touch. It is where living descendants and the ancestors commune. It is where the unseen and the seen share one ground.

Once I learned to slow down, quiet my mind, and surrender myself to the thin places and the mist-filled spaces, something ancient would draw close to me. This practice was always part of my childhood, yet things would often occur in ways I did not fully understand and could not articulate. I just knew that these mist times felt familiar and that they fed me in ways that nothing else did.

In my childhood I developed certain skills and leanings, such as the ability to enter into deep meditative states and otherworldly states of consciousness. In the contemporary milieu such states are spoken of as trance, nonordinary reality, or SSC (shamanic state of consciousness), to use anthropologist-cum-shaman Michael Harner's term. In the fold of these holy times I was shown that I was living in two worlds: the modern world, a world that has become exiled from the rich green realms of nature, and the mist-filled spirit world, inhabited by wise spirits, great beings, and luminescent people that love us and yearn for us to know and have goodness. A third world, the world of nature, served as an intermediary between the modern world and the world of the spirits.

As children, many of us were fluent in the language of these worlds. Perhaps you have a lingering childhood memory of being aware of thin places or presences that occupied the borderlands of consciousness. Now, when I watch children, it appears that they still have passports to travel back and forth across these borderlands between the mechanistic and the animistic. Moments after helping an adult program the VCR, a child can be just as swiftly in touch with beings of light in the forest just behind their home. Known as "walking between the worlds" in the Scottish traditions and as "walking with the spirits" in other traditions, I think of this phenomenon as having mist consciousness. It is the ability to flow and pass backward and forward at will, to move from the complexity of modernity to the profundity of a sacred world still dripping with the dew and mist of a continually renewing earth.

Mist consciousness is what stirred within my soul that day that the mist enveloped me. As it embraced me, I felt not only that I belong in the forest but also that I belong *to* her. After this experience of being at one with the mist-filled forest I would step from the supposed comfort and security of our home as often as I could to commune with these powers. In doing so I became aligned with the peacefulness of the place, what the old Scottish and Irish traditions speak of as *sitchain* (a state of peace), or becoming *an sith* (pronounced ahn-shee), as Celtic mystic Tom Cowan speaks of it.

It is no accident that in the Irish and Scottish traditions peace (*sith*) is the same word used to speak about the faery people. These beings, spoken of anciently as the Sith (*shee*), are also called the "people of peace," the "quiet folk," or the "shining ones." Sometimes they are spoken of as the "people of the hills" or mounds. Some old people today still believe that the spirits of the dead go to join the shining ones either below the earth, "in the hill," or in a parallel world only a hairbreadth away from this one.

There is no uniformity to such cosmologies, as evidenced by the wide-ranging cataloging of Celtic beliefs in W. Y. Evans-Wentz's *The Fairy Faith in Celtic Countries.*[3] A classic work as meticulous in scholarship as *The Tibetan Book of the Dead,* which he also translated, Evans-Wentz discovered not one Celtic tradition but innumerable strands of belief and practice with differing cosmologies depending on local tradition and custom.

Traveling to Cornwall, Ireland, Wales, Scotland, the Isle of Man, and Brittany, Evans-Wentz found a vast range of faery and ancestral beliefs that were not homogenized. In certain areas of the Celtic world, faery beings and ancestors have merged into a unified realm that continues to be related to and communed with through a variety of practices. In other areas, such as Brittany, the old spiritual mysticism of the druids continues to survive as an undercurrent in certain death cosmologies, even among old people who still hold that certain great ancestors are reborn as souls in newborns — a belief not unlike that governing the Tibetan lama system.

In becoming *an sith* we align ourselves with what I call the shimmering peace of a place. We open ourselves to its mysteries, not in some romanticized Tinker Bell way but in an authentic dialogue with the holy energies, with the spirits. By entering into such a dialogue with the spirit of peace in a place we are able to experience firsthand the results of inner transformation. We begin to take on and embody the essence of a place of power. Indeed, over time we can become so profoundly merged with a place and identified with its energy that we become part of its spirit, its voice.

There are many ways of becoming *an sith,* of becoming the peace: Engaging in deep meditative states within the natural world.

---

3 W. Y. Evans-Wentz, *The Fairy Faith in Celtic Countries* (New York: Citadel Press, 1990).

Hillwalking and going on pilgrimage. Making ablutions in a stream or spring. Sleeping on the side of an ancestral cairn (ancient burial places of actual ancestors) or a faery hill (sacred mounds considered to be special "fey" or faery places). Sitting in a tree. Doing a prayer fast (or what many Native American shamans call a vision quest). Communing with the mist created within a sweat lodge (ceremonial sauna), be it Nordic, Finnish, Celtic, or Native American. All these are ways of entering *sitchain* (a state of peace).

The emphasis on peace within the Celtic spiritual traditions is not always obvious. An old Irish proverb states, "The peacemaker is never in the way." In other words, in any natural setting and within any human circumstance the peacemaker, one who has become *an sith,* is someone you want around. Their presence promotes harmony and healing. Their essence engenders trust and instills a sense of the spirit of peace in a place.

Fostering peace and forming deep bonds to the peace of a place are touchstones of the Celtic spiritual traditions. The Celtic road of life is about sourcing our lives deeply in this discipline of encouraging and engendering peace rather than discord. In making it a central aim to become attuned to the guiding spirit of peace, in effect, we are able to become peacemakers. It is by taking time to commune with the mist that we are able to cultivate this path of peace and peacemaking.

I was always astonished at the things I experienced in the peace of these mist-filled states of consciousness. Within the spiritscape of my childhood, when the mist would draw near to our home, my otherworldly senses would take over. I was keenly aware that just beyond the wood beams and mortar that formed the old walls of our house were "high-traffic" areas where presences of various kinds moved beside our home. Some of these presences were not complete with their time on this earth, disembodied spirits who had passed from earthly life but who were still working out unfinished business.

Other presences seemed to be more of this earth than anything else. I look back now and perceive them to be the "fey," the faery folk, as well as other nature spirits of various kinds.

On more than one occasion I encountered spirits inside that old house. Usually they were just passing through — here one minute, gone the next. Sometimes they seemed to linger. As a child I was often intrigued by their presence, curious about what their stories must be, but seeing them was not always a pleasant process. More than a few times I saw rather frightening energies or spirits move through the house. They seemed lost and sometimes filled with grief and rage. On nights when these more frightening presences were around, I would force myself to stay awake all night long, keeping myself in bed for fear of encountering them, often resulting in my wetting the bed.

On one misty winter night I got up and tumbled from my bed. As I emerged from my room into the hallway near the living room I saw the spirit of a girl standing by the fireplace. To my astonishment, however, I was not the only one seeing the ghost. My maternal grandmother, Nonnie, who was visiting us for Christmas asked, "Do you see her?" I replied, "Yep." Moments later the spirit was gone, but something priceless happened for me in that moment. It was the first time I remember an adult validating the invisible world and its ability to make itself known. Over time I realized that my Nonnie, like other women on the maternal side of my family, had a real propensity for seeing spirits and for "feeling the chill." It was in our blood, inherited, no doubt, from our Scots-Irish ancestors.

For myself, I learned at a young age that when the mist descends upon us, the veil that ordinarily separates the unseen world from the visible world is drawn back, fostering a fluency of movement between the two worlds. The mist becomes a visible cloak that conceals that which is ordinarily seen, while another invisible cloak is removed, making that which is usually invisible

visible. Although in the Celtic conception of the "sight," it usually occurs at random, beyond the actual control of the seer, I have personally come to associate the presence of the mist with the conditions of otherworldly sight. It is as if the presence of the mist makes these states of consciousness all the more accessible, somehow ushering in the parameters typical of "thin times," opening up the thin spaces necessary for authentic otherworld contact.

It would not be until much later on in my life that I would comprehend more clearly what had happened for me back then. The visionary dispensation of my Celtic ancestors was at work within my childhood spirituality. It was a presence that slowly evolved, mostly without my being fully conscious of it or having an inherited vocabulary for understanding it. A somewhat unconscious process of committing to a lifetime path of mysticism and learning was initiated in those trees in Georgia. It was unconscious in the sense that it simply became a leaning of mine, and I did not consider it as anything very formal. I knew the spirits and these various other presences existed. I made note of that. The natural world was also holy to me. I made note of that too. This knowledge was always part of me.

My formative mysticism as a young lad would later involve the forests of my native Mississippi (once we had moved back there), the hills of North Carolina in my later youth, the birch woods of northern Wisconsin, and, eventually, the Scottish Highlands. I feel that I also have a standing appointment in Wales and Ireland, where I still have not been, yet which served as ancestral source grounds for some of my later experiences.

MIST AS GUIDING METAPHOR

Mist is a beautiful natural power. This old spirit is an ambassador of the in-between. Not entirely water, not entirely air, the mist is a unique dancing marriage of these two elements. In effect, it is a shape-shifting element. At times it nearly resembles a light rain. At other times it is more like a heavy fog. Either way, the mist is a blending or a weave of the moisture of water and the fluidity of air and represents a profound and creative dance of elements that are otherwise thought to be separate. This kind of synthesis is also a quality of the Celtic spirit.

It is no wonder that mist has come to be associated with the Celtic people, for in virtually every Celtic landscape one encounters certain mist-filled places. From the Orkney Isles in the north of Scotland and the forested glens of Wicklow in Ireland all the way down to the Isle of Man and Cornwall, mist is a prominent presence. It goes without saying that the mist also figures heavily in the lore of the Celtic people as well.

Mist is also an apt metaphor for the Celtic spiritual traditions, for the mist is not a static and unchanging form. It is not like the other elements of earth, air, fire, and water, which are usually in some fixed form or another. Mist is ever changing, always shifting its form as it moves through the landscape in serpentine fashion. Similarly, the Celtic traditions cannot be pinned down. These traditions enjoy the dialogue that comes with encounter. In the words of Celtic scholar Nigel Campbell Pennick, "Through-out history there is a continuous process whereby culture develops and changes according to the needs and prevailing beliefs of the times. Celtic culture has been through several stages where new influences have been absorbed and reinterpreted according to the Celtic genius."[4]

The Celtic spiritual road is contextual and always open to wherever the beautiful mystery of the Soul of Life may reveal herself. Because of this there is no unified Celtic tradition. Some Celtic descendants work more with ancient customs and technologies of the sacred that dwell within the fold of rural folkways.

---

4 Nigel Campbell Pennick, *Celtic Sacred Landscapes* (New York: Thames & Hudson, 1996), p. 9.

These descend from Druidism, a sacred natural philosophy of life whose followers love and revere nature.

Others consider themselves adherents to an earth-loving contemplative Celtic-Christian mysticism that looks on the Creation as filled to the brim with the effervescent and illuminative influence of a loving, wakeful God. Scholars such as Jean Markale and Peter Berresford Ellis strongly suggest that these streams within the Celtic tradition are kissing cousins, ensured by the good works of certain Celtic sages such as Morgan of Wales (Pelagius) and John Scotus Eriugena (John the Scot).

These days, in the United States especially, many people are unfortunately caught up in the constrictive trap of overdefinition and separatism. Our lack of assurance about mystical reality, and the ongoing realization that we, in the end, cannot define or pin down the unknown, cause some to cling to rigid ways of asserting what is and what is not spiritual, what is and what is not Celtic. We can simply utter the words *Celtic spirituality,* and those within earshot may assume we are talking about pre-Christian Celtic tradition, shamanism, or Celtic-Christian tradition, depending on their viewpoint. The need to categorize is not as strong among Celtic rural people, be they people of the shore or hill people.

Often the spirituality of Celtic descendants in the homelands represents a unique and sophisticated form of spiritual syncretism that may weave elements of the pre-Christian earth-based animistic tradition with facets of a rural folk Christianity, not unlike the Japanese people, who often blend Shinto nature customs, Buddhist prayers, and certain Confucian concepts to form the basis of their daily spirituality. What freedom of spirit! How beautiful to stand on a misty moor and orient oneself to a loving universe rather than to some wrathful conception of predestined darkness (Calvinism). The Celtic spirit does not avoid darkness, or shadows, or struggle, resting in a quiet assurance that even within the darkest of the dark lies a flickering flame of goodness.

The Celtic soul and culture have an incredible propensity for change, adaptation, and innovative spiritual evolution. The fact that a desert tradition, such as Christianity, could be adopted and blended with the mist-filled indigenous tradition speaks to this. The fact that certain cultural traits, customs, and ways of relating to the land could survive the Celtic diaspora (primarily Scots and Irish migrations to North America) and evolve into a unique Appalachian form of earth mysticism is an equal testimony to the resiliency of the Celtic soul.

Today, as mistwalkers (rather than as sleepwalkers), we continue the journey and dialogue of sacred encounter with the world, even in settings never glimpsed by our ancestors. The deep and abiding Celtic-Christian vision returns in the hearts of practitioners who now sit and share silence with the Buddhists. The natural farseeing wisdom of the Celtic shamanist tradition stirs again and actively discusses nature connection with ecopsychologists and Native Americans. The potent and soul-stirring word power of the Irish bardic tradition raises its head once again in the form of people writing bestsellers and facilitating radical transformation in American corporations. You only need to read the work of modern Celtic vision-poet David Whyte to know this is true. I especially recommend *Crossing the Unknown Sea: Work as a Pilgrimage of Identity.*

Let there be no doubt: the Celtic soul is alive and well. It beckons us to awaken to our inheritance of aliveness, yet one does not have to be of Celtic descent to benefit from the insights of this ancient tradition. Everyone hails from an earth-honoring tradition if you trace the legacy of the ancestral lines back in time. As a guiding spirit, in essence, the Celtic traditions can serve as a potent model for assisting people of all backgrounds to remember the yearning of their ancestral souls, their own link to the primal source of their ancestral earth wisdom.

So much of our aliveness is rooted in whether we make room for the spirit of joy in our lives, a joy that is connected with ancient, collective ways of loving the earth, but we must actively seek to remember this. If we do not approach nature with love, if we do not embrace our transpersonal and spiritual history with the same mythopoetic and animistic eyes of our ancestors, whoever our ancestors are, we will always stand outside our cultural and spiritual inheritance (which transcends Cartesian models of time). The Celtic spiritual pathways of animism can be a reliable mentoring spirit for reminding the collective human family of these things, but one of the first steps is to begin reconsidering the Celtic mystical traditions as living, thriving pathways rather than as lost customs.

To speak of a people, a tradition, or a spirituality in the past tense is to unconsciously attempt to keep it quarantined to the past. For the various kinds of animistic Celtic people, time flows in a circle, not in a straight line, and, truly, what goes around can, and does, come around. Celtic spirituality as a soul path of life and as a lived presence invites us to reinvest our lives with a mythopoetic sense, one that is aware of and inspired by our numinous ancestral past but not frozen in it. After all, we live now, and we must apply the same level of fortitude and ingenuity to our present circumstances as the old ones did in their time.

The spirit of the mist, in its ever-widening circle of encounter and blending, invites us into a living, breathing opportunity of opening ourselves, once again, to soul, to heart, to truth, and to whatever patch of earth we live on. When we welcome into our lives this kind of openhearted view, we suddenly find ourselves enveloped in a spirit that is not crippled by fear but that is rooted in the heart and engaged with life.

Like the mist, the Celtic spirit seeks to weave in and out of places, to touch the edges of all things. Perhaps it is pagan, perhaps it is Christian, or perhaps it is even a unique expression of dharma, in the Buddhist sense. Perhaps it is simply a kind of naturally earned knowledge, called *eolas* in Gaelic. Perhaps it is all of these things; perhaps it is none of them. Like the mist, the Celtic spirit defies categorization. It is pure soul and pure mysticism. Be it the healing energy of a tree, a time of silence at a river's edge, or a moment of prayer at the hearth, the heart of the Celtic spirit is about blending with direct experience. It is about an activated awareness of the presence of Cruithear, the Great Shaping Power of Life in all things and at all times. And sometimes, just sometimes, a deeply soulful experience can be very simple.

The image of the mist serves as a constant reminder that the Celtic spirit is a blend of things. It is partially a tradition that hails from a legacy of ancestor-based nature mysticism that is at least five thousand years old (and probably much older), while another part of the tradition is fueled by the ancient monasticism and Celtic-Christian wisdom that eco-theologian Matthew Fox has termed "green Christianity" or "Creation spirituality." That which we seek to label as Celtic spirituality is above and beyond all these things.

Partially air, partially water, the mist dances, blends, and dwells in collaboration. It is in the spirit of the mist that we are shown the healing that can be found in dialogue: dialogue with nature, dialogue with one another, dialogue with ourselves, dialogue with the rhythms of two people in relationship, dialogue between druid and Christian, dialogue between Catholic and Protestant, dialogue between Israeli and Palestinian. It is through the in-between-ness of the mist and the complex in-between-ness of ourselves as wanderers, exiles, and seekers that we will find our togetherness and come home to ourselves.

The mist teaches us that the road of life can be a road of peace, awe, and wonder. It whispers to us that our path of seeking comfort in and movement between these worlds is crucial. These sacred realms exist below us and beside us, and they overlap one another. An awareness of these worlds is, in fact, an unbroken holy tradition, what R. J. Stewart calls the "underworld tradition." Truthfully, it is a collective human tradition, one that is anciently steeped in an awareness of a primal land. We may be in a different land than our ancestors, laboring in different ways than our ancestors labored, but the same dedicated path of deep love for the natural world and the natural wisdom of the spiritual world are our birthright. On this matter, from a Celtic animistic and shamanist perspective, we merely need to open ourselves to the same numinous way of seeing the world and the same patterns and practices that our earth-honoring ancestors knew, be they Celtic, Nordic, African, or Asian. This vision of life, and these ancestral patterns and practices, offer an important antidote to the rampant loss of soul in the world today. They can assist us in rediscovering the sacred shape of the soul.

Chapter 2

People of the Shapes, Children of the Mist

Many followers of shamanist traditions view the soul as having different parts. This is why it is possible for us to continue functioning even when one part of our soul has become hidden away or eclipsed. Although *soul loss* is a shamanic term, the phenomenon has also been recognized by contemporary psychology, which uses words such as *dissociation* or concepts like post-traumatic stress disorder (PTSD). Whatever we choose to call it, the individual who is suffering from soul loss does not have full access to their soul's energy, vitality, memory, or inspiration for living.

Some traditions perceive the different parts of the soul as luminous strands or cords that are woven into the Soul of the World. Sometimes these strands can become snagged or even severed in extreme cases of trauma. Other traditions perceive soul parts like a strand of pearls, with soul loss resulting in the loss of the pearls that form the cohesive and healthy energy body.

In the old Irish traditions the soul is perceived as having three parts, represented by three different cauldrons, with three distinct powers or functions that maintain the health of the soul and the soul shrine (the body). If an imbalance or dysfunction is present in one of these cauldrons of the soul, the unified flow of the soul's energy becomes compromised, and we open ourselves to a whole host of things, such as disease, depression, or even psychic attack (what can sometimes simply be the mismanaged energy of others with whom we may come into contact, or to more intentional expressions, such as the "evil eye").

Essentially, these traditions hold that the soul is formed and fueled by the cauldron of warming (life force), located in the belly, the cauldron of vocation (calling), located in the heart or solar plexus, and the cauldron of knowledge (wisdom), located in the head.[1] When these cauldrons are in alignment, it is as if all the necessary parts of a transistor radio are in attunement. It has "juice." It is a reliable conduit for the flowing energies of life. In this way, the cauldron of knowledge, the seat of spiritual health, the cauldron of vocation, the seat of psychic health, and the cauldron of warming, the very ground of our physical health, form a potent holistic weave that results in an orb of energy around the body.

Irish shaman and scholar Caitlin Matthews, ever the lore-keeper of the primal vision of these pathways, has assisted us greatly in reminding Celtic descendants of this ancient topography of the soul. Hailing originally from a fifteenth-century text in Ireland that describes the spiritual mechanics of poetic inspiration, I think this primal notion of the soul in the Irish tradition is helpful in considering the phenomenon of soul loss.[2]

In the following practice I invite you to take some time to scan your soul. This practice, which I call Walking the Time Line of the Soul, will allow you to become aware of whether or not you have

---

1 Caitlin Matthews and John Matthews, *The Encyclopaedia of Celtic Wisdom* (Rockport, Mass.: Element Books, 1994), pp. 218–37.

2 Matthews, *Encyclopaedia of Celtic Wisdom.*

total access to your soul's energy. It is built around a traditional prayer posture known anciently in the Celtic world. The posture itself appears on a variety of Celtic artifacts, such as the well-known Gundestrup cauldron. Considered widely to be of pre-Christian druidic origin, this posture was also used by Celtic-Christian monks in certain parts of Ireland for prayer practices. An integral part of the Celtic-Christian *Rule of Tallaght,* the posture was believed to invoke protection.[3] For our purposes I will simply refer to it as the Druidic Prayer Posture.

Trance postures such as this are a universal tradition, part of our shared heritage as humans. They are our inherited legacy of using the body as a direct means of altering consciousness. The Druidic Prayer Posture is simple. Raise your arms out to your sides to shoulder height, forming a T. Bend your elbows, palms facing forward, fingers pointing to the sky. Each of your arms will form something of an L shape out to your sides. This is a good posture for centering, for showing reverence to a tree or shrine, or even for greeting another person in a sacred manner. Traditionally, in the *Rule of Tallaght* of the old Celtic Church, the monks would assume this posture and would face each of the four directions, hinting at the druidic undercurrent within this Christian meditative practice.

The Walking the Time Line of the Soul practice is also meant to help you become aware of your past. Before beginning the practice allow yourself to choose a direction that you associate with your past. In the Irish movie *The Secret of Roan Inish,* there is a scene in which the grandmother announces, "The past is in the west, the future is in the east." You may want to use this notion of the past dwelling in the west as a guiding template for this and other spiritual work. It speaks to the cyclical nature of all things as perceived of in the Celtic spiritual traditions.

---

3 Philip Sheldrake, *Living Between Worlds: Place and Journey in Celtic Spirituality* (Cambridge, Mass.: Cowley, 1995), p. 38.

Finally, you may want to have someone read this practice to you, slowly, giving you a few extended moments for each phase of the process. You can also record your own voice on a tape if you prefer. Additionally, you may also want to listen to *Origins,* track 5, "The Face in the Fire," by Steve Roach (available from the Timeroom or www.steveroach.com) to accentuate this practice. I find that Steve Roach's music is particularly effective in facilitating the states of consciousness necessary for the inner work discussed in this book.

PRACTICE: WALKING THE TIME LINE OF THE SOUL

- Stand upright, facing whatever direction you feel drawn to when thinking about your past.
- When you have selected the direction, take three breaths, with your hands hanging straight down at your sides, and face in that direction. Look into this direction and see your past floating off on a distant horizon. Take three more breaths and visualize the first breath as filling a cauldron in your belly. See your second breath as filling the cauldron in your heart. See the third breath filling the cauldron in your head.
- Now assume the Druidic Prayer Posture.
- Feel this posture fully, making note of how it feels. Hold this posture for a few moments as a simple means of showing reverence for the road you have walked in your life. When you are ready for the work of this exercise, simply turn and face in the opposite direction, the direction of your future.
- Take three more breaths, keeping your head and spine in comfortable alignment. Make note of how this posture opens your chest, opens your heart, and opens you to the universe. Now take three more breaths, and on the third exhalation slowly lower your arms to your sides again. You will not move

from this position, so allow yourself to become anchored energetically.

- Now imagine a golden light descending on you from the heavens, while an emerald green light slowly ascends from the earth through your legs and up your spine. See these two energies meeting and blending, first in the area of your belly, then in the area of your heart, and then in the area of your head. Take three more deep and slow breaths.
- Take a moment to become aware of your soul. See all the way back in time to when you were an embryo, floating within the watery world of your mother's womb. See this time as existing along a time line that begins somewhere behind you. Standing with your back to your past, see your past as a field of energy and memory existing as a station in time that runs toward you in the form of a thin cord of light. Pay attention to any images or sensations that come to you as you remember your formative time in the womb.
- Now see the actual moment of your birth. Whether it was an easy birth or a hard one, you were brought into the world as one of the many holy shapes of life. The light that lights the world is a light inside you. See yourself as the newborn that you were and welcome yourself into the fold of this greening life of power and beauty.
- Slowly move yourself along the time line now. Move forward in your memory to the time when you finally mastered the art of walking. It has taken you a while on your pilgrimage from the way of crawling to the way of walking. Stand there for just a moment and feel what it is like to be up on your legs and feet for the first time. Take three more breaths.
- Now take a few moments to simply be aware of the thin cord of light that flows from your childhood self to who you are now as an adult. Take a few moments to shift your perspective. See your childhood self. Now see your adult self. Now shift

back to your childhood self. Shift back to your adult self. Look at the space in between. What do you notice? Simply make note of it. Take three more breaths, filling the cauldron of your belly, the cauldron of your heart, the cauldron of your head.

- From the time of your childhood self to now you have encountered many things, met many people, and taken many developmental steps in your life. Some of these life experiences have been profoundly nourishing to your soul. Other experiences may not have been healthy for you, while some experiences may have been traumatic.
- Allow your consciousness to slowly move forward on the time line from the time of your childhood, walking to your adult self now. As you slowly move forward, allow yourself to become aware of any points along the line where the thin cord of light may have been threatened. When you reach these points along the time line, simply bring awareness to them. You might choose to "see" your hands slowly "touching up" or reweaving the cord at these places that were a challenge to your soul. If you experience a charge of memory at different points along the time line, there is probably unfinished business there, issues or wounds that are incomplete and need resolution. Simply make note of this. It will be something to return to in time.
- When you have reached the present in the time line, take three more deep breaths, one breath filling the cauldron of your belly, one filling the cauldron of your heart, and one filling the cauldron of your head, and then turn around, facing the direction of your past. Scan backward along the time line.
- Allow yourself to become aware of whether you have full access to your soul's energy. Let your mind, your visioning eye, slowly discern whether a part of your soul may have been left somewhere along this time line that has been the road of your

life. Become aware of the time in life when this soul part may have been hidden by your soul or perhaps even taken from you. It sometimes presents itself as a feeling of gaps in the line or pockets of memory that feel particularly stirred and need attention.

- Send a conscious prayer or message to any soul parts that have been hidden that it is safe for them to return: Standing in the Druidic Prayer Posture, again with your arms raised upward, take three more breaths and *seid* (Scots Gaelic, "blow") outward, strongly on the last breath, sending out your breath with power as a way to seal this work. See this sealing breath in your visioning eye as a visible breath, as if you were blowing a column of mist, light, or fog to your missing soul parts. Blowing outward like this is a way of activating, consecrating, and sealing with sacred breath. You have made a Mist-Filled Path for your missing soul parts to use on their journey home to you.
- In the next few weeks you may notice certain things coming to you. You may notice sensations and memories from the past. You may feel that you have more access to your energy than ever before. You may notice emotions such as grief, anger, or joy. You may feel profoundly enlivened. If strong emotions arise from this process, that's good. It means that the force of these emotions was already there, awaiting release. Release is cleansing and makes space in the interior world for healing. Note that you can reinitiate this process of calling the soul parts home whenever you feel the need.

Many people can experience spontaneous soul retrieval simply by extending energy to those exiled soul parts and inviting them back. However, depending on the circumstances under which a soul loss has occurred, it may be necessary to seek the counsel, guidance, and shamanic services of someone who can facilitate the soul-retrieval process with you. In other words, if you find that despite your efforts you are still haunted by a trauma in your life, or that you are lacking energy or find it impossible to concentrate, you may need a formal soul retrieval with a seasoned practitioner. Such an individual can be one who practices within a specific cultural tradition, such as Larry Peters, a Westerner authentically initiated as a Tibetan shaman, or someone who practices core-shamanism, such as Sandra Ingerman, author of *Soul Retrieval: Mending the Fragmented Self.*

PEOPLE OF THE SHAPES

I am certain that the water, the water of the seas
and of the lakes and of mist and rain,
has all but made the Irish after its image.[4]

— WILLIAM BUTLER YEATS

Celtic spirituality is a courageous path because it is about agreeing to be shaped by the powers of life. It takes courage (from the French *coeur,* "heart") to open oneself to life in such a deep and powerful way that we surrender to the life-affirming shaping powers of the universe. Ultimately, it takes trust.

In the ancient days of the early Celtic Church, an extraordinary group of individuals embraced a life of being shaped. Monks exiled themselves from their homelands to travel in other lands and preach, and it was said that they took on the mantle of white martyrdom. Others, though they did not exile themselves from their homelands, entered into the uncharted wilds of the natural world and surrendered their lives to the ancient rhythms there. This is called the green martyrdom. The white and green martyrdoms, as

4 William Butler Yeats, *The Celtic Twilight* (Dorset, U.K.: Unity Press, 1990), p. 70.

opposed to the red martyrdom of actually being killed (dying for God), was a life of wandering, of perpetual exile of living in nature, of seeking closeness to God, the Creator. Such a lifestyle was a profound act, because it was a choice of removing oneself, permanently, from the human community to enter into a deep communion with the sacred.

Kevin of Glendalough, who was a green martyr for a time, is one such figure found in the Celtic-Christian inheritance. Born sometime near the middle of the sixth century, Kevin was a child of Leinster, in Ireland. Around the age of seven he entered a monastery. A precociously wise boy, Kevin received a vision as a novice monk that eventually sent him into the forests near the Wicklow Mountains. During this time he turned his back on human companionship and lived as a wild man, deep in the trees and caves. Even today there is a cave in southeast Ireland called "Kevin's Bed." A number of amazing things took place during Kevin's green martyrdom, almost all of which speak to his intimacy and connection with animals.

Some tales suggest that he carried on daily conversations with a blackbird. Irish oral tradition speaks of other animal companions, such as a wolf and a deer, that would draw near to him. In another story we hear that Kevin had a custom of making ablutions in cold water. He would stand in a lake and read from "a most precious book of holy words." One day the cold numbed Kevin's hands so much that he dropped his book into the water, where it immediately sank into the depths.

Kevin was heartbroken over the loss of this special book, which some say was a gift from a wise teacher. His eyes filled with tears, and he lifted a sudden prayer. When Kevin opened his eyes he noticed that an otter was swimming in front of him, with his precious book in its mouth. Kevin took it from the otter and looked inside. Not a drop of the ink had been smudged, not a line was unreadable. Kevin wept with joy, and throughout the rest of his days, even after he went on to establish the great monastery at Glendalough, it is said that Saint Kevin prevented the killing of otters.

Many modern people, on hearing such a story, would immediately consider it just a quaint fairy tale. Through the lens of primal Celtic tradition, however, we see it in a different light. We see that if we lean toward life willing to give ourselves over to being shaped, as the many druids, Celtic shaman-poets, and saints have done over time, that life also leans back toward us, as in the example of the otter helping Kevin.

A contemporary example is the story of Linda Kohanov, author of *The Tao of Equus.*[5] A horse trainer and equine-facilitated therapy practitioner (someone who fuses psychotherapeutic work with clients and horse riding), Kohanov is a person, like Saint Kevin, who has leaned toward the sacred shapes of life and experienced the sacred shapes of life leaning back toward her. Instead of an otter or a blackbird, the sacred shapes of life that have leaned back toward Linda have names like Rasa. They are particularly sacred animals to the Celts: horses.

Linda shares with us the profound dimensions of the relationship attainable between horse and human, an ancient relationship undoubtedly known, cherished, and cultivated by our horse-riding ancestors. From her shamanic dreams and her direct physical encounter with horses through riding, to the profound dimensions of subtle emotional healing and clairsentient communication from the spirit of the horses, she offers us an example of the kind of holy dialogue between living things that no doubt was known by the old shamans, druids, and horse-whisperers. *The Tao of Equus,* in effect, is a shamanic account of the potential alliance between the

---

5 Linda Kohanov, *The Tao of Equus* (Novato, Calif.: New World Library, 2001).

human and animal realm, and within this mutual alliance we clearly see a potent healing and shaping consciousness at work.

In this encounter with the sacred world we meet the many shapers of life and, in turn, learn that we too are shapers. As shapers we direct energy. As I have said, it matters a great deal where we choose to place our awareness, because where we choose to place it often shapes reality. Are you overly negative? Gossipy? A skeptic? Are you always seeing the faults in others and yourself? Are you unable to suspend the trap of the one-dimensional literalist mind for the millisecond required for an experience of the ineffable hand of the Great Mystery shaping your life?

We shape ourselves by the thoughts we hold in our minds. Modern allopathic medicine is just now beginning to catch up with the ancient traditions of shamanic energy medicine that have always worked from the premise that many physical diseases originate in the mind. The mind that is contorted begins to contort the body. And the mind that is contorted begins to contort nature by destroying it.

We also shape one another by our actions, by what we choose to say to one another as well as by what we do not say to one another. I remember receiving a kernel of wisdom from my mother once when I was a little boy, living in Mississippi. I was in a rather foul mood one day. I looked at my shoes and said, "I don't like my shoes." A little while later I had made my sixth or seventh attempt to paint a picture and what my hand had created did not match my inner vision. I grew very frustrated and said, "I don't like this picture!" Not long after this I looked out of the window at the rain falling on the road and declared, "I don't like this day; it is too rainy!"

Very gently, my mother took my sour demeanor as an opportunity to assist me in shifting my perspective. She asked me, "Frank, what do you like?"

I responded, "I like Mr. Green Jeans. I like my Lincoln Logs. I like Rocky (our beagle). I like you and Da."

"Very good. Now, what do you notice after saying all of the things you like?"

I pondered her question a moment and responded, "I feel better, Ma. I feel better," smiling, surprised at this interesting discovery.

"Good. Try to remember this. If you pay attention to the things you like you will look for the good things instead of always looking out for something else you do not like."

I went back to my ~~painting, and I have preferred rainy days~~ ever since.

Great inventions have come about via our shaping powers. Financial ruin has taken place because of the influence of shaping. Whole countries and nations we never have imagined would change have fallen apart overnight, shifting irrevocably to new forms. These have been the product of lone individuals and collective groups, all in the process of shaping and being shaped.

In addition to having the power to shape — both others and ourselves — we also have the power to be shaped. Though we may resist it, we are all shaped, whether we like it or not. Even in the act of resisting something, we are being shaped by it. We were shaped by our mother's womb and our father's seed. We have been shaped by language, by the media, and by the spirit of the times in which we were born. We have also been shaped by innumerable forces we will never fully comprehend. One of these forces is the actual building blocks of Creation: the elements.

The Shaping Power of the Elements

Many indigenous people believe that different cultures and tribes on the planet have been shaped by a particular element. There are "fire people" and "earth people." There are "people of the sand"

and "people of the ice." Sometimes we hear this in the names for certain tribes. The Sami of Finland, Norway, and Sweden, for instance, are sometimes referred to as the "people of the sun and wind." Likewise, certain Scottish clans in the Highlands and islands, such as the MacCodrums, originally from the isle of North Uist, are spoken of in the oral traditions as "people of the sea." The belief is that they are descendants of the union of a man and a *selkie* woman, a seal woman who could take human form.

A unique perspective is offered to us in the teachings of the Dagara (West African) shaman, Malidoma Somé, author of *The Healing Wisdom of Africa:*

> Different cultures represent the profound influence of certain elements. Take Western culture, for instance. Western culture is a Fire culture. Its emphasis has been on firepower. It is a culture that has harnessed fire in ways never seen before, and sometimes in very destructive ways. But a problem arises when a culture becomes imbalanced and does not have equal parts water, mineral and nature to balance out the fire. Witches, for instance, are Nature people in Dagara cosmology. The nature people preserve the knowledge of nature and teach the knowledge of nature. They are often the holders of the knowledge involving the healing power of plants. The time of the witch burnings in Europe and America represents the beginning of the imbalance in Western culture. It is the time when fire was used to overpower nature and it has been the same ever since.[6]

Celtic people, at their very core, are a water people. Within the various expressions of Celtic culture and spirituality there are hill people, shore people, and island people, but in each expression

6 From a lecture given by Malidoma Somé at Naropa University, 1998.

there is a deep and abiding orientation to the holiness of water. Something of the spirit of water has gotten right down into our soul, into our bones. Water has shaped us.

The water of Celtic lands is a penetrating force, and its presence is felt in a number of ways. It has shaped not only the people but also the daily rhythm of life. The ebb and flow of tides, the coming in and moving out of strong storms, the presence of healing springs gurgling up from holy ground — all shape the lives of the water people. The water's edge is also a shaping feature for many Celtic people. Ireland, the Isle of Man, and the Inner and Outer Hebrides of Scotland are completely surrounded by water. The people of western Wales, Brittany, and Cornwall are people of the shore. We hear of the "bonny, bonny banks of Loch Lomond" and the shores of Nova Scotia, where Gaelic culture, music, and language survive today in full force.

In the Scottish Highlands a number of places are forever shaped by the legacy of water. One such place is the area of Loch Awe and Ben Cruachan. Now converted into a power generator inside of the mountain for the Scottish Power Company, Ben Cruachan is the home of a powerful hag spirit known as Cailleach Bheur. As Highland oral traditions tell us, at the top of Ben Cruachan was once an ancient well of youth. Cailleach Bheur is the guardian of these waters. In addition to placing a capstone over the well to keep the water contained, it is said that she maintained her beauty by taking regular sacred ritual baths in its waters.

One day Cailleach Bheur fell asleep on a long walk and forgot to replace the capstone. When she returned she discovered that throughout the night the waters had run from the well, flooding the lands below the mountain, thus creating Loch Awe, still there today. It is said that she then turned into a powerful hag. Even today Cailleach Bheur is considered a powerful old woman tutelary spirit. She is experienced in different ways by different people. Some have felt her atop Ben Nevis. Others report her presence in the mountains of the Glencoe Valley and near Ballachulish. Hillwalkers dare not tread on certain parts of Ben Cruachan for fear that the hag will let loose with thunderbolts and hail, for she is sometimes referred to as the "witch of storms."

The late great F. Marian McNeill, author and Scottish folklorist, states: "Many a mountain has its Cailleach (hag). The Cailleach nan Cruachan, for example, dwelt on the summit of Ben Cruachan. 'When anything ruffles her temper, she gathers a handful of whirlwinds and descends in a tempest, steps across Loch Etive at a stride, lashing it into fury, and prevents all passage at Connel Ferry.'"[7]

Other features of Celtic lands hold the presence of water. Holy wells and healing springs dot the Celtic landscape and serve as a testament to the importance of water in the Celtic spiritual consciousness. Some of these wells and springs are still very active and worked with by Celtic pilgrims from all over the world. We leave offerings and prayer flags ("clooties") and sometimes even seek healing in the attributes of the waters. These places are alive with power, alive with presence, and something of this presence leaves an indelible mark on the soul of the visitor.

The fact that a pre-Christian Celtic form of baptism (water blessing, purification, and initiation) existed is intriguing. Even the name of this ancient druidic rite, *baisteadh geinnleidh*, which translates as "the rain wedge of protection," speaks of our most ancient relationship with the spirit of water.

In the following practice I invite you to return to a primal memory of our ancient lineage in water. This practice is inspired by an Irish custom, still practiced today by some, of offering a visitor a bowl of water when he or she enters your home. While most

7 F. Marian McNeill, *The Silver Bough: Volume One* (Edinburgh: Canongate, 1956), p. 124.

people will accept this custom as simply a nice invitation to wash one's hands, the truth is that it hails from much older practices. It is not merely washing one's hands; it is a moment of returning to oneself and the knowledge of shelter after traveling. It is a moment to feel the Great Sheltering Spirit that provides for us.

MEDITATION: COMMUNION WITH THE SPIRIT OF WATER

Preparation:

- Place a small cloth on a table, perhaps a piece of tartan or some kind of altar cloth. It can be a cloth place mat, a hand towel, or piece of Irish lace. Whatever you have will work.
- Get a small bowl, preferably earthen or pottery, but, again, if all you have is a metal bowl or a glass bowl, use it. It does not need to be a big bowl, just large enough to put your hands in. When I travel I use a rather small earthen bowl made by my mother's hands. It is blue-gray, tan, and speckled and reminds me of the western view over the water, from the woods below Dunollie Castle, in Oban. You may also want to use a similar bowl that connects you to lineage or family.
- Fill the bowl about halfway with lukewarm water. It can be tap water from the sink, or it can be from a bottle of mountain spring water at room temperature. I have, on occasion, brought sacred waters back from Scotland to use. Do not overfill the bowl, leaving a few inches from the surface of the water to the top of the bowl.
- Now drizzle a bit of salt or sea salt into the water. Salt is a sustaining force, and in the medicine traditions of the Gaelic people it is frequently used to purify the home. In the old days each young couple moving into a new home would be given a

"flitting box" or a "salt box" for such purposes. Salt is the power of life. It can be used as a shamanic tool for banishing negative energies or evil spirits. In this meditation our purpose is merely to acknowledge our ancient source in the salt tides of the sea.

- When you have added the salt to the water your bowl is ready to use.
- Put on *Strata,* track 4, "The Grotto of Time Lost," by Steve Roach and Robert Rich (Hearts of Space).
- Meditation: Take just a few moments to clear your mind. Hold your hands up in the Druidic Prayer Posture to simply set the space and acknowledge the influence of the sacred. Take three slow and deep breaths, letting go of any extraneous thoughts or concerns. See the three cauldrons filling up with life force, first in the belly, then in the heart, then in the head.
- Now, slowly place your hands into the bowl of water.
- Feel the water on your skin. Become aware of your heartbeat. Take another three deep breaths.
- As you breathe, allow yourself, in your visioning eye, to envision the moon. Be aware that the saltwater that your hands are resting in is, in essence, the same basic makeup of the saltwater in the oceans and seas.
- Take three more breaths.
- Be aware with every breath you inhale and exhale that a similar salt solution as the ocean percolates, traveling up and down our spines as we breathe. Just as the planet's surface is mostly water, we too are made up mostly of water. Be aware that the salt tides of the sea are pulled by the force of the moon, and that we too are affected by the powerful medicine of the moon.
- We do not stand outside the influence of the powers of the universe.
- Take three more breaths, filling each of your cauldrons.
- Allow yourself to remember when you, as a precious embryo within your mother, floated in a watery world of nourishment.

- Now feel the ties that connect you with water-filled places in the natural world that hold meaning for you. Perhaps you have a favorite stream, spring, or loch. Maybe you have been to a place like the Isle of Iona, and the water in your bowl facilitates a remembrance of a pleasant time you had. Perhaps your spirit longs for that most holy of places where the waves of the ocean collide with the shore.
- Slowly move your hands around inside the bowl, allowing your skin to inform you of all the various sensations connected with the water: the roughness of residual salt granules, the smoothness of water, the cool or warmth of it. You are not a stranger here.
- Take just a moment to contemplate:
  What does it mean to be a person of the water?
  How did my ancestors view water?
  What was their relationship to water?
  Are there places in my life where I need to call forth the flowing energy of water?
- Now go pee and then drink two glasses of water. These are such common things we all do, yet these commonplace things can remind us, just like a morning shower or an evening ritual bath, that the spirit of water moves around and through us. We are the water.

THE WANDERING SOUL OF THE CHILDREN OF THE MIST

There are many kinds of water people. There are ice people, such as the Inuit. There are rain people, such as some of the tribes of the Amazon, like the Jivaro. There are also river people and loch people. Many of the ancient Scandinavian tribes, such as the Norse and the Danes, for instance, are undoubtedly people of the sea, the Vikings traveling as far as North America and the Middle East.

In contemplating my own ancestors, I have arrived at the conclusion that Celtic people are not only a people of the water but also, and even more so, we are the consummate children of the mist.

Children of the mist is a term often used by Scottish historians to refer to a very specific Highland clan, namely the MacGregors. The MacGregors earned this appellation in part because they were victims of the expansion of the Clan Campbell, who ousted the MacGregors from their ancestral lands. After they became dispossessed of their lands, it is said that the MacGregors lived largely from raiding the lands of others, thus earning them an even more precarious position in the history of the Scottish Highlands.

We learn from Highland oral tradition passed down into written history today that, under stress as an outlaw clan, in 1603 there was a significant battle between the MacGregors and a clan from the shores of Loch Lomond known as the Colquhouns. On a tree-lined field at Glen Fruin we are told that the battle was rather one-sided, with a vast majority of the Colquhoun men being slain. The MacGregor surname was then officially proscribed, making it illegal to bear it.

Many members of the Clan MacGregor intentionally hid themselves within other clans for safety. Some MacGregors assumed other surnames, such as Grant, White, and Black, while some historians suggest that certain Scottish surnames, such as Greer, represent a process of Anglicizing the name for protection. Because this particular group of Scottish families was forced to live on the run, to hide and cloak themselves, they were eventually labeled with the appellation "children of the mist." In time this term came to be used to denote any of the clans or people who were caught in between, wandering homeless or on the run. Historical accounts speak of some of the MacEwens living such an existence when they became known in Scottish clan lore as a "broken" clan (a clan dispossessed of its hereditary lands and its chief).

In the final analysis, the majority of Scottish Highlanders became children of the mist during the Highland Clearances of the latter half of the 1700s. It was during this time when many of the Highland chiefs turned their backs on their own clans because of economic conditions imposed by the British Crown, forcibly evicting, removing, and relocating many ancient families to Ireland, North America, or Australia. An ancient way of life came to an end during the Clearances, as well as during the Irish Potato Famine, one hundred years after the Highland Clearances, when hundreds of thousands of Irish families were both starved and evicted from their homes by the British.

These events ushered in an enormous Celtic diaspora, with hundreds of thousands of people forced onto ships bound for "some unknown shore." Many did not make it, either because of disease on the ships (resulting in the nickname "coffin ships") or because the ships never actually made it. During the Famine forty-nine ships, with hundreds of travelers, were lost at sea between 1847 and 1853 — a birth by water and a death by water.

These displacements uprooted an ancient people from lands that they loved and from waters that they communed with, and exacted immense cultural soul wounds, the effects of which are still felt today, consciously and unconsciously. The spiritual legacy of the Celtic people runs backward through time, to the time of the saints and the Celtic-Christian Church, to the time of the druids, and with these forced relocations a severance from the land that held these memories took place. In the words of Elizabeth Sutherland, a Scottish writer from Ross: "The Gael has inherited a talent for poetry, a knowledge of natural lore, and an affinity with and deep respect for the physical world. This strong, abiding love for a countryside peopled with rock, wells and mountains all with personalities of their own was one of the reasons why the

Gael suffered so deeply during the eighteenth- and nineteenth-century evictions."[8]

For many Americans it is a vast stretch of the imagination to contemplate cultures and people who have a history that goes back more than our country's mere 225 years. Nevertheless, the Celtic people, and the living descendants of these cultures today, actually hail from lineages that can be traced back at least six thousand years and probably much further when we consider the research into the Indo-European cultural tree, of which the Celtic cultures are but one branch. The people that we think of as the living descendants of the ancient Celts are the Irish, the Scots, the Manx, the Welsh, the Bretons, the Cornish, and certain groups of the Galician people of northwestern Spain, and yet it must be mentioned that there never was a unified or distinct "Celtic" people.

Celtic presence, traceable now through archaeological and linguistic sources, is now well documented in parts of Turkey, the steppes of Russia, northern Italy, the Swiss Alps, present-day Austria and Germany, as well as in Spain. Some scholars, and even Sarangerel, a shaman of the Buryat-Mongolian tradition, have said that the ancestors of certain branches of the Celts may have possibly originated with the Dilling people on the western edge of Lake Baikal, not far from the Sayan Mountains (in Asia south of Russia). Westerners are sometimes criticized for studying and practicing shamanism, and told that they are "stealing" traditions from tribal groups, when it may well be that many of us actually hail from a part of the world considered the cradle of shamanism.

Other interesting pieces begin to bubble to the surface as we peer through the mist of Celtic history. In contemplating a more far-reaching transpersonal history of the Celtic people we slowly realize that the wanderers among the ancient Celtic ancestors have

---

8 Elizabeth Sutherland, *Ravens and Black Rain: The Story of Highland Second Sight* (Guernsey, U.K.: Constable/Corgi Books, 1987), p. 25.

consistently been in a process of entering into dialogue with others, experiencing a cross-fertilization of ideas and integrating those elements that fit with their sensibilities. Here are just a few points worthy of consideration:

- The bagpipes, stereotypically considered a Scottish instrument, actually originated in the Middle East, most probably in Syria or Egypt, and expressions of this ancient instrument are also used in Northumbria, Brittany, Ireland, England, and even in Galicia.
- The ancient Indo-European ancestors of the Celts experienced a cross-fertilization of ideas with the Brahmins of India, leading some to suggest that the pantheons of Hinduism may have influenced aspects of the pre-Christian pantheons of the old Irish tradition.
- As far-fetched as it may seem, some theorists and folklorists have suggested that Ireland may have experienced Buddhist missionaries at one point in its history.[9]
- There is a ninth-century Celtic cross in Ireland that bears the Arabic inscription: "Bismillah, er-Rahman, er-Raheem," the first line of the Qur'an and a common prayer phrase in the mystical practices of the Sufis.[10] For many, including Celtic musician Loreena McKennit, an ancient relationship between the mysticism of the Celts and the mysticism of the Sufis is not an outlandish thing to consider. One can easily hear echoes and strains of Middle Eastern musical note structures within Celtic music.

The land we call Ireland today has not always been the indigenous home to the modern-day Irish; the land we call Scotland is

---

9 James Bonwick, *Irish Druids and Old Irish Religions* (New York: Barnes & Noble, 1894, 1986).

10 Robert Graves, foreword to *The Sufis* by Idries Shah (New York: Anchor Books, 1971), p. xi.

an amalgam of different cultural influences such as Gaelic, Norse, Pictish, and Norman; and the entire Celtic world is dotted with standing stones (such as Callanish and Stonehenge) and burial cairns that are pre-Celtic in origin.

The fact of the matter is the primal ancestors of the modern Irish (the Milesians) actually migrated from northwestern Spain, what is known today as Galicia, or what the Romans called Celt-Iberia. The Galician people are, in essence, the cousins to the Irish who stayed behind and kept their villages, while many of the Irish today are descendants of the immigrants who left present-day Spain and migrated to Ireland. A poignant celebration of these ancestral connections, a veritable "coming together of cousins," can be seen in the glorious recording project entitled *The Road to Santiago,* with the Chieftains and Galician piper Carlos Nuñez.

Of course I am oversimplifying here, for there were pre-Celtic predecessors in all of the now-Celtic countries, and there were successive waves of cultural migration from continental Europe to these places over the course of many generations. The point here is to expand our affixed perceptions of history to encompass a wider view, a wider view of our ancestors, if you are of Celtic descent, as wanderers; a wider view of the Celtic people in particular as seekers; a wider view that affords us the understanding that, as children of the mist, we Celts have always been migrating. We are a wandering, searching people by nature.

Sometimes this wandering was born of the spirit of exploration and voyaging, as in the case of Saint Brendan the Navigator, or Sir Henry Sinclair and members of Clan Gunn from Caithness, Scotland, who landed in the "New World" almost one hundred years before Christopher Columbus. At other times this wandering sprang forth from necessity, as in the case of the Highland Clearances and the Famine. In all cases, we have always been like the mist, slowly moving across the landscape, perpetually in-between and always seeking for that place we can call home. An ancient spirit drives the perpetual search of the Celtic soul. This ancient spirit is the spirit of longing.

Chapter 3

The Spirit of Longing

Tell me, men of learning, what is Longing made from?
What cloth was put in it that it does not wear out with me?
Gold wears out, silver wears out, velvet wears out, silk wears out,
every ample garment wears out — yet Longing does not wear out.
Great Longing, cruel Longing is breaking my heart every day;
when I sleep most sound at night Longing comes and wakes me.

— Excerpt from an old Cymric (Welsh) poem[1]

Longing is one of the most human of qualities. Like breath, blood, and water, we all share it. All people have a longing for something, and that longing is always a dynamic process that we must follow if we want to be led into our deeper life. Sometimes our longing calls to us from off in the distance. At other times it may get behind us and push us toward something. In any case it is something to pay close attention to, for to disregard it can only be to our detriment. We conjure great risk when we ignore the powerful prompts of the longing in our souls.

1 Kenneth Jackson, ed. and trans., *A Celtic Miscellany* (New York: Penguin, 1971), p. 261.

Celtic culture and spirituality were birthed from longing, the kind that the old Welsh poem points to. You will notice that the word *longing* is capitalized in the old verses, and I think the reason for this is that Celtic people have such a longstanding familiarity with it. In some sense, we refer to the longing almost as we would a person with whom we have a relationship. Longing is a presence in life and is therefore to be reckoned with as an entity unto itself. It is why nearly every Celtic poet, writer, teacher, mystic, and musician mentions it. We could also call it the spirit of longing.

What we long for speaks volumes about who we really are. Although surrendering to our sacred longings can sometimes be quite a painful soul-stretching and soul-tempering process (for this process always requires that we move beyond our comfort zone), our longing, with its unique quality and energy, is also a magical state to befriend, for it is a trustworthy guide. Longing calls us to actively place our awareness and attention onto things that are inseparable from the fabric of the deeper life of the soul. For some people this may be a version of financial stability, such as the ability to support worthwhile causes through spiritual or environmental philanthropic initiative. For other people it may be the passionate pursuit of mastering a particular art or skill such as writing, dancing, or playing the Irish harp. For others the longing may be profoundly rooted in a desire for birthing a family and making a home. *True* longing is anchored in our souls, and when it comes and wakes us in the middle of the night, it often chips us down to our most humble, innocent, and childlike selves — the very place where all of us can meet one another.

THE LONGING OF THE CELTIC SOUL

One of my favorite stories of the spirit of longing comes from the contemporary Scottish Highland tradition. Many Scottish clans have similar stories that exemplify the path of cultural survival and recovery, but the case of the MacLeans of Duart is one of the most poignant.

The Scottish Clan MacLean, known as *Mac Gille Eoin* in Gaelic, is an ancient clan that has long held lands on the Isle of Mull, off the coast of Oban, Scotland. Throughout history the castle of the MacLeans has been attacked by Vikings, other Scottish clans, and eventually by the Hanoverian forces allied with the English Crown. In time the castle of the MacLeans fell into disrepair, so much so that whole walls toppled. At one point all that remained were the skeleton of a once proud home and sketches of the original floor plan.

One day a young boy named Fitzroy MacLean, related to the line of the chiefs, was taken to the ruins of the castle. It is said that he was overtaken with great emotion at the sight of the abandoned castle. With one hand over his heart and another placed on the old stones that once formed a complete archway, young Fitzroy declared, "It is going to be my life's ambition to restore the castle as a family home and as a gathering place for the MacLeans all over the world."

It was not until the age of seventy-six that Fitzroy MacLean was able to begin the work of restoring the castle. Twenty-four years later, after spending a small fortune of his own money, Fitzroy MacLean turned one hundred and reopened the newly restored MacLean of Duart castle. MacLean's childhood vision is one unique expression of the Celtic soul trying to reemerge from an eclipsed state, and MacLean of Duart castle stands today as a testament to an action birthed from the spirit of longing.

CONTEMPLATING THE LONGING

What is your longing? What would your longing say if you gave voice to it? These are powerful questions to hold within our awareness. Very often the thing we long for feels like something that was lost or taken away. Because our soul aspires to commune with our longing, a heartfelt approach toward whatever our soul longs for is a process of healing and deepening of our collective humanity. You may have a longing to heal relationships with loved ones or family. You may have a longing to reclaim qualities you had as a child but that you let go of as you were socialized in school. You may have what the poet and modern Celtic *filidh* (poet-seer) David Whyte calls "the longing for belonging," or you may have the archetypal and perennial longing for the Beloved (God) as is so eloquently spoken of in Sufism, the mystical branch of Islam.

On some mornings I awake from my dreams and am absolutely saturated with the spirit of longing. Most mornings my spirit longs to be in a misty forest somewhere or to be near an old friend or relative. But at other times, I am aware that my whole being is suffused with an even more powerful longing that has come and pulled me from the respite of sleep. This longing is to be able to look out onto a very different world than the one we have right now. A world of peace. A world in which the human soul and the soul of nature are integrated. I have had this longing all my life.

Undoubtedly, longing fuels some of the most potent and beautiful expressions of the human soul. Longing (and the devotion that arises from it) were what led the monks of Ireland to create the beautiful *Book of Kells* and the ancient Picts (Cruithne) of Scotland to carve zoomorphic designs in standing stones throughout the Highlands. Longing leads hundreds upon hundreds of people on an annual pilgrimage up the side of Crough Padraic (a holy Irish mountain) to pray. Hundreds more follow their longing to a small island off the west coast of Scotland called Iona.

I think this may be where the dharma of Buddhism and the dharma of the Celtic spirit may meet in holy unison, in the belief that although the desires of the ego almost always lead to suffering and separation, the longing of the soul always strives toward peace and beauty. The thing to remember is that the longing is something we can trust.

The longing has an ancient allegiance to the evolution of our souls. If we want to discern the difference between the desires of the ego and the longing of the soul we can always rest in the knowledge that the longing that calls to us will always facilitate a deepening relationship to our lives, while ego-driven desires only serve to separate us from our potential. The longing promotes a glorious life journey of shaping and being shaped that results in holiness and wholeness, whereas the ego almost always leads us into the land of distraction, disconnection, and fragmentation.

The longing is a spiritual force that will lead us to where we need to be and to connect with those whom we need to know. This is what the Mist-Filled Path of Celtic spirituality is really all about; it is a proactive and provocative path of fostering a deep relationship to the life we are meant to lead.

LONGING FOR THE HOMELAND, LONGING FOR SPIRIT

Longing and the Celtic soul are forever linked. We might say that longing is a Celtic pastime. The spirit of longing is what led the ancient Scottish and Irish bards (and later the Celtic-Christian monks) to employ very powerful visionary "technologies of the sacred" to produce a plethora of poems and visionary verse. Many of these poems and verses are like overgrown pathways that can be followed backward through time, leading us to discover the same qualities of vision and mind states of the seers, prophets, and visionaries of the Celtic traditions.

Longing is the force behind the ancient Druid religion, with its emphasis on merging with the beauty and healing powers of the natural world. Longing has driven warriors fearlessly into horrific battles and seers to sleep in ancient caves and graves for the sake of receiving guidance from *Tir nan Sinnisir Mbeo,* the Land of the Living Ancestors (sometimes spoken of as the Celtic Otherworld). Indeed, talk to most any Celtic descendant — in America, Canada, Ireland, Britain, or Australia — who is even faintly aware of his or her roots, and the conversation will quickly turn toward our longing for the wide-open spaces, the wooded and mist-filled places. This dynamic is often true even for Celtic descendants who remain unconscious to the spiritual and cultural process presently churning in the deeper strata of the Celtic soul.

The spirit of longing for the homeland is interesting to observe. This deep longing for home arises in the hearts of many people who are of Celtic ancestry but who do not live in Celtic lands. These Celtic descendants are, namely, the offspring of those Celtic people who were forcibly relocated from the homelands or who were forced to leave due to inhumane religious and economic conditions. Many of these people who report a deep longing for the homeland, a longing for the ways of our ancestors, have never been to Ireland, Scotland, Wales, or other parts of the Celtic world. Yet something very ancient, very deep, and almost mournful exists for many modern Celtic descendants whose families have been separated from the ancestral lands by several generations.

Something of their Irishness, their Scottishness, their Welshness — their Celticness — has endured the trip and weathered the storm. Despite years and distance, despite generations of separation from the homeland, the Celtic spirit has survived. This kind of sentimentality and reflection on roots is unfathomable to some, yet it is very real to those who experience it.

West African Dagara shaman Malidoma Somé states: "No matter how many miles or how many years separate a person from their homeland, we still carry the village in our hearts. Something of this spark is always passed on." This is certainly observable in the "heritage tourism" of Celtic North Americans traveling to the lands of their ancestors. Although some are critical of the romanticism of Americans of Celtic heritage who travel to the homelands (a criticism obviously leveled by those not surviving on much-needed tourist dollars), these travelers are fueled by something very potent: the spirit of longing. With what we know of the ancient Celtic practice of pilgrimage and ancestor worship, we must admit that this activity is also fueled by very Celtic propensities and leanings. The Celtic soul has sprung up again from the moist roots of our past, and the spirit of longing now travels like a restless ghost seeking embodiment, expression, and manifestation.

BEFRIENDING THE LONGING

You are already familiar with the longing. You may not have consciously thought about it or had elaborate discussions with anyone on the subject, but this energy is present in your life nonetheless. The spirit of longing is a universal force that is linked to moods and dreams, ponderings and hopes, fears, and visions of the future. The longing is deeper than a desire for a better-paying job or more money, deeper than the plethora of distractions that modern culture offers us. The longing of which I speak is a rumbling in the deepest layers of our humanity, a longing for simple things like beauty, silence, connection to nature, story, rites of passage, peace, and initiation into our fuller selves.

We are all thirsting for a sense of lineage, a sense of place, a sacred community, an affinity with the natural world where we live. Just as we all share collective wounds, we also share this collective longing. For those who believe that what they are longing for is material success and fame, I challenge you to think about whether this is true. What is the true longing stirring beneath these transitory hopes? Picture yourself on your deathbed with only days to live. Are fame and fortune the true elements that will sustain you when you are in this state? When you make the "Great Crossing," will material gains serve as the necessary preparation for such a journey? Now imagine that you have already passed on. What do you look forward to now? Very often when we long for some material object, or objectified material state, we are overcompensating for some emotional lack or wound. What we truly long for goes back to a basic list of needs we all share as human beings, such as love, acceptance, health, belonging, daily peace, beauty, none of which is the same as an object.

Humanistic psychologist Abraham Maslow, in his classic theory of *The Hierarchy of Needs*, stated that all humans must have certain basic needs — such as for shelter, food, and warmth — met, and that once these needs are met we develop a deeper longing for spiritual ideals, altruism, aesthetics, beauty, and peace. He called these higher needs "B Values." Following our longing for these B Values provides us with a potent experience of a process known by the ancient Celts, who were ever seeking to know God, ever yearning to connect with divine inspiration (*imbas*), and ever longing to live a life of beauty imbued with connection and spirit.

We are also on this path, and the fulfillment of our collective task as a human community lies in the process of actualizing a deeper communion with these same life-affirming powers. Celtic spirituality is an ongoing initiation into a life of beauty and a mindful preparation for the passage of death. The ancient spirituality of the Celtic peoples has always been a dynamic orientation to the ebb and flow of the seasons, daily practices that foster an awareness of the passage of our lives and of thanatology (a vision and study of our death and dying). This vision is of life ending in a wondrous death journey toward a home we have all been away from. When death is really an experience of going home, what is there to fear?

In the end, the Celtic spirit is not concerned with fame and fortune, knowing that neither of these temporary states can travel with us at our passing. The enduring quality of who we are on a soul level from day to day is the only thing that will travel with us into other forms and into other realms at death. Our quality of mind, heart, and daily experiences is extremely important. From a Celtic mystical view, we are simply laying down the pattern of our death passage within this life. It behooves us to pay attention to how we are shaped, because we are simultaneously shaping the energetic processes and states that we will revisit at the time of our passing.

When we become aware of the thin permeable membrane between the land of the living and the land of the spirits, our emphasis on material things fades dramatically. Whether gained through spiritual practice or near-death experience, a daily awareness of the thresholds changes how we go about living. It fosters a path of heart, of being present, of compassion for self, earth, and other. Suddenly everyone, regardless of who they are, becomes part of our clan, because in befriending our own death we also befriend all forms of life.

A life path such as this is walked with a sense of extended kinship. Following our longing and working with death creates openhearted human beings who want to assist others with their particular longings. It is why we are all here. When we have a tangible heartfelt sense of the pain and joy of our personal longing, a powerful force that seeks to serve others becomes activated in our souls. This force is intolerant to bigotry, racism, sexism, homophobia, and the destruction of the natural world, to all human attitudes that maim, harm, and restrict. Who and what we do not love says nothing about them; it only serves to illuminate our own limitations. Limitations such as these are washed away if we are living a life steeped in the spirit of longing. In the words of a kinsman, David Henderson, of the Clan Henderson Society of North America:

> People surmise that because I am in a clan I must be Scottish. I think that is quite an understatement. I am in a

> clan because it means that I care about the common man. It is not that I just care about Scots, or even Celts, but if a person can care about someone that they have never met it is possible for that person to love anyone in this world. That is the true legacy and hospitality of the Scottish clan. That is the legacy that I hope to pass on to my visitors and to my kith and kin.[2]

Celtic spirituality awakens us to these dimensions of being. Our focus becomes caring for the spirit: spirit of the clan, spirit of the hearth, spirit of the earth, spirit of the open heart, spirit of the purpose of our work, spirit of service and healing. Ultimately it takes great courage to face the spirit of longing. Longing is a powerful force, similar to hunger and need for warmth and shelter; it is a force that makes all human beings equal. It places us all on the same level: the level of the heart.

MEDITATION: ATTUNING TO YOUR LONGING

- Take a few moments to access a deep state of relaxation. Breathe deeply, taking three breaths and filling the three cauldrons. Meditate for a few minutes on your life's longing.
- What is your longing made of? Pay attention to what emotions, sensations, and images arise as you turn your awareness to what your soul longs for.
- If desires for more money, a bigger house, a flashy car, a new job, and so on arise, write these down and then proceed by asking yourself the same question again: "What is the longing of my soul?" This is a potent way of peeling back the layers

2 From the Clan Henderson Society of North America website, (www.msu/edu/~hende117/).

of personality and ego and getting to the heart of what is true for you and your life.

- Continue breathing, meditating on this topic, and recording the second layer of what arises for you when you hold this question. Again, upon writing these down in your journal, peel back another layer by asking yourself the question a third, a fourth, and even a fifth time, recording the different layers of answers that arise.
- What is the longing of your soul?

Reviresco: Longing to Grow the Soul Green Again

The longing, in the Celtic sense, originally surfaced in my awareness as a deep desire to be connected to some sort of earthcentered village or community existence. I seemed to have been born with an unquenched need in my soul to witness the holiness of sacred community, of people gathered in the name of earth and spirit.

As a boy I would receive what I will call "glimpses of memory." Sometimes these visions would be of a tribal lifestyle in a forested land. At other times I recollect seeing imagery that bordered on hermetical, where community came in the form of local stones and streams, rather than in the form of people. At other times, I am aware that in some of the scenes I was living alone but knew that I was also in deep connection to some kind of community nearby. I remember being aware in some of these glimpses of memory that everyone I loved lived in one place. In these memories I am aware that life was characterized by certain orientations. Meals and dreams were shared. In the autumn the community would rally around bonfires to sing and to dance. From a very early age I had memories of people gathering together simply to chant in the trees.

As a child I could open myself to these cellular memories and for many hours bask in the orange wood-smoky glow of a life that seemed to stand on the edge of my awareness like a dream I could not quite remember fully. Though my memories were particularly strong in the autumn, I was aware of them at all times in one way or another. I still feel some of them, and, in looking back to my childhood, I realize that these experiences were a way for the spirits to prompt a deeper longing within my soul.

As I grew older, this longing for a sense of village, clan, and tribe slowly took on the added element of yearning for rites of passage in my life. Eventually, as you will see, I came to discover why I had such a longing for my tribal ties. I had not been raised with any overt awareness of the ancient tribal traditions or histories associated with my Celtic bloodlines, yet my lack of awareness of these things did not negate their ability to exert their influence on my psyche as a child. These things have always been inextricably tied with the spirit of longing in my life. They have always been with me.

Much later I discovered an image that truly captures the process of the Celtic path of longing for me, namely the clan crest and motto of one of my Scottish Highland clans. All clans from the Highlands have three components that express our affiliation and kinship: an ancient crest, something called a plant badge (a sprig of a plant often believed to have mystical properties in the lore of the clans), and an accompanying motto around which the clan rallies and draws strength. Some of these symbols and emblems are rooted in particular events from history, such as battles or tales involving great ancestors, while others hail from a totemic and druidic past.

We MacEwens (MacEoghainn) are an ancient Scottish clan, originally from Ireland. Our bloodlines, along with those of our cousins the MacLachlans, the Gilchrists, the MacNeils, and the Lamonts, are traceable back to the High Kings of Ireland and, even farther, to the original Milesian Gaels who landed on the shores of Ireland following their druid-shaman, named Amairgin, from the hills of Galicia (northwest Spain).

Around 500 C.E. these ancient Irish families were then part of a migration from Ireland to present-day Scotland, where our ancestors founded a kingdom by the name of Dalriada (present-day Argyll in the west of Scotland). The MacEwens in particular were known anciently as bards, poets, and *seanachies*, or tribal historians. Being a poet was originally a druidic role in Gaelic culture, and the MacEwens became attached to other Highland clans, such as the MacDougalls, serving the chiefs of the clan.

The crest of the MacEwen clan depicts an old oak tree that has been cut down yet which is growing new saplings from its wounded stump. Like many other Scottish clans, the accompanying motto is in Latin: *reviresco.* This word has many derivative translations, all of which capture the real spirit of the intended guiding principle of the clan. I have heard it translated as "we grow again," "we are born again," "we grow strong again," "we grow green," and "we grow green again." In all cases, you can feel the power of what is held in those words. There is a sense of renewal, of regeneration and return.

What is not as obvious, however, is that when you combine the image of the clan crest with the guiding principle of the motto, the end result is something of a prophecy regarding both the condition of the clan and the Celtic traditions in general. The oak tree has long been a symbol of the old druidic beliefs of Celtic lands. Alternate translations of the word *druid* suggest that the tradition has always been comprised of "oak-seers" or "people of forest knowledge." However, just as the MacEwen crest suggests, the powerful oak of the original Celtic spiritual ways (both pre-Christian and Celtic-Christian) was eventually cut down, first by Roman incursions, then by patriarchal expressions of Roman Christianity and Protestantism and, finally, in the attempted genocide and mass extermination of the people and culture by the English Crown. In all cases, the tree became wounded, the full expression of the traditions eclipsed.

There is a profound message of hope here, however. If we turn our attention to both the motto and the image of the greening saplings growing from the wounded stump, we quickly see, with the emerging saplings, the spirit of the oak trying to reassert itself. Drawing great power from the roots that still dwell deep in the earth, the eclipsed energy of the tree is beginning to push its way upward toward the sun, growing itself green again. I feel that this potent image is a powerful commentary on what we are currently involved in as a collective cultural process as both homeland and diaspora Celts. More generally, I feel that this image speaks to many people from a variety of backgrounds and cultures who are feeling the quickening call back to an earth-honoring spiritual path. We are all waking up, regardless of heritage, to our collective human path of longing, which ultimately is rooted in a desire to "grow the soul green again."

We are all being extended an invitation. We are being asked by the spirits of the ancestors and the spirits of the crying earth to:

- work through both the wounds and the shadow elements of culture (the wounded stump);
- to remember the true power of our ancient ways (the roots still deep in the land);
- to rekindle the life-affirming cultural elements, characteristics, and orientations that are so much a part of the view of our primal ancestors (the greening saplings emerging).

These saplings are the cultural soul elements that were eclipsed by the traumas that *all* our ancestors have endured. Latino friends, even Catholic ones, are looking once again at the wisdom contained in the tradition of Mexican shamanism (*curandisimo*). Chinese friends who have become largely Americanized are once again rediscovering the wisdom inherent in their ancestral Taoism. Middle Eastern friends who have experienced a great deal of personal wounding at the hands of fundamentalist Islam are now discovering the mystical branch of Sufism, with its unique interpretation of the Qur'an and the beautiful vision of certain teachers such as Rumi and Hafiz. Indeed, some Irish cousins who may turn pale at the mere mention of Christianity ("recovering Catholics") are finding great solace and homecoming in the Celtic-Christian vision of nature.

At the heart of these various traditions dwells a collective natural path that we all need to walk. We not only need it, but we need to be able to recognize it in each other. For all of us, the very antidotes to our own modern state of cultural soul loss are the roots of our cultural soul: the values, ways of seeing and being, and customs that predate the cultural traumas our ancestors endured and/or the cultural aberrations that occurred when our ancestors may have strayed from a life-affirming path.

For many of our ancestors the experience of forced emigration and diaspora is akin to that of the animal that gets its foot caught in a trap and then chews off the paw to get away and survive. We have survived, because we are here now, but vital soul elements of a sacred way of being have been left behind and need to be "re-membered," literally, as if we were reattaching a severed limb. All too often we forget these vital parts of ourselves, and then we slowly forget that they have been forgotten.

Vital cultural soul elements in the Celtic traditions, to name only a few, are:

- the love of nature and therefore the protection of her
- the hearth as an altar of family, clan, and otherworldly passage

- a powerful sense of respect for and hospitality to all peoples
- a sense of honoring the feminine, the balanced masculine, the elders, and the spirits of the ancestors through observances and rituals of remembrance and communion
- perceiving and relating to the divine in nature and all living things, which characterizes both the Celtic shamanic and druidic path, the folk traditions of faery lore, and the Celtic-Christian traditions
- the importance of myth cycles and sacred stories as a means of orienting to spiritual reality and a mythopoetic history
- an inherent understanding of the value of dreams and an active process of working with them
- an observance and active participation in the cycles of life as perceived of in the seasons and rhythms of the earth

Because of our disconnection from many of these basic ancestral values (what one of my ancestors in a dream called the "mother root"), I find that much of what characterizes our contemporary culture is a state of separateness. We are disconnected from ourselves and from one another. We are caught in a strange and exhausted half-sleep, suffering from thirst, hunger, and forgetfulness, attempting to rest our weary hearts against the stump of a wounded tree that once sustained us and provided shelter.

We do not yet realize that feeling a sense of shelter in our lives, and providing a sense of shelter to others, is rooted in our ability to "grow the tree" again that provided shelter to our ancestors. This flowering tree extends solace to all people, a sense of protection of the earth that is our shared home. As I look back at my childhood visions that were connected to my longing, I now realize that the quality of some of these glimpses of memory has always been with me. The same things I had a deep longing for as a child, that is sacred community, peace in the world, a sense of shared spiritual practice that transcends our differences, rites of passage, and deep communion with nature are formative strands of the longing that form the tapestry of my life now. I am now able to see that, from my childhood to now, there has never been a time when I have not been working on these themes in my life in one way or another.

Longing is a constant companion. I invite you to listen closely to it. It often comes in a dream. It may call from the trees outside. It often quickens at the hearth within our homes and beckons us to come closer. For some the longing may emerge as an undeniable nagging sensation, as if we have an unfulfilled appointment with a destiny that is waiting for us. If we forget to listen to the voice of longing, just as the old Welsh poem suggests, she will often come and wake us. Sometimes this reawakening to our longing occurs in trying times of great difficulty, in which all previously held notions of ourselves and the nature of reality are melted away. When we find ourselves in conditions such as these, we know that we are in the midst of an initiation.

CHAPTER 4

RIDING THE WIND

Initiation and Awakening to the Celtic Spirit World

Sometimes we have to travel
to the edge of ourselves to find our center.

— BUCK GHOSTHORSE, LAKOTA MEDICINE MAN

Nearly all initiations, if they are truly centered in the life of the soul, are about stepping into right relationship with the spirit of longing. Initiation is the process of defining and refining one's role in the life of our longing, determining how we can be conduits for its influence in our lives and world. Regardless of the number of visions, tutelages, advanced degrees, or sacred objects that may have entered our lives, if we forget to listen to the voice of longing, we will get nowhere.

In late October 1991, around the time of *Samhuinn* in the Celtic tradition (the ancient Celtic New Year and time of the ancestors that coincides with All Hallows' Eve), I found myself in a situation that was directly linked to forgetting my longing. I was suffering from a powerful illness. Arising from both a physical ailment and deep emotional struggles, it was an illness that the classical tradition of shamanism has referred to as the "shaman's death" and the contemplative Christian tradition has called the "dark night of the soul."

Like a black cloud, my illness seemed to blow in over my life. Yet unlike a cloud, my illness did not move on. It settled in around me and elected to stay. I slowly began to visualize this illness as a large serpent that had slithered into my life, attaching itself to gaping holes in my energy body, slowly but surely sucking the life from me.

I was struggling through both a deep-seated depression about my life as well as the thick torment of a case of double-lung pneumonia. The conditions mirrored each other. I felt as though both my body and soul had been engulfed by a dark force. Both my lungs struggled against being engulfed by the fluid created by an illness that had already taken my spirit and that worked round the clock, intent on claiming my body. I look back, with what I know now, and call such a psychosomatic ordeal *an nela dubh,* Gaelic for "the black cloud."

For two months I struggled with this sickness. Different antibiotics and the opinions of various physicians proved fruitless. At times it appeared that I might recover. After ten days on one antibiotic, we thought the illness had been defeated. Within a few days, however, my immune system would waver like a buoy in the sea, and I would be back to where I had started. Nothing seemed to work.

I had intentionally kept my illness from both sides of my family, because I had no desire to worry them. Southerners are natural-born worriers and I originally did not think that my illness was that serious. In time, however, I began to sense from the tone in my doctor's voice that my condition was far more precarious than I had thought. When the physician asked me if my family knew about my illness, I knew it must be bad. I contacted my mother, who has studied with a variety of alternative healers, including First Nations people and Peruvians, and told her what was happening. She immediately put me in contact with an old Cherokee medicine man in North Carolina named Chief Two Trees, whom she trusted a great deal. He had, in fact, assisted her in shrinking a problematic tumor in her throat with the use of herbs.

Two Trees was an astonishing character. I had met him once before in the hills of North Carolina when I was much younger. I didn't quite know what to make of him. My early boyhood stereotypes of Native American people were smashed on Two Trees's old porch. I saw no feathers, no drums, no beaded vests or feathered war bonnets. He wore a simple flannel shirt and was an avid collector of different kinds of pinecones and plants. Two Trees saw a number of people for diagnosis all at the same time, barking his findings and instructions as if he were the emcee at an auction. Another thing I remember from this earlier encounter with Two Trees was the framed honorary doctorate in pharmacology from an Ivy League university hanging on the wall of his rustic cabin. Two Trees was the real thing.

Two Trees was widely known for his unorthodox treatment of everything from acne and yeast infections to cancer and even HIV. I eventually learned that medical residents from renowned universities had been coming to study with him to learn more about his diagnostic techniques, as well as his methods of treatment.

We talked on the phone. He listened carefully to my description of what was happening, including my resistance to antibiotics. He instructed me to look in the mirror, while on the phone, and tell him point by point the color of my tongue, what the edges of my eyes looked like, as well as my temperature reading, which hovered steady at 104 degrees.

"You've got parasites!" was his brusque diagnosis. "Yep. You've got little nasties in you. They're eating away at you. They're in your ears, your sinuses, down in your lungs. But, your real problem, boy, is you're not 100 percent sure you want to be here, or these things would never have set up camp inside you. They're eating away at you because something in your own spirit is already eating away at you!"

His words hit me between the eyes. How in the world could he diagnose any of these things accurately over the phone?

"Your mother is going to send you some things for you to take," he continued. "Cherokee bitters and other nasty-tasting things. To get rid of the nasties you've got to hit them with something nasty. But, no amount of ol' Indi'n medicine is going to help you if you don't decide you want to be alive. No amount." Chief Two Trees hung up the phone with no formal good-bye. What mattered to him was the business of medicine.

While I questioned the theory of an infestation of parasites, I also knew that his assessment of my emotional state was flawless. He picked up immediately that I was engaged in a serious spiritual crisis, which included depression, lack of motivation, and even intense dreams filled with suicidal imagery. I had enough training in psychology and counseling to know that people often become suicidal when they desire a ritualized and symbolic death of an old way of being, of an old life or identity. But at that point, within the dark cloud, clear thinking failed me.

The Rough-and-Tumble Nature of the Call

For about six months leading up to my bout of pneumonia I had experienced a whirlwind of mystical experiences I did not quite know how to integrate. Rather than finding enlightenment, I seemed to find myself plunged deeper and deeper into spiritual difficulty, what I would later hear referred to by Stanislav Grof as a "spiritual emergency."

In the phase preceding my pneumonia I experienced a complete and unequivocal "blowout." A number of powerful energetic processes had been activated within me with no closure in sight. I was experiencing the classic "shamanic dismemberment," or what Jung called the "night-sea voyage." Years later I would see the pattern of my process eloquently portrayed in the Celtic *immrama* stories (harrowing otherworldly sea voyage tales in Celtic tradition), in which sea-faring Irish wanderers, such as Maleduin, are guided to thirty-three different islands representing thirty-three different gates of power, thirty-three psychospiritual states of consciousness and initiation. These otherworldy encounters were not always pleasant but always led the voyagers to new levels of awareness.

Wisdomkeepers in the Celtic tradition have suggested that these initiatory *immrama* stories are, in essence, our "Celtic Book of the Dead," mirroring the same patterns found in Tibetan texts and Bön shamanic lore (the indigenous shamanism of the Tibetans that predates the arrival of Buddhism). Perhaps if I had had a Celtic psychopomp (a type of shaman who aids the dying on their death passage) reading or telling me of the old islands, I would have known that eventually there is solace, peace, and a sense of home at the end of the journey. At the time, I knew only fear.

Fear, like silence, is one of our most powerful teachers. Though it hardly feels like it in the moment, fear is an ally, a guide, a friend. It is also a bit of what the Lakota people call a *heyoka,* a contrary clown spirit. Whatever fear tells us regarding our inner life, you can bet she really means for us to do the opposite. In this way, fear alerts us to what we need to be aware of (that we don't want to be), of what we need to face (that we don't want to see), and where we need to go (because it is a place that will make us stronger).

Immense fear arose when I tried to sort through some of my experiences. I did not know what the various mystical states might mean. Was I crazy? What was all of the imagery rooted in? Was any of it leading anywhere? I was looking for the off switch or the mute button to my experiences. There was none. As a result, I made valiant attempts to ignore these energies. I tried to avoid any direct confrontation with these experiences. I tried to go about leading a "normal" life, and yet I had forgotten what a normal life looked like.

If we want to be whole human beings, we really have no choice, if we are in the throes of an authentic initiation, but to enter into the process and travel its full circuit. Initiation, whether shamanic or mystical, is about giving up and handing over. It is about dying to an old life that no longer serves the soul. Initiation is about having everything stripped away — everything. The smaller definitions we hold of ourselves, the tiny confine of the box we have labeled our "life" are swiftly and assuredly placed on the fires of transmutation within an authentic initiation.

Initiation is part of every great religion and mystical tradition. If you are called to be a monk you "leave all worldly treasures" behind. In Sufism, if you are called to the way of the dervish, you are "plunged into fire" only to emerge in the "healing waters of the heart." If you are called to the shaman's path through the traditional or classic call of near-death or shamanic illness, you do not decide when or how this occurs. For the shaman, the monk, the druid, and the mystic, initiation is not something scheduled in between your vacation and a trip to the grocery store.

When an authentic initiation is activated it becomes paramount. Ideally everything should be put on hold. However, all too often our nine-to-five world does not stop long enough for us to complete our process of initiation. Contemporary society rarely understands the importance of the process underway. The process of authentic initiation asks us to give ourselves over to deeper forces within us. Our psyches are the seasons. Our biorhythms are the seasons. Our many moods mimic the ever-shifting weather. We are summer's abundance, and we are the death and dying of late fall and early winter.

This is probably one of the main areas in which the indigenous, contemplative, and shamanic worlds are at odds with the industrialized world: rhythm. Earth-based people think that we industrialized people are crazy because of how we live. I think they are right. Indigenous people, knowing the deeper mysteries associated with a woman's monthly cycle of menstruation, for instance, support women in taking this sacred time for themselves. Even today among some of the Canadian Ojibway people, women are supported in slowing down, in honoring this rhythm as one of the different seasons of the inner life. Earth-based people also support individuals who have recently experienced a death in the family to take a significant phase of time to work through their grief and loss before they are expected to return to normal functioning within the community, as has been spoken of by Sobonfu and Malidoma Somé of the West African Dagara.

Can you imagine a society in which women were supported in taking four days each month to attune to their "moon time," as the time of menstruation is referred to by First Nations people? Can you imagine having three solid months to dedicate to dealing with the unresolved feelings of loss from the death of a friend, a child, a spouse, a parent? The industrialized world is currently rooted in clock time and business, not the soil of the spiritual life. Women must deny their natural rhythms and show up for work, and despite the sadness in your heart over a recent death or tragedy, you have three days of personal leave for such things.

Heeding the Call

In the years leading up to my illness I closed myself off from the mysticism that I had nourished in my childhood, largely because of personal pain, socialization, and the demands of my life as an adult. Attempting to deny the flow of spirit, however, only causes difficulty. I encountered spirits and experienced deep mystical states, yet I immediately turned my back on anything I had seen, heard, or felt. I endured a number of psychic openings in which I began to "see" scenes from other times as well as beings or people that I had no context for understanding. Some of this imagery or these activated streams of information were at times quite overwhelming and debilitating. I did not have the training to understand what was happening or the wherewithal to push forward and attempt to integrate these experiences. Instead I expended an incredible amount of energy in closing the door to any potential knowledge about them. I forced myself, in essence, to become a sleepwalker, merely going through the motions of my life, lacking any true awareness, forcibly trying to portray the image of normalcy.

As is often the case, however, when we knowingly (or unknowingly) dedicate ourselves to a life path that keeps us limited, small, and fearful, the influence of the sacred world will come along with what I call the "cosmic two-by-four." Sometimes someone or something gives us a gentle reminder, like a Rinzai Zen priest waking a drowsy meditator. Other times we can get hit rather hard, and sometimes repeatedly, if we do not learn from the lessons and see these moments for the wake-up call that they are.

Some of my experiences involved glimpses into the spiritual reality of my Celtic heritage, but I did not know that these visions or energies were streaming into me from such sources. Things would occur in my daily life in ways that were profoundly shocking. And I had no words for these experiences at that time.

I had one experience while I was attending to the very mundane task of taking out the trash. I was living in a large apartment complex at the time. All residents were required to carry all trash and recycling to the far end of the building. As we all do with daily chores, I proceeded with this task rather mindlessly, not paying much attention to my surroundings. I sorted my bottles from my cardboard and placed a trash bag in a large brown dumpster.

Then I turned and decided to walk the full length of a long

grassy patch of ground that stretched behind the apartments. I stepped from the asphalt onto the damp green earth and instantly slipped into a vision. I was walking in a line of men toward another line of men at the far end of a field. It was obvious to me that a skirmish of some kind was about to take place. I made note that we were armed with very primitive weapons: staffs, clubs, some swords, even a few farm tools.

As the two columns of men drew closer, there were war cries, and the two groups headed for one another in a full run. Just as swiftly as this vision had absorbed me, it left me. I found myself standing nearly halfway down the grassy park toward another parking lot. The images still whirled in my head, but I had returned to ordinary reality. To this day I do not know the source of this visionary flow, but every cell in my body senses an ancestral and historical relevance to my gaining this awareness.

I fell into a similar visionary stupor a few months later. Some dear friends of mine knew that I had done gardening before and had asked me to prepare a field with a rototiller. At a certain point I took a break from the plowing. Other friends had gathered to assist, and someone let go of a shovel, which fell to the ground, striking some of the other tools that lay there. This simple sound of clanking metal tools seemed to split my head open.

I had a vision of a small croft (farm) in what I would later realize were the Scottish Highlands, though I did not know that at the time. It was almost as if I were surveying the scene through the eyes of an ancestor. I could still see ordinary reality, namely my friends standing around the tools, drinking beer and eating watermelon, yet I also caught a shimmering glimpse of a nonordinary scene, specifically that I was a middle-aged farmer with two teenage sons. They were wrestling and laughing near an old stone wall. I could see a small stone cottage with a thatched roof and a cow, and a horse standing nearby. Suddenly one of my friends asked if I wanted something to drink, and my consciousness was swiftly brought back from Celtic soil to Colorado.

I still do not know, to this day, whether I was having a composite ancestral memory or a glimpse into some kind of past life. In the end, it does not matter. What matters is that I was being made aware of the power of the sacred world, and the only obstacle to being able to fully receive this gift was my own conditioning and the limits of my consciousness.

In animistic cultures it is understood that the spirit world leaks through to this world in a number of ways, times, and places. In reality the spirited dimensions permeate our physical universe, so the influence of the spirits (or the Spirit, depending on your cosmology) is never very far away. As John O'Donohue once said, "The spiritual journey is only as far as the end of your own nose."[1] The holy powers that wake us up to our life (and to other lives) are that close.

In some shamanist traditions it is understood that in the process of an initiation, the spirit world can reach through the permeable membrane between the worlds. Sometimes these forces gracefully touch us, like a warm southerly wind. Sometimes they throttle us! Stories abound in various cultures, from the Inuit to the Inca, of people receiving the shaman's call who are then "dismembered" by spirit animals and then put back together again by these spirits. In my case, I felt that the influence of spirit forces, ancestors, and the matrix of the spiritual world itself initially attempted to coax me gently to wake up. Then the process became steadily more intense until I began to listen with the proper ears.

In various traditions, a similar energetic process occurs for poets, artists, and sacred musicians, who can become so engulfed by the power of the *imbas* (divine inspiration in the Gaelic bardic traditions), the muse, and the creative powers that they are blown

---

1 John O'Donohue, Anam Cara: *Wisdom of the Celtic World* (Boulder, Colo.: Sounds True Audio, 1996).

apart. They experience a divine madness. These inspired people are only "put back together again" through close contact with the healing power of the natural world and through the natural closure of a creative act. Over time, just like shamans and mystics, they learn to master this powerful fire, and their experience becomes much more integrated.

During many first initiations, people have experienced potent ancestral presences draw near to them. Other knowledge sources suddenly become available. An awareness of other times in history forcibly impinges on their current place on the spiral of time. For the unguided these revelations can be quite disorienting, destabilizing, and sometimes frightening. They certainly were for me.

For me these events, or "flares," as I came to think of them, involved imagery and energies I did not understand. I liken this process to being in a foreign country, trying to make my way through unfamiliar terrain, a terrain whose landmarks and road signs we have only read or heard about. Upon arrival to the foreign shores of initiation, however, we suddenly realize that we really aren't able to read the road signs at all. We are lost, without direction. We slowly lose our sense of grounding in where and who we thought we are.

During this period before my illness, I saw flashes of people's faces in dreams. I felt spirits and other beings draw near me and then disappear. I began to have brief visions of symbols I would later find in Scotland, in books about Ireland, and even in other tribal cultures. I had no real context for extrapolating the purpose or meaning of these experiences at that point. I felt like I was blindly running through a forest, hitting every tree on my way through. With the onset of my illness came an overall sense of being consumed from the inside out. I had no sense of clear direction in life. I was living day in and day out feeling that my life energy had been drained from me, siphoned off by an unseen force. I groped and grasped for my center. It was not to be found.

Without any real way of articulating or understanding what was happening, I simply withdrew from life and became more and more depressed. *Depressed* may even be too light a word. I felt beaten. A deep sense of shame washed over me during this time. I clung tenaciously to outworn notions of myself as a person who had always stoically "done it alone." I was the guy (in my own mind) who always had it together, who never missed a beat. Not anymore.

Suddenly, the weave of my identity, the ego-centered (and often egotistical) representation of how I hoped to be seen by the outer world withered as I withered. My life began to unwind. I was unclear, angry, depleted. I did not maneuver the terrain of my inner turmoil with much fluency or grace. As if this were not bad enough, my relationship to a woman I loved with all my life began to fray at the edges and, then, slowly closed in on itself as I closed in on myself. I snapped at people. I boiled. I had the archetypal "fire in the head" of Celtic tradition but not the know-how to direct its power to wholesome aims.

I distinctly remember the moment when I gave up. I awoke one morning and stumbled into the bathroom. The room spun beneath the weight of my fever. I splashed water on my face in an attempt to cool my flaming brow. Suddenly, a tremor rippled through my every cell. My hold on reality was gone. I no longer cared. I wept at this realization. I looked in the mirror and trembled at what I saw. I did not recognize the face of the chap staring back at me. The face and the self I had known myself to be had disappeared.

THE OLD TRADITION

Under the oak of the druid
we wait by the stream at Cwm Buchan.
Discovering its shadows and silence,

its secret falling water
turning toward night.

And deeper even than the stillness of night
is this quiet, now given over to water,
the faint whisper of rising wind
and the first rustle of leaves on the oak.

Here we study the old tradition
— giving up what was never possessed.

Here we run our fingers along the sharp
strange edge of silence
feeling the blade that cuts away the self.

And the man I was, just a moment before
is also there in the silence, cupping his hands,
drinking deep draughts with the thirst
of one who is wounded.

My voice insistent, I startle him.
"Stop drinking,
I forgive you your selfish life."

One astonished moment of surprise
then the cupped reflection
swaying beneath his face
slips between the interwoven fingers
drops to the surface and dies.

— FROM *WHERE MANY RIVERS MEET*, DAVID WHYTE[2]

---

2 David Whyte, *Where Many Rivers Meet* (Langley, Wash.: Many Rivers Press, 1990), pp. 74–75.

I continued to lay awake every night, unable to eat, wheezing violently, my incessant coughing preventing my girlfriend from sleeping. I was caught in a psychosomatic state of paralysis. Meanwhile, my partner was beside herself, not knowing what to do or how to help me. Even the doctors were becoming frustrated by their attempts to figure out what could effect real change in my condition. Their approach was to treat only the body; yet the source of this powerful illness had its roots in another reality.

A few days after my phone conversation with Two Trees, a small box arrived in the mail. Inside were a variety of brown jars, some with pills, others with strange gelatinous materials that smelled like roadkill on a hot Texas highway. There was a bottle of silica gel, something Two Trees had called "Cherokee bitters," and a few other things that were so "nasty," to use Two Trees's words, that no one had bothered to name them. They were just called the "green bottle" and the "small brown bottle."

That same day I began my strict regimen of ingesting herbs, such as mullein tea, as well as various other concoctions and nectars, following the nearly encyclopedic instructions that had been written out for me. With a fever that fluctuated between 103 and 105 degrees at any given time, I was willing to try anything, including Cherokee bitters. I've often said in hindsight, "Cherokee bitters will either make you better or kill you." I think they did both.

THE SPIRIT OF THE WILD GOOSE

Three nights after beginning to take my medicines, it happened. I had an experience that has changed the way I view my life. Even now, more than a decade later, I am still only gradually beginning to integrate this experience and its ramifications into the larger trajectory of my life. In a single night my life path went from being one of great suffering to one of great relief and knowing. With this knowing came the understanding of how little I really knew about the spiritual life and the sacred world within which the spiritual life occurs.

On this particular evening my fever was high. I had been awake for a while, but eventually fell off into a strange half-sleep at around 1:00 A.M. By now my partner had adopted a new sleeping routine of lying beside me until I drifted off at night, and then she would go into the living room, where she would collapse on the couch to get some uninterrupted sleep, devoid of my thunderous coughing and mumblings. I had begun to experience auditory hallucinations of various kinds associated with my fever, and apparently I was answering them.

Some time around 3:00 A.M., my spirit slowly arose, and I found myself standing beside the bed, looking back at my frail body clinging helplessly to the sheets. Although I had experienced fleeting moments of involuntary astral travel (out-of-body experiences) when I was younger, when I looked down at my body I knew that this was different. I was dying. I looked closer at my chest, my torso contorted from the discomfort of feverish sleep, and I saw that I had stopped breathing. I tried to rouse my body for several minutes but was unsuccessful. The weight of what was happening hit me and, suddenly an enormous wave of fear overtook me. "What have I done wrong?" I thought. Slowly the fear was replaced by an odd sense of peaceful resignation. "I'm going to die."

I wandered through my apartment and stood beside my girlfriend for a moment, watching her as she slept peacefully. I looked down at her with deep remorse in my heart for not having been a better companion, always self-absorbed and rarely emotionally available to her. I wished that I could tell her how much I loved her, but I knew it was too late. I bid her farewell in my own way, and then I continued on.

I found that if I conjured the image of a location that I had been to in my mind (in what I call the visioning eye), within a matter of seconds I could be there, spirit traveling faster than the speed of light. I traveled quickly to my mother's home, then to my father's, then to my grandparents', and even to the homes of different friends around the country. I stood next to their bedsides and attempted to stir them with my thoughts. In all cases my presence was not felt.

I wept over the sight of my mother, wept that I would not speak to her again, that I would not be able to thank her for all that she had done for me. My heart was seared by sharp pain upon realizing that I could have been a better son to my father, a better grandson to my grandparents. I had said so many hurtful things, and now I would not be able to heal these wounds. So many things had been left unsaid. Death grants no leniency, and I felt so powerfully the truth that one of our worst fates is to die holding a grudge against a loved one.

As I thought about my life, deep feelings surfaced that I had not made something of myself. The feeling that I "could have been more" continued to flash through my soul. I found that the only thing I could do was to hope that the people in my life would know that I loved them and that somehow I would make more of my life the next time around.

After a while I found myself back in my apartment, in Boulder, Colorado, and returned to my own bedside. I looked down and saw that I still was not breathing. My body was in the same position as it had been in before. Our cat had taken up a spot at the foot of the bed and was studying me attentively. Suddenly, to my sheer horror, I realized that something was different. My body still lay there, motionless, and then it dawned on me: I was not alone in the room. I could feel that very near me was a presence. It was my first experience of visually perceiving a disembodied entity since my childhood.

As I've mentioned, as a very young child in Georgia I would see ghosts, spirits, and other unexplainable things moving about our house at all hours of the night. This experience was not out of the ordinary for me then, but as I grew older I lost this ability. Perhaps I lost the ability, or perhaps it was socialization. Truthfully, I think I ceased to really pay attention to such things and, like unused muscles, these senses atrophied.

Now, in the moment of this out-of-body wandering, something struck me as very different. The shifting energies of the room finally settled like swirling dust. I could feel the spirit standing right beside me. The thought of encountering a spirit was not unnerving to me until I realized that I too was disembodied and very much in the element of the spirits. Somehow I felt unprotected, completely open, vulnerable.

I turned to my left, very slowly, to find that the spirit was an old man. He felt oddly familiar to me, but on closer examination of his features, I knew I did not recognize him from this life. He had long silver hair, a beard, and a scar that ran straight down his face from forehead to chin through the area of his right eye. He was clad in some kind of black robe. The old man winked and smiled at me and then held his finger up, pointing to the sky. As he did this, I heard a sound from far off in the distance to the west. It was the sound of a flock of honking geese slowly approaching. The sound grew increasingly louder as the flock drew near.

As the geese reached the air space above the apartment, the old man and I were suddenly whisked up and away, as if we had been sucked up by some warm unseen wind. We were enveloped in the eerie sound of the honking geese, clothed in the light of twilight. I was astonished. Our spirits were flying with the geese, miles and miles of landscape passing underneath us.

The next thing I remember is the sky becoming illuminated by the dawn sun. The old man directed my attention to some sort of structure on the ground below us. At first I could not really make out what the place was or why I would be there, but as we drew closer, I realized that the ancient circle on the ground in front of me was a traditional northern plains Sun Dance arbor, used for the annual Sun Dance ceremonies of the Lakota, Cheyenne, Crow, Mandan, and Hidatsa.

I looked at the old man and then back at the Sun Dance grounds. I could see people dancing inside the arbor, bobbing up and down to the sound of a drum. As I scanned the faces of the various dancers, much to my surprise, I noticed that one of the dancers was me, completely decked out in traditional Sun Dance regalia, holy prayer pipe in hand, head crowned with a sage wreath.

In a style of communication I can only describe as a transmission of thoughts and guidance, the old man began to tell me how I was being given an important choice. I was being shown that if I wanted to live I could, but that it would require a decision on my part. I was also told that if I wanted to die, this was also possible and, again, would be determined by my choice. Like life, death is very often a matter of a choice made by the soul. I had to choose, and with this choice I would have to lean fully into whatever I decided.

I was told that if I chose life, my life would no longer be my own. I would live a life in service of something much greater than I. I was told that if I chose life, it would be a life under certain directives. In other words, my life, as I had known it before, would be over. If I chose death, then my lungs would remain the same (nonfunctioning). I would already have taken my last breath. I would be carried forth to another place by the old man.

Largely because of my emotional state of the time, I actually spent what felt like a long while pondering my choice. The faces of loved ones floated in front of me. Scenes from my childhood came to me. Glimpses of possible futures unfolded before me. The images, thoughts, and impressions that came to me were woven in with deep churning emotions that were quite overwhelming. I felt powerless, gripped by unresolved anger that seethed and splashed on others. Yet these very heavy emotions were countered with images of the faces of loved ones and even loved ones yet to come, including the faces of my unborn children. I saw future friends, some of whom I have now met. I saw future colleagues, some of whom I now work with. I saw other people who would play an integral role in my life later on, including some I have yet to cross paths with.

Like a woven cord, these visions kept me tied to my life. I realized the full weight of the decision. I thought about the physical pains my mother endured to bring me into this world. I thought of the many sacrifices that my parents, my partner, and other friends had made for me along the way. All these things were very present in my awareness when I made my decision.

Life.

I remember the sense of relief I had even at the thought of the word: life. Life. Making the decision to live after being so close to death was a visceral experience. Deciding to live, even though my life would no longer be my life alone, was a highly somatic sensation of shifting my will into the "on" position, so to speak. I was told (again in a streaming surge of thoughts and images) that I needed to express my commitment to my decision outwardly in some way.

As Above, So Below

Like all shamanistic or mystical traditions whose initiates have received the call through death and ancestral intervention, I was being given my first instruction about the shamanist path. The ancient Mist-Filled Path was telling me that *the act of embodying in the outer world through ritual gesture what has already taken place in the heart or in the spirit world is a crucial and necessary step in forming a power-filled relationship with God.*

I looked back down at the Sun Dance arbor and spoke my oath to the old man, telling him that I would dance in the Sun Dance the following summer. With this, the old man moved closer to me, reached inside my chest, and removed a large mass of tar-like material from my lungs. He broke this thick ball of dark sludge into four pieces and cast each piece into the four directions, declaring something with each throw in a language I did not know but that felt deeply comforting to me.

The old man turned back to me and placed his left hand on my visioning eye (in the center of the forehead). When he did this I "saw" what he saw. For a fleeting moment I saw what must have been hundreds of thousands of images, all flashing across my mind in rapid quicksilver fashion. Some of these images were of places I would visit later, such as the hill of Dunadd in western Scotland. Other images I would find in picture books later on, such as the Grianan of Aileach on the Inishowen Peninsula in northern Ireland or a tree-ringed hill fort in County Tyrone, Ireland, called Tullaghoge. I have never been to Ireland, and I know a pilgrimage to places of such importance in my ancestral lineage will be powerful.

Though I could not integrate many of these images, I knew that this initial information had been transmitted to me in such a way that I would have access to it later. Most of the time I do not even remember some of these images until I encounter something that serves as an outward reminder. I will be remembering for the rest of my life.

One vision was of the old man sitting in a circle of people, surrounded by old trees. This image stayed with me for a much longer time than the others and had more the quality of memory than of anything else. A fire was burning in the center of the circle, casting a warm and inviting glow on the faces of all the people. At first sight I assumed they must all be Native Americans, but slowly I began to notice that all the people sitting in the grove of trees looked like me. I had a deeply healing realization that all the people in the circle were somehow connected to me. These were some of my ancestors.

Even within this vision I remember feeling confused, the image of these non-Natives as well as the Sun Dance arbor held tightly by my awareness. The vision faded gradually and, with this, the old man moved closer to me again. Suddenly he hit me in the center of my chest very hard. With a gasp, my spirit, or what the Scottish tradition refers to as a *taibhs,* returned to my body, and I sat upright in bed with a start.

I wiped a night's worth of sweat from my forehead and rubbed my eyes for several moments. Gradually coming into a fuller awareness of my bodily sensations, I realized I could not initially remember many of the details of the night's events, though I had an eerie sensation that something significant had transpired. I took a deep breath as my eyes were drawn to the dawning sky outside my window.

The sun filled my heart as a deep, life-fulfilling breath filled my chest.

With a sudden jolt, I realized that I had taken a completely unobstructed breath of fresh air into both lungs. I could breathe! For what felt like eons I had not breathed a normal breath, so this experience was the closest thing to heaven I had known. I jumped from the bed and scurried into the kitchen. I grabbed a mug, made myself a cup of coffee, and took the fresh aroma into my nostrils. The simplicity of this action was profound. I could have been filmed in that moment for a coffee commercial! I was filled with the purity of gratitude.

What happened in the next moment snapped my soul like a rubber band.

As I stood drinking my coffee, looking out the window at the rising sun, a flock of geese from a nearby park flew directly by the window. Everything collapsed into slow motion. My mug slipped from my hand as this synchronicity rippled through my awareness and brought into my mind the full knowing of what had taken place for me in the middle of the night. As if I were suddenly remembering a dream previously forgotten, all I could do was lean against the windowsill and whisper, "the goose, the goose."

I had walked with the spirits. I had flown with the spirit of the wild goose and with a spirit I now take to be a shaman-druid ancestor. I had stopped breathing. I had been given the choice of life or death. I also knew that I had chosen life. Coupled with the remembrance of all these elements came the horrifying memory that I had made an oath to the old man, a vow, to dance in the Sun Dance the following summer. Immediately I began to interpret my experiences as merely symbolic. I tried to rationalize away the importance of this spirit journey, saying to myself that everything must have been a dream. Surely the many images I had seen had been only an expression of an intrapsychic phenomenon that did not need to be acted on literally. Certainly these experiences were just metaphorical, a dream symbol to decode, right?

CHAPTER 5

DANCING THE SUN

Before the coming of Christianity, the religion of Scotland was Druidism, a form of sun-worship peculiar to the Celtic peoples. Like all sun-cults, it was based upon a universal doctrine regarding the two states of existence — the one in the visible world, and the other in the invisible or lower world.

— F. MARIAN MCNEILL, SCOTTISH HISTORIAN[1]

I was very quiet about my experiences. I had not completely come to terms with them, so I did not have the impulse to share my latest foray into the realm of the spiritual with anyone. I was especially quiet with my partner. I was quite content to allow her to think that my problems had been resolved by Two Trees's remedies alone. I was extraordinarily quiet about the events of that month with the Indian people I knew. Largely through introductions by my mother, I had been attending ceremonies with various First Nations people since my midteens, including

1 F. Marian McNeill, *The Silver Bough*, vol. 1 (Edinburgh: Canongate, 1956), p. 12.

Cherokee, Iroquois, Ojibway, and Lakota people. I had learned how to be a "good guest" and did not want to seem like an "Indian wannabe" by sharing these experiences. I also did not know what the ramifications would be of relaying such an account in more traditional circles. Despite my silence I was eventually "found out," you might say, and it was then that I realized that there is no getting around destiny.

In early December of that year, about a month after my near-fatal soul flight, I was sitting in a traditional *channunpa* (pipe) ceremony with a group of people. As the pipe was passed from hand to hand, each person lifted prayers of smoke and sat in silence. At the end of the ceremony, as the pipe was pulled apart and placed back inside its sacred home (pipe bag), suddenly I was met by the stares of three people. I looked at them blankly, not knowing what was happening. Had I forgotten some crucial aspect of the ceremony?

The primary facilitator of the pipe ceremony looked at me sharply and asked, "Do you have something you want to tell me?" My whole body was jolted, and my stomach churned, as if I had fallen some great distance suddenly without control.

"I, I, don't really know what you mean?" I replied shyly, seeking to be respectful, but also feeling both truly perplexed by and afraid of the question.

Another person involved in the pipe ceremony, a mixed-blood Native American/African American woman named Judy Fatu Henderson, squinted her eyes at me as if to say she knew something I did not. I remained quiet. The medicine person continued putting the pipe away and then stopped in the middle of tying up the bundle and looked at me again.

"Well, you may not have something to tell me, but I've got something to tell you. The spirits say that you are going to be in the arbor this summer. They say you're going to the Sun Dance."

The Sun Dance, known as *Wiwanyag Wacipi* in the Lakota, Dakota, and Nakota tongues, is considered the most holy ceremony of all those that form the Lakota cosmological complex of ritual life.

Preparing to Dance

A month after the pipe ceremony I found myself before a circle of traditional elders in South Dakota, pledging that I would be a dancer in the Sun Dance that next summer. We met in an eight-sided roundhouse, a kind of modern hoganlike structure made of aluminum siding and a concrete floor, on a traditional family homestead near Kyle, South Dakota, where the Sun Dance would take place. One elder in particular talked at length about the Sun Dance path and the importance of making it "an everyday path, not just four days in the summer."

To be part of a traditional Sun Dance one must pass through a few "gates," you might say. First, it is required that you be sponsored by someone already within the inner circle of the traditions. Second, you must make an oath on the pipe that you are going to prepare yourself and dance with integrity. Third, after passing through the first two gates, a prospective Sun Dancer enters into a phase of preparation that lasts all the months preceding the actual ceremony, sometimes as much as a year in advance. These preparations, the details of which I do not have permission to reveal, also include going on prayer fasts (known as *hanbleceya* in the Lakota tongue), participating in sweat houses (*inipi*), and getting a variety of materials ready, such as a ceremonial half-robe called a Sun Dance skirt.

About halfway through my preparations I encountered an incredible wall of resistance in myself to Sun Dancing. I was sponsored to dance by the assistant to the primary medicine man of the

Sun Dance. I had made an oath to prepare myself accordingly and to dance with integrity. However, midway through a vision quest (a traditional rite of praying and fasting alone in the wilderness to seek guidance or a vision) I had a breakdown.

I was sitting inside my vision-quest circle. Some time on the second day I was praying intently, occasionally singing a prayer song to beseech the guidance and protection of the spirits, when I opened my eyes to find the old man sitting just outside my circle looking at me. His face was beaming. He smiled at me in recognition and had only one thing to impart. He declared, "If you do not own all of who you are, you will die in the Sun Dance."

As if lightning had just struck me, I fell over in my prayer circle and began shivering with an intense fear. In reality I had made great strides in processing my near-death experience. These experiences generally produce a heightened state of fearlessness in the person who has survived such an ordeal. Up until that point I had noticed this kind of fearlessness in my own life. However, for some reason, with this statement from the old man, my soul was split open by both paralysis and horror. I had chosen life when I was *walking between the worlds* with the old man. Now it seemed that there was a change and I could have my life taken away again.

I glanced upward from my place in the circle, where I lay in a fetal position, shivering. The old man smiled again and turned into a deer. The deer looked down at me for a moment longer and trotted off into the Colorado scrub pine forest surrounding my vision-fast circle.

If I do not own all of who I am, I will *die* in the Sun Dance?

What did I need to own? What had I disowned?

I did not know what his words meant, and I was not sure I wanted to know. I could barely breathe again, and this shortness of breath brought back into my awareness the vow I had made to the old man. My life was over as I understood it, and it was now guided by the prompts of a sacred world around me. But now I was horrified by the thought of what might be in store for me.

When you go on a traditional Lakota *hanbleceya,* you must stay in your circle. On that day, I did not. I stood up, made a final prayer to the four directions, and left. As I stumbled along slowly in bare feet over rocks and pinecones, I began to experience waves of intense nausea.

"What am I doing dancing in a Lakota Sun Dance? These are a warrior people. They are genetically designed by the South Dakota landscape to be able to Sun Dance. I'm a white boy. I'm going to die!" I rambled on and on in my mind, continually coming up with deflective thoughts and justifications of why I should not be dancing.

"I'm from the oppressor culture. I don't belong in their ceremonies. They don't want me there. I don't come from a warrior people. Surely I will die."

As I made my way from my vision-quest circle back toward the vacant sweat lodge area we had used earlier, I stepped right on top of a ground cactus. I fell over onto the earth, successfully embedding another four cacti into my left shoulder and hip. Cursing under my breath, I pulled myself up and began removing the small cactus spines from my sunburned foot and side. Luckily no one else was around to witness my embarrassing moment, though I thought I heard even the trees laughing at me that afternoon.

The cactus spines, as they entered my body, pierced my awareness as well. This pause in the incessant ramblings of my mind caused me to reentertain the challenge put forth by the old man. I needed to own all parts of myself, or I would die. I never told anyone about this visitation and I never told anyone about leaving my circle. I simply slinked back to my humble seat in that circle on the earth and prayed to be guided through the next few months.

When I returned to my home in Boulder, Colorado, I called

up my sponsor for the Sun Dance and informed him I was not going to South Dakota. I was not going to be a Sun Dancer. He, of course, inquired about the reasons, and I told him that I did not feel ready, that I did not think I had what it takes — physically or psychologically. The discussion was short, and he did not have much to say to me, although it was evident that he was disappointed.

Our second call was harder. He had spoken with the elders, including the primary holy man who was to lead the Sun Dance for which I had been preparing. None of them was happy that I was thinking of not attending. When I asked my sponsor what the response had been, he replied, "They prayed about you, and the spirits said you are being swayed by unnecessary fears. You are living from your fear right now." He had called to inform me of this.

He went on to inform me that if I did not come to the Sun Dance, to fulfill my oath of dancing in the ceremony that year, that he would have to take on my commitment and dance in my stead. I began to get a sense of both the political and spiritual ramifications of my absence. It made him look bad in the eyes of the elders. It also offset the energetic signature of the ceremony in its preparation because I had been "woven into the altar." They were expecting me, and my lack of follow-through made it appear that he had sponsored someone who was taking the whole thing very lightly. I was not taking it lightly, however. Rather, I was profoundly aware of the weightiness of the matter and scared to death because of it.

In time, both through more dialogue with my sponsor and with our mutual friends, I decided that I could not let him stand in for me on an oath I had made. It was not his problem or fault that I was afraid. But the definitive factor that caused me to go was a brief exchange I had with my friend Fatu. Our conversation was my saving grace. Her words were something to trust in, and I clung to them as if they were a shield. However, psychologically I also began to prepare myself for what felt like a real possibility: death by the Sun Dance.

The words that changed my mind were these: "What do you think the Sun Dance is really about?" "I don't know. Prayers? Power? Spiritual development?" I responded, feeling like a deer in the headlights of an oncoming truck.

"It is about love, *kola.* It is about love, my friend," Fatu explained. "Until you learn to love yourself, you will never fully love your life."

A Sleeping Lineage Awakens

Growing up, I knew very little about my Celtic roots. Like many of us who are part of the Celtic diaspora, I remember bits and pieces of my childhood that hinted at our Celtic origins, but my family never spoke of them overtly.

I now realize that there were elements of our Highland and Irish heritage that seemed to pour through to us quite strongly. My childhood memories of both sides of my family are filled with storytelling, cooking, hunting, hillwalking, fly-fishing, poetry, and woodworking, as well as more spirit-based qualities such as moments of the "sight." Now I know that these leanings come to us from our Celtic ancestors. This description of my family may fit many post-diaspora Celtic families today. Let us celebrate them.

From time to time I also remember my paternal grandfather speaking about "our ancestors, the Irish kings," the "Welshmen" in our lines, and on a few occasions his barking out "when Saint Patrick chased the snakes out of Ireland it was our people he was chasing away." I knew that we descended from "hill people," but I did not have a clear sense of what this meant. My grandfather had heard these things all his life from his Irish aunts, who were convinced they were Irish royalty. Later I came to learn that the story of Saint Patrick banishing the snakes from Ireland was, in fact, a way of speaking symbolically about his challenge to the authority of the druids. Of course, the only thing that was banished was an organized presence of institutional druidism. In its stead we see both a culturally sanctioned rural bardic tradition and, in many cases, the theological mantle of the druids being thinly covered by the mantle of the Celtic Church. So, in effect, the druids did not go anywhere; they merely transformed.

These anecdotes eventually made sense to me. The old family sayings now hold a great deal more meaning for me than they did when I first heard them. Although only partially historically accurate (our family did not come to America until the Famine, long after the decline of the druids in the time of St. Patrick), suddenly a quaint family story felt like a living stream of knowledge that flowed backward into time.

I would also learn that part of our pedigree descends from the U'Neill High Kings of Ireland. Our Ewing/MacLachlan/MacEwen blood places us along an ancient line known for its Celtic poets, along with a number of well-known primal ancestors and kin, such as Niall of the Nine Hostages and Columkille (Saint Columba) of the Celtic Church.

On my maternal side there is an equal amount of Irish, Welsh, and Scottish Highland and Scottish Borders blood, mixed with some Northumbrian as well. Again, this side of my family did not consciously celebrate or participate in our Celtic roots when I was younger, but we were distinctively a Southern storytelling family. We would gather around the fire and tell story after story. I remember my maternal grandmother, Nonnie, declaring one day that "we'd fought for the Stewarts." Another day I heard a story about a desk still in the family that had been in Borthwick Castle and had been used by a house servant of Mary Queen of Scots. Our Scots-Irish family traditions governed that "the oldest daughter or oldest female cousin always inherits the desk." It had come over from Scotland and was passed down through the family when we were still "hill people." The desk was constructed using only wooden pegs, no nails, and even to this day people say there is a secret compartment in it.

This was the extent of my knowledge of our Celtic roots. I remember that whenever I asked relatives on either side of my family about "our people," I would hear simply, "We are Scots-Irish." So you can imagine that I did not completely know what I was supposed to do in approaching the work of "owning all of myself," as the old man had put it. Without any real sense of direction, I found myself naturally turning toward some deeper understanding of my cultural roots.

About a month before the Sun Dance I was able to trace and confirm some of our family names in the genealogical records on both sides of my family. By initially studying the etymological roots of our particular family names, I learned that our ancestral lines hailed from the Scottish Highlands, the Scottish Borders, Ireland, Wales, the Isle of Man, Cornwall, Brittany, and Orkney. These ancient family names poured into my soul as if they ached to be remembered. The more I discovered about these Celtic names and their locations, the more a powerful surge of energy began to vibrate within my being, both when I was awake and when I was asleep.

Some of the mystical experiences that had led up to my illness began to make sense to me. The images that had come and that had held so much potent energy began to feel comfortable and, indeed, familiar. A kind of cellular knowing washed over me, and it was as if even the smallest mention of something Scottish or Irish or Celtic would spark something deep and familiar inside me. Suddenly, the process of "owning all of who I am" was not nearly the fear-ridden process I had imagined it would be. I started to feel quenched, soothed, embraced by something.

At some point during this brief research phase I encountered an article that talked about the Scottish Highlanders being the modern-day descendants of various ancient bloodlines. Some of the Highland clans are of Norse descent, others of Irish Gaelic ancestry, others are considered Strathclyde Britons, while a few are the living descendants of the ancient Pictish tribes. A statement in the article read, "The Scottish Highlanders and Caledonians were a warrior people who turned back even the armies of Rome."

"They were a warrior people, like the Lakota?" I gasped. I wrote these latest findings from this article down in my journal and began to contemplate them. Why had I not been told growing up that I was not just a cultureless American and that I did, in fact, have bloodlines that went back to something powerful, such as a culture of warriors, a culture of druids, a culture of bards, poets, saints, and midwives? I had internalized the notion that to survive the Sun Dance one must be a strong warrior. It was something of a relief to feel that I had descended from a people who could endure intensity.

Even deeper, however, I began to come to a profound realization about my life with this newly discovered sense of my ancient Celtic ancestry. For nearly a decade I had identified with the tribal perspective of First Nations peoples. I had learned their songs. I had studied how to lead specific ceremonies, such as the purification lodge. I had also identified with the political struggle of indigenous peoples in North America and was involved as an activist at one point. I had harbored anger at the U. S. government for all the treaties that were signed but that have never been honored. Something ancient inside me boiled with rage that it took the U. S. government until 1979 to formally grant indigenous people in this country religious freedom. If it were not for Jimmy Carter, who signed the American Indian Freedom of Religion Act, native people might still be having to hide and meet in private to worship the Creator in their way.

As I examined the underpinnings of my connection to First

Nations people, however, I realized that two things were happening. One is that I was connecting vicariously and unconsciously with my Celtic roots through my time "behind the buckskin curtain" of Native America. Second, I felt so much guilt and pain about what the U. S. government, and perhaps even some of my own ancestors in the South, had done to the First Nations, that I began to identify more with Native American culture than with my own white background, about which I knew very little.

I had been playing a psychological trick on myself by over-identifying with Native Americans and denying my European background. It was too painful to admit to myself that I hailed, at least in part, from the culture that had been responsible for crushing an ancient way of life. And yet, with the realization that my own ancestors hailed from an ancient way of life that had been equally displaced by incoming raiders my empathy and, therefore, my actions could be rooted in the true spirit of solidarity and not in my clinging need for them to accept me to absolve me of my "whiteness."

Turning to the oppressed for absolution to feel okay about our presence in this land has its problems. It denies who we really are and prevents a new alliance from forming. For us to bow down before the archetypal New Age rendition of the "wise old Indian" in hopes that he will say, "It's okay. We're glad you're here" is a fallacy. We are here. There is no changing this fact. But there remains the potential of changing things politically and socially between the dominant culture and the surviving indigenous people in our own backyard by voting in ways that will begin the reparation that needs to be done. The problem is that these issues are not even in the consciousness of most North Americans, as evidenced by the continued incarceration of Leonard Peltier (Ojibway-Lakota).[2]

---

2 Despite appeals from the Dalai Lama, Coretta Scott King, Nelson Mendela, Desmond Tutu, members of Congress, former FBI agents, and the U.N. Commissioner of Human Rights (Mary Robinson), Peltier remains in prison after twenty-five years.

It is too comfortable to simply reap the rewards of American Indian spiritual wisdom without regard to the political plight of most Native Americans. It is only from standing in our own selves, as descendants of a northern European tradition (or Latino or Asian or African, etc.) that we can bring about any of the needed changes in relations between the U. S. government and Indian America, or indeed between any ethnic groups where wounds still exist. If you are a Celtic descendant, one who hails from ancestors who faced racism, forced removal, and exile, it is a dynamic travesty, especially in the face of our own ancestral wounds, to hold fast to a worldview that maintains racial division and oppression in our communities.

For myself, as a non-Indian, I came to realize that I can only truly love my Native American brothers and sisters, and participate in their ceremonies if invited, if I connect to them as a post-diaspora Celtic person — an American, yes, but also the living descendant of an ancient earth people who were forced to relocate. At this point on my path I became aware that I was a descendant of a sleeping lineage that was beginning to stir. But before I delved much further into my thoughts about these matters, I was on the road to the Pine Ridge Reservation in South Dakota to see if I had owned enough of myself — or if I was going to die.

Drawing Back the Veils

When one enters into the Sun Dance arbor, a Sun Dancer is ushered in by the deafening sound of what the Lakota singers call the "big drum." The powerful thwack of the four-foot drum sends a tremor through one's whole being. You feel as if you are on a death march. In hindsight, I can say that this is the most appropriate music for the ceremony. Everything I knew of reality melted like butter on a hot sweat lodge stone in the Sun Dance. It was very much a dying that took place, a dying of an old way of seeing. But it was also the rebirth of an even older way of seeing.

Most of the dancers who enter the Sun Dance are dancing for four full days, fasting from food and water, in a scorching 112-degree South Dakota sun. When I danced I was a "new dancer," a "one-timer." The Lakotas would say I was dancing a *wopila,* a thanksgiving. I had been fasting for three days when I entered the Sun Dance arbor on the morning of the last day. Pipe in one hand, eagle feather in the other, I also held an eagle bone whistle in my mouth. My head, hands, and ankles were wrapped in sage wreaths, and I wore a cobalt-blue Sun Dance skirt that my mother had sewn for me as part of my preparation.

There is no way to fully articulate the experience of the Sun Dance, both because words fall short and because I cannot reveal all the inner dimensions of the ceremony out of respect for what I was taught. Suffice it to say, however, that the Sun Dance is an intense and grueling ordeal that pushes the dancer past every known boundary.

Starting at dawn and ending near dusk, I danced in what turned out to be the western gate of the Sun Dance ceremonial arbor, a direction often associated with vision, the spirits of the ancestors, and the healing power of water and mist. As I bobbed up and down in my place in the circle of Sun Dancers, my consciousness began to change, induced by the heat, the fasting, and the prayers of those around me. Very subtle shifts began to occur, and I had a variety of experiences through my otherworldly senses. I was aware of certain transmutations of sounds, which only served to put me into an even deeper altered state of consciousness.

At one point, the big drum's rhythm, tone, and beat began to change dramatically. The usual single beat and one-two, one-two rhythm of the Sun Dance drum started to come through in my ears as a polyrhythmic one-two-three-four-five, one-two-three-four-five. Looking back, I realize that what I was hearing was the ancient rhythm of a Celtic drum, known as the *bodhran* (pronounced bo-rawn) in Scots Gaelic and Irish. As I heard these rhythms my mind flashed back to my near-death vision of the people sitting in the trees around the fire.

The second transmutation of sound occurred whenever the medicine man raised his eagle wing fan and all the dancers were expected to blow vigorously through our eagle bone whistles. For almost the entire day I noticed nothing of particular importance about the shrill of the whistles, but as I entered into a deeper shamanic state of consciousness, their high-pitched squeal turned into the sound of the bagpipes. At that moment I began to have the eerie sensation that something was about to happen to me, not just on a spiritual or visionary level, but also in my body. I tried to anchor myself in my senses, but they failed me. Being a firm "see-it-to-believe-it" kind of guy, I thought that my mind was just playing tricks on me.

On the heels of this very doubting thought, I suddenly had the bizarre sensation that all around my feet was a moist and cool air, as if mist had slithered in and around my place in the circle. This, of course, did not compute, since the tops of my feet were sunburned from the same sun that bakes the South Dakota earth.

Soon it was my time to participate in the piercing, an intense and widely misunderstood dimension of the northern plains Sun Dance religion. Piercing is an art form and involves the male dancer approaching the central tree of the Sun Dance ceremony and lying down on his back on top of a buffalo robe that is on the ground. Once the dancer is positioned properly, two medicine people then make two incisions in his upper pectoral muscles. A chokecherry skewer is then placed through each of the two incisions, and large ropes are affixed and tied to the skewers.

Many people do not understand this ritual. They mistakenly think that it is some sort of puberty rite or a macho endurance test of one's manhood. All these assumptions are incorrect. The Sun Dance tree is like an antenna to the spirit world and to the Creator of Life. The ropes, which are tied to the tree and then affixed to the dancer by the skewer and incision, is like a spiritual umbilical cord. In the cosmology of the Lakota Sun Dance religion, the belief is that this ritual gesture symbolically and energetically ties the dancer to the people of the tribe, the people of the world, and to the Great Spirit.

The Sun Dancer's pain is also meaningful, for in enduring pain the dancer takes on the pain of all those who are suffering in the world. The pain of the Sun Dance is about waking up to life. It is about coming back into alignment with a balanced, refined, and empowered sense of warriorship. In essence, Sun Dancing is the northern plains expression of the path of love, service, and sacrifice, not unlike the path of Christ or of Buddha. It is a ceremony in which one becomes a conduit for sacred energies. Some elders say it is also a way for men to be humbled and to know that the pain they endure is but one ounce compared to the pain women undertake in childbirth.

After I had been pierced and tied to the tree, I was helped up onto my wobbly legs and ushered back over to my place in the ceremonial circle. I resumed the rhythmic dancing shuffle that a dancer keeps up throughout the ceremony. It is not a dance of entertainment. It is a dance of beseechment and humility. Bobbing up and down, while other male dancers were pierced, I fought back waves of nausea. At first my eyes were closed and I was very "out of it," simply trying to get strength back into my legs. Gradually I became used to the intensity of the pain, and I used the power of my mind to move beyond the threshold of these feelings. I opened my eyes for the first time since being pierced, and the doorways of my limited reality were blown wide open.

I looked around the arbor, and I could see that the ceremonial energy of the Sun Dance is essentially a vortex, a doorway, that is established by a variety of complex ritual variables set up by masters of ceremonial space. Without them, the Sun Dance would be a purely devotional and liturgical experience; with them, the veil separating this world and the world of the spirits is drawn back and the dead walk among the living and the living among the dead. In essence, the Sun Dance, like any empowered ritual, is the creation of a thin place, a liminal threshold or gate.

Realities collided within the arbor, and as I danced tied to the Sun Dance tree of the Lakota people, a warrior people, I met my own ancestors, also a warrior people. I encountered the ancient past, my present, and a vision of a bright future rushing forth to greet us. As I looked to my left, I saw the old man, complete with facial scar, clad in a black robe. Other ancestors drew close to me, providing energetic support. I could also see many other spirits dancing in the arbor. Some were native spirits connected to certain dancers, while others felt more like formless, faceless guardians and tutelary spirits, some connected to me, others connected to other people in the arbor, others of an even older, more ancient world that seemed to loom just at the edge of the arbor.

My ability to see and feel all these things was not just a result of my fasting. It was also not just rooted in my prayers. Rather, my visions were largely a result of the impeccable ceremonial container that the Lakota elders held that day. They are true masters. It was because of the subtle energetic mastery of the Sun Dance intercessor and his medicine helpers that I received an involuntary experience of the second sight within the arbor. I had activated within me a steady flow of awareness that is quite common in the Scottish Highlands and other Celtic lands. This awareness is that of *an da shealladh,* or the two sights.

Ancestor Transmission and the Echo

Innumerable thinkers and anthropologists have discussed the process of initiation in the life of the shaman or seer. From Holger Kalweit and Michael Harner to the more classical reflections and accounts of Mircea Eliade and Joseph Campbell, the flow of events associated with indigenous spiritual initiation vary greatly, depending on the individual undergoing the event.

Eliade was probably the first to really focus on how initiation into shamanism and various indigenous priesthoods occurs. In some cases there is a hereditary transmission of powers or skills, meaning that a student undergoes tutelage with living shamanic elders, who pass on the tradition to the student. Eliade described this transmission in depth in his work *Shamanism: Archaic Techniques of Ecstasy.*[3] In other cases, the call to the path is spoken of as "spontaneous vocation," meaning that the shamanic candidate receives a powerful call and may be elected directly from the spirits of clan and/or ancestors, or even from sources in nature, such as lightning or a totem.

In all cases, the initiate is expected to orient his or her life to the wisdom tradition, not only as a means of shamanic continuance but also as a means of surviving one's ordeal. The wisdom tradition itself holds certain safety locks, so to speak. The person who is able to truly follow the instructions about psychic safety becomes a keeper and transmitter of the deeper reality of the sacred world.

In my own experience of initiation into the mysticism of my Celtic ancestors, the ancestors themselves have been an inseparable part of the process. It is as if the ancestors are standing at the very center of a large spiral, while my place is on one of the outer rings of this spiral. At first, in almost a visual assault, information comes from the realms of the spirits. Insights, knowledge, impressions, body sensations, empowered images, and certain practices have come to me via what has felt like an echo from the old ones deep in time, reaching out to me.

This echo was well known in Scotland and Ireland. In the Highlands of Scotland it was called the *taghairm* and involved setting up very specific ritual elements to receive guidance from the ancestor spirits. There are also variations of the *taghairm,* which seem to have been governed by local custom. In some cases a seer

3 Mircea Eliade, *Shamanism: Archaic Techniques of Ecstasy* (Princeton, N.J.: Princeton University Press, 1972), p. 13.

is wrapped in the hide of a white bull, or perhaps a deer, and is set out in a mist-filled place or on a hill known to be a spirit place. Sometimes the seer enters a thin place, such as a cave, where the spirit world is accessible. These seers, even as late as the 1700s, would undertake this ordeal for knowledge and guidance. It was a way of keeping the flow of the traditions alive, of staying in tune with the echoes of the ancestors.

In a conversation we once had about the ancestors, Alberto Villoldo, a Cuban-born *altomesayoq* shaman in the traditions of the Inca had this to say:

> In the medicine traditions there is the understanding that you embody a lineage that continues to live through you. Your sense of personal identity begins to merge with an identity of a lineage of men and women who have come before you and will come after you. And it is very destabilizing psychologically, or it can be, and this is why you have to be very grounded and connected to the earth to be able to have this merging of souls that happens within you, which increases your individuality but appears to be undermining it at the beginning of your work. A lineage can be interrupted and can even come to an end. Yet even if it is interrupted for hundreds of years, it is like a fire that disappears: you rub two sticks together and the fire is there, intact again, and the same.

During the portion of the Sun Dance in which I was pierced and tied to the sacred tree, I experienced a phenomenon that I have since coined as ancestral transmission, as opposed to the hereditary transmission that Eliade described. As I danced in place, ropes tugging at my flesh and muscle, I entered into a powerful state of trance in which certain spirits of my ancestors communicated directly to me and imparted a great deal of information and knowledge about my various bloodlines. Some of this information I have managed to verify through research and genealogy, while some strands are more otherworldly, verified only via quiet communion with the primal earth.

Although this process may sound very exciting or seem like a wonderful and uplifting experience, part of this kind of initiation entails what the Celtic tradition calls the "keening," which is characterized by very intense grief and catharsis. Keening, from the Gaelic word *caoineadh,* is fully embodied grief. During my experience of ancestor transmission I was shown both the wound and the healing powers of the Celtic spiritual traditions. I had to travel through the wounds to understand the cultural and spiritual richness that is still accessible. But first and foremost, I had to see and feel the profound and heart-wrenching loss of the ancestors.

The Lakota big drum continued to sound like the quicksilver beat of an Irish *bodhran,* while the sound of the eagle bone whistles shifted into the sound of *piborach,* an old form of bagpiping. With these sounds mixing in the arbor, along with the cool and shimmering sensation of mist around my ankles, I began to see my ancestral lineages, as well as even more ancient images from an ancestral reservoir of imagery I had never before encountered.

I was shown the wound, the shadow, the underbelly, if you will, of my heritage. This presented itself to me in a variety of overwhelming images of events I knew nothing about but that felt extremely familiar to me as I witnessed them. The word *seeing* is a bit of a misnomer, for my experience was more akin to my cells and blood "seeing" and then informing my visioning eye, rather than the other way around.

I saw deeply painful imagery. I saw what I can only describe as textural impressions of what I now believe were of the Irish Potato Famine, the Highland Clearances, as well as other clan battles and massacres. At another point I saw images of horrific scenes of people being decapitated, what I now believe were composite ancestral memories (as opposed to past-life memories) of village massacres and perhaps even of druids being killed by Romans. This process caused me to wonder how many people currently receive such images and mistake them for past-life material, when in fact they are the composite cellular reawakenings of the ancestors trying to communicate with us.

At times the imagery was profoundly congruent with my emotional state, as I also began to feel very powerful feelings of lack, hunger, pain, alienation, and a sense of not feeling at peace or at home. These were my own feelings arising from the visions, yet they were emotions that were all startlingly familiar to me, and I now believe them to be the unresolved grief and rage of my ancestors. I suddenly realized that those of us who are living descendants of those who suffered from these events have all been influenced, shaped, and molded by these unhealed traumas, though we remain largely unconscious of the symptoms. All these things churned deeply inside me, and I felt a combination of grief, rage, and nausea all at the same time.

I began to cry deeply. The muscles of my torso rippled with sadness as I received a deep-seated knowing that I descend from a beautiful, powerful, and life-affirming culture that has been profoundly smothered. Certain female spirits gathered close to me at this time, and I could hear them wailing and crying at the tops of their lungs. These were the "keening women," often spoken of in Scottish Highland and Irish tradition. Their fully embodied grieving edged me toward my own full catharsis. As this dimension of knowledge moved through me, it slowly began to decrease in intensity, as if in experiencing it I was able to dissipate or transmute the wounding into healing.

Very gradually there came a shift, and the images were more of the Celtic mystical and visionary tradition and less of the wound.

Again, in a barrage of imagery flooding my awareness, information was transmitted to me via a cellular knowing and feeling about the earth-based essence of Celtic ways, and even of the template of their more ancient origins. The energies rumbling through were connected to what I took to be the rural folk mysticism and faery tradition, the druidic dimension as well as elements of the early Celtic-Christian monastic tradition. In any case, these visions emphasized the inherent divinity of Creation and the sacredness of the earth.

I cannot even hint at the fullness of the material that was being transmitted to me, as it was so rich and vast that I know I will be living, embodying, and aspiring to understand it for the rest of my life. I became aware of ancient practices my ancestors were involved in, accessible to us now, many of which I have verified as actual traditions. I encountered specific ancestor spirits whose lives had been inextricably linked with the faith of the druids, as well as certain functions within Celtic culture, such as those we would call midwifery and healing. Others simply sat by quiet forest pools and prayed, content. Throughout this time the old man stayed very close to me, while other ancestors seemed to swirl around me.

R. J. Stewart, a well-known and very talented Celtic seer of both Scottish and Welsh extraction, who works tangibly in the Celtic Underworld Tradition, speaks eloquently of this process in a manner that captures the mood of my own experience:

> The Ancestors awaken within the individual psychic and body complex, through the triggering of a series of biochemical changes within the bloodstream. Initially the communion with the Ancestors is a purgative experience; once the encounter has been fully absorbed and understood, it may be repeated at will without the catalytic shock.... In many cases, the Summoning creates a deeply empathic and emotional response, holding the seeds of memories

> of past events, often of extremely distant historical or pre-historical periods. During this early stage, the predominant memories are of difficulties, disasters and acts of injustice upon a large scale. At a later stage, when the initial ferment has come under control, material can be selected for comprehension.[4]

My Sun Dance experience was, in essence, a powerful doorway to reactivating a bond with the spirits of my ancestors and the Spirit of Nature. It was a restoration of a much-needed dialogue with the sacred world in my life. Tracking our lineages, whoever we are and wherever we may come from, we eventually get to the primal ancestors, those who were the first to place their feet upon the Mist-Filled Path of loving life and Creation. They are the first shamans, the first seer-poets, the first druids, the first midwives, the first healers, the first mystics, the first hillwalkers, primal ancestors who lived much more attuned to the rhythms of the earth, who held their hands up to the rising sun and prayed:

> Hail to thee, thou sun of the seasons,
> As you make your way across the shining sky.
> Your steps are strong on the wings of the heavens.
> You are the grandmother of the stars.
> You lie down at twilight in the deep green ocean,
> without fear, without loss.
> You rise up, brilliant, on the peaceful wave
> like a regal woman blooming with life.

— ADAPTED FROM A SCOTTISH HIGHLAND SUN PRAYER

---

4 R. J. Stewart, *The Underworld Initiation* (Lake Toxawy, N.C.: Mercury Publishing, 1990), pp. 131–2.

The next year I did not return to Pine Ridge for the Sun Dance. A full year had passed, yet I was still heavily engaged in the work of integrating my experiences of the previous year. Nonetheless, every night, the week of the next year's Sun Dance, I would light a candle, drum, and send prayers for the Sun Dancers, the men and women who "take on the pain of the world" during the ceremony.

I heard a few weeks later from friends who danced that on the evening of the third night the sound of bagpipes could be heard inside the Sun Dance arbor. My friend Fatu remarked, "Out of nowhere, we could hear the sound of the pipes coming from the center of the arbor near the area of the tree." When I heard this I wept with gratitude. The old ones in my lines had made their presence known to the dancers as a gesture of support. It was an auditory manifestation of my deep prayers from home and of my "warrior people" praying for another warrior people.

Walking this road, this Mist-Filled Path, has taught me that these primal ancestors are dynamic and real. They love us and support us. They want a better world for us, where all the earth is our Holy Land, where all people are the chosen ones. These primal ancestor spirits, regardless of culture, have always met the world with beauty. They have always entered into dialogue with the Spirit World, the Soul of the World, in the multitude of thresholds of our everyday reality and within nature. The Celtic ancestors, as exiles, wanderers, and seekers, have always been driven forward by this relationship to the world as sacred.

The same can be true for us now.

Chapter 6

The Shape of the Sacred World

We lie in the lap of immense intelligence,
which makes us receivers of its truth and organs of its activity.

— Ralph Waldo Emerson

The foundation of druidic thought is the universal harmony
of beings and things in perpetual realization.

— Jean Markale

Celtic spirituality is rooted in a deep love of life. It is a practical path that enriches us by instilling into our daily flow of awareness a sense that we dwell within a place and that we have also been *placed* in a spiritscape in which many other beings dwell. The soft yet enlivened eyes of Celtic spirituality foster a profound view of our life journey on this earth as moving through a spiritscape of holy shapes. There is purpose to this movement, purpose to these many shapes of life, although the meaning of life may sometimes appear to leave us.

Even more important than this profound view is the profound experience of living in a sacred world that enjoys greeting us. We might call it a "tenderized" orientation. It is tenderized because it softens us to life, from the inside out. This softening is an induction and an attunement of all our faculties to be more aware of the mystery rather than thinking we have it all figured out. How boring life would be if we had it all figured out. The mysticism of the Celtic soul puts to rest the monkey mind of analysis and urges us to fall back into the arms of the unseen, unnamable power that instinctually moves all things toward wholeness.

The Celtic spiritual approach fosters wholeness because it seeks to rekindle holiness. Part of this holiness, or of any holistic spirituality, is the deeply felt sense that all living things are ensouled — filled with the Soul of Life. This belief, formed from experience, is called animism, a belief system of indigenous, shamanist, and earth-based tribal people the world over.

Animism is a way of experiencing life so that we are constantly awakened to the preciousness of our moments on this earth. While not a religion per se, animism is an informed spirituality characterized by handing oneself over to the authentic, untainted experience of the universe from the vantage point of sacred eyes, sacred senses, and an open heart. Animism is a powerful healing path, especially in this day and age, for it not only counters mechanistic cosmologies currently at work in the world, but it also ushers in a primeval experience that the world around us is inhabited by innumerable beings that are alive, aware, and intelligent.

In essence, animism is a path of reclaiming a relationship and dialogue with an earth that is aware of us. The Celtic spiritual tradition is rooted in relationship and the ongoing awareness of relationship. The following practice invites you to go into the natural world for the purpose of connecting to its storied and ensouled nature. In the shamanic traditions, when a person makes a pilgrimage into nature, one of the first things that she or he does is to identify the "keepers" or guardians of the place. Perhaps it is a large boulder or a tree. Perhaps it is a grove of trees or a hill. There are also very ancient Celtic traditions that perceive and interact with a dimension or realm below the earth. Pivotal sites for engaging in this dialogue are often places where these keepers or guardians can be found.

PRACTICE: EARTH AWARENESS

- Dress appropriately for the weather so that you are warm or cool enough, but dress in clothes that can become soiled with mud or wet.
- Go to a natural place that feels special to you. Step into the spiritscape of the land and begin by identifying the ancient guardian of the place. Approach this tree, stone, or hill as the enlivened and ensouled living being that it is. See the particular boulder as an ancient rock filled with story, or an ancient tree saturated in memory.
- Allow yourself to perceive a particular tree or coupling of trees as a liminal gateway. Walk toward this gateway of trees and consider that on "this side" of the gate you are in ordinary consciousness or in the ordinary world, but on the "other side" of the gate you will have entered a nonordinary flow of spiritual awareness. Open yourself to the images of the land and the teachings to be found therein.
- Expand your spirit, the energy of your soul, and open yourself to the guardian of the land. If the moon is up, open yourself to the moon. If the sun is up, open yourself to the sun. If there is a mist or a slight drizzle, allow your face to be kissed by the flutter of light water on your skin and open yourself to

its presence. Allow yourself to discern the shaping intelligence of the soul of the place. Allow yourself to relate to the multiple intelligences and spirits in the landscape from a vantage point of sacred encounter, dialogue, and awareness of relationship.

- What do you notice? Are you really just a lone human getting rained on? Are you really just a solitary person standing by a big stone? Are you able to discern some of the many presences in nature, or within the primal earth? To feel and enter into dialogue with inspirited citizens of the sacred world in this way, we must perceive ourselves as inspirited as well.
- Record your findings and repeat the practice regularly. Return to the same keeper or guardian. Ask to be shown how to merge with the "land beneath the land." Record your findings with each visitation, and pay close attention to what happens on the level of your senses, your mind, and your heart.

REVISITING THE SHAPE OF THE SOUL

The word *soul* has become a buzzword, not unlike the word *Celtic.* Yet I see great value in the fact that so many people are now feeling drawn to such words as *soul, fire, earth, wisdom, sacred, Celtic, shaman,* and *spirit.* That these words have become part of our common lexicon speaks, at least to a certain degree, of where we may be headed.

In the primal Celtic view, the soul is not inside the body, but rather around the body. Or, as John O'Donohue reminds us, "the body is inside the soul." This is not just some fanciful belief. It is something that can be known. It is a direct and visceral way of coming into relationship with the holy shapes of the sacred world. It is an experience that can be felt through the communion of holy contact with our sentient planet. Connecting with the Soul of Life through the various doorways of Creation is an act that can guide, purify, and realign us with our purpose for being here. It is also a proven path of personal healing, both psychological and physical.

Soul energy can be felt around the tree, around the stone, around the plants within a small garden. Soul surrounds a newborn baby. Soul is around the loved one who grapples with dying. Soul is around the friend or stranger beside you. Whenever two entities come into contact, there is dialogue between souls, an unspoken discussion of our mutual placement in the ebb and flow of things.

SENSING THE HOLY SHAPES

Nonanimistic cosmologies do not allow us to experience a multidimensional relationship with the holy shapes of life. The nonanimistic view perceives everything as unfeeling. Stones, trees, even some people on the planet are viewed as "less than." At best the nonanimist may evolve a kind of conservationist or preservationist ethic that suggests we must save things because we may need them later. Yet this view fosters a perspective of the planet as one big treasure chest or pharmacy. The planet has a right to exist of its own accord, devoid of our directions. We, as a species, must cultivate a global understanding of the inherent rights of nonhuman life.

Those who live according to a nonanimistic cosmology relate to the planet as if it were inert matter that has no sense, no intelligence, no feeling, no consciousness. Cohabitation is countered with ownership and fellowship with an imbalanced and violent warriorship. If we are unfeeling we cannot perceive the feelings of the living earth. If we do not feel her we cannot love her and her many shapes. If we do not love her we will not protect her. The only antidote is to reeducate ourselves and one another about the feeling dimensions of the earth beneath our feet. Our planet is not only an intelligent planet but also a process of dynamic formation and organic beauty that continues to shape and be shaped. Our survival as a global community is directly linked with whether we can rekindle this kind of reverence.

Traditions, religions, economies, and systems of governing that do not acknowledge the sentience of our planet cannot be sustained. For us, as individuals and communities who comprise the microcosm of these greater systems, it is an act of mental health, a humanitarian investment in healing the future, to openly question the wisdom and sustainability of these antiquated institutions. We must shake ourselves free of the myopic view that our individual choices do not have an impact. Part of this waking up is about reclaiming our primal senses, which are at the heart of animistic spirituality.

The Celtic spirit leans toward the world through activated senses and, in doing so, finds a sacred world leaning back toward it. If we open ourselves to the sacred dimension of reality, as it is experienced and worked with in so many animistic traditions, we will soon find that we are extended an important invitation. It is an invitation of memory and belonging. It is an invitation of recollection and recognition. When we enter the holy circle of this invitation we inaugurate a profound relationship with the Soul of Place in which we live. We begin to appreciate the world again. We start to feel the landscape, and what is done to her, right here on our own skin, in our own hearts.

From this experience we stumble on a secret that has actually never really been a secret. We come to see there is no separation between us and the world around us. Like the soul that envelops the body, the world is a soul that envelops the individual and the community. From a Celtic and druidic view, the Soul of the World is currently sick, dwelling in a state of soul loss, with vital soul parts hidden away and forgotten. We have all come under a strange and illusionary spell, one that causes us to falsely assume that our planet can sustain unchecked population growth, that our economies will somehow continue to expand, that there will always be enough for everyone despite our unsustainable approaches, and that our planet can withstand our abuse.

Celtic earth wisdom knows full well that what befalls the soul soon befalls the body within the soul. Similarly, what befalls the Soul of the World will eventually befall its individuals and communities. There is no such thing as a permanently troubled world unless we consciously or unconsciously choose this for ourselves. We have a choice about our lives, and the world, and how they will be shaped, which is all the more reason for us, like our ancestors before us, to reclaim a soulful and practical spirituality of aiming goodness, love, and yearning at the world through the presence of our soul. In this matter, the old saying stands: If we aren't part of the solution we are part of the problem.

The problem can sometimes feel quite heavy. I know for myself that when I listen to the news about Palestine, Northern Ireland, the clear-cutting of the rain forest, or the drilling for oil in the Alaskan wilderness, I am astonished by the overarching sense of helplessness that can wash through me. These feelings, however, do not have to stay with us. We can feel them, fully, and then move through them, enabling us to be informed by the depths of what is happening in the world and then act to address these things. Enduring wave after wave of helplessness, we eventually armor and callous ourselves so as not to feel the despair. This is a natural human response. It is our way of coping, of shielding ourselves. But an armored heart does not love fully. A closed soul no longer sees the world as a place it wants to be.

We must do everything we can within our lives and in the world to reverse this condition. One of the first steps might lie in the courageous act of purifying ourselves of the toxic, yet contagious, sarcasm and unfeeling cynicism one finds oozing from every crack and crevice in our concrete world. This cynicism and sarcasm morph and mutate us into people with slumping bodies cut off from the heart and the breath, leaving us with nothing but glazed eyes that can no longer see clearly. It is time to reclaim a more ancient breastplate for the road ahead, one that stands upright in the morning and declares:

> I arise today
> Through the strength of Heaven:
> Light of Sun,
> Radiance of Moon,
> Splendor of Fire,
> Speed of Lightning,
> Swiftness of Wind,
> Depth of Sea,
> Stability of Earth,
> Firmness of Rock.[1]

You Do Not Have to Do It Alone

We become paralyzed if we contemplate the darkness and negativity as if we alone must solve it all. We cannot breathe, imagine, feel, act, or be activists from such a place. We must educate ourselves about all the various places of imbalance in the Soul of the World, since this is simply something we do as part of our citizenship in the sacred world. In keeping with the words of Thich Nhat Hanh, "Do not turn your eyes from suffering." This instruction is very important. We should think of it as part of our collective job description.

---

1 An invocation known as "The Deer's Cry" or "Saint Patrick's Breastplate," believed to be older than Patrick and probably of druidic origin.

However, we must also realize that as individuals we are not going to solve all problems by ourselves. To hold this kind of unrealistic expectation over ourselves strips us of our true power and effectiveness, our true ability to respond. But the abiding truth of the matter is, in waking to the world as sacred, we come to understand that we can effect change with one cause, one problem, one moment in life that has fallen out of harmony. We can be shapers.

Take Julia Butterfly Hill, author of *The Legacy of Luna* and executive director of the Circle of Life Foundation, for example. She did not try to solve all the problems of the world. She did not even take on a whole cause at first. She chose one tree — or rather, it chose her. Within the holiness of their encounter, embrace, and dialogue, Julia and the spirit of Luna (a California redwood) brought back an aching soul part to the Soul of the World, namely a model for how to slow down and listen deeply to the wise directives of an ancient tree while simultaneously protecting her. Julia, a Celtic descendant, is, in my mind, one of the true Druid spirits in action within the Soul of the World. When she speaks about the forest she wakes people up to a potent greening spirit. She is a shaper of the world, dedicated to the holy shapes and to the practice of holy shaping.

ENTERING SACRED WORLD

The greening spirit that Julia and others before her have tried to remind us of isn't just found in old-growth forests. The greening spirit that is the shape of our sacred world is ever present, ever near to us. Our daily life can start to feel like a daily grind, causing us to forget this precious greening spirit of life.

The old land-based Celtic way of being has always been one that banishes the heavy energies of a banal existence by sanctifying every moment with soul energy and purpose. In following this way, we can resist the unfortunate forgetfulness that can overtake us. We can remember the holy powers of life in the food we cook, the water we drink and bathe in, in the pets that share our homes, and in the people with whom we are connected. Common tasks and everyday chores, when approached with sacred eyes and senses, become brief moments of conscious communion with the Soul of Life. Even the simplest of tasks can become invested and imbued with sacred energy.

A fisherman ties his knots in holiness. A woman tends to a garden in holiness. A grandmother tells a tale to grandchildren in holiness. A woman cooks a meal for extended family in holiness. A grandfather and grandson walk an old forest trail in holiness. Modern Celtic people who still practice crofting, who cut turf, who gather sheep, who knit, who bring their wares into town, do so in the spirit of a tradition of holiness. In a Celtic way of being everyday tasks are tendered gestures that are not separated from the deeper tapestry of life. Rather than a series of unconscious hoops to jump through with each passing day, the Celtic soul is driven by a kind of spiritual code written in the interior life. The spirit of the mist says, "This is your life. Blend with it. This is the Soul of the World. Seek to accommodate opposites." The Celtic code of living states, "Your life is a gift and a pilgrimage; see every day, every event, every moment, and every act as a renewable point in time offering you a new beginning."

If we listen to the spirit of the mist and apply such a code to our lives, a sense of a vast and unexplored terrain opens up to us. The first few moments of morning become another dawning of Creation. We open our eyes and are born anew. A silent walk on a beach, punctuated by saltwater gusts of wind and gossiping gulls, becomes a kind of soul massage. We feel invigorated, washed from the inside out. Two people who have never met look into each other's eyes and experience an ancient recognition of their bond. And, at the end of our day, our lying down to sleep at night becomes a textured template for how we can approach our death and passage into the world beyond this one. We shut our eyes, and the journey begins.

One of the greatest proponents of reactivating atrophied senses, a teacher who taught prolifically about working with the sacred world, was Chögyam Trungpa. Originally known as Dorje Dradul of the Tibetan highland clan Mukpo, Chögyam Trungpa Rinpoche was a lover of the world. His approach to life was very animistic, no doubt influenced by both the Bön-Po shamanist traditions and the Buddhist traditions of Tibet. Trungpa Rinpoche was a great lover of Celtic culture. He often asked that bagpipes be present at various events, including at his own funeral. Likewise, he was known to don a kilt in the Nova Scotia tartan from time to time, believing that the kilt is a regal garment expressing the principles of sacred warriorship of the Shambhala lineage. Some have said that his wearing of the kilt and his communing with the sounds of the bagpipes was a way for him to invoke the Scottish *dralas* (primal energies) of the Celtic traditions.

Dorje Dradul of Mukpo would have been recognized by the old druids and Celtic seers for what he was: a warrior, a divine child of earth, a sensualist, a friend of the earth spirits. His secular teachings to the Western world, known simply as the Shambhala teachings, share a great affinity with the primal Celtic vision, which cannot be confined. It is a living, breathing tradition that is able to turn an eye (and even more important, an inquisitive heart) to many faiths, traditions, customs, and practices to see the common thread that runs throughout.

Similarly, Trungpa Rinpoche was deeply in touch with another tributary of the Celtic spirit: the importance of the natural world as an expression of the sacred world. In his own words:

> When human beings lose their connection to nature, to heaven and earth, they do not know how to nurture their

> environment or how to rule their world — which is saying the same thing. Human beings destroy one another. From that perspective, healing our society goes hand in hand with healing our personal, elemental connection with the phenomenal world.[2]

Embracing heaven and earth means being aware of multiple realities all at the same time. It means holding both the highs and lows of life: the joy in a child's face on seeing a butterfly for the first time, the anguish of a friend dying of cancer. One thing opens, another closes. The Mist-Filled Path is about touching all these moments and being present to them. A life oriented to this kind of wakefulness demands a great deal of us. It leads us down twisting, winding roads into dark valleys of intense exploration (and sometimes grief) and back up the other side to cairned vistas of remembrance and glee. It is a path of embracing the many shades and nuances of life, and within this embrace coming to realize — animistically speaking — that the Soul of Life holds us.

Celtic spirituality is a practical path of reinvigorating a connection to life, a tangible experience of the spiritual underpinnings of majestic waterfalls, the deer running, and the face of the person in front of us. In effect, there is nothing without soul, and Celtic spiritual seekers hold a sustained memory of this ancient celebration of place bonding. Indeed, the Celtic way is to see God in all things, the Goddess as a wakeful shaping power. In such a world, all things are steeped in beauty. Morgan, an early Celtic theologian from Wales (whose name was Romanized as Pelagius), states:

> Look at the animals roaming the forest: God's spirit dwells within them. Look at the birds flying across the sky: God's spirit dwells within them. Look at the tiny insects crawling

2 Chögyam Trungpa, *Shambhala: The Sacred Path of the Warrior* (Boston: Shambhala, 1998), p. 125.

> in the grass: God's spirit dwells within them. Look at the fish in the river and sea: God's spirit dwells within them. There is no creature on earth in whom God is absent. Travel across the ocean to the most distant land, and you will find God's spirit in the creatures there. Climb up the highest mountain, and you will find God's spirit among the creatures who live at the summit. When God pronounced his creation was good, it was not only that his hand had fashioned every creature; it was that his breath had brought every creature to life. Look too at the great trees of the forest: look at the wildflowers and the grass in the fields; look even at your crops. God's spirit is present within all plants as well. The presence of God's spirit in all living things is what makes them beautiful; and if we look with God's eyes, nothing on the earth is ugly.[3]

The diversity of the expressions of life, the different creatures, the differences in landscape, and the various cultures and peoples on the planet are all the faces of the Creator and the elemental shapers. Within *every* expression of life's sacred shapes is an opportunity to commune with the Divine, including our own unique expression.

THE MEMORY OF OUR MANY SHAPES

It is healing for us to remember our sense of place with the holy shapes of life. When we make it a point to remember the holy shapes, we in turn remember our own divinity. When we truly know the ancient shape of our own heart, we can then attune to and understand the shape of other things around us. We can become "at one" with a certain tree or an animal, or we can strive

3 Robert van de Weyer, ed., *The Letters of Pelagius: Celtic Soul Friend* (New Alresford, Hampshire: Arthur James, 1995), p. 71.

to understand another person with whom we may be in conflict or who may be suffering.

The ancient shamanic art of shape-shifting is essentially the bioenergetic practice of attuning the rhythm of one's own shape to the rhythm of something in the natural world so that we may share its consciousness. When we begin to discern the grand shape of things, we become one with the forest, the stream, the raven, the earth. This may sound far-fetched, but even some scientists are beginning to articulate a paradigm of physics that mirrors the perennial vision of druidism and shamanism. Jean E. Charon, a French physicist, for instance, has this to say: "An electron that was successively part of a tree, a human being, a tiger, and another human being will thus remember for all time the experiences it has collected during these different lives. The electron will maintain within itself all of its experiences as tree, as human being No. 1, as tiger, and as human being No. 2, to whose organisms it belonged at certain times."[4]

These are astonishing words to come from the mouth of a physicist, and yet more and more physicists are beginning to espouse a similarly animated perception of reality. This perception is one long held by shamans and mystics of various traditions, now being rekindled, rediscovered, and harnessed today by various shamanic practitioners and visionaries. This is not supernaturalism; rather, it is naturalism, and the words of this scientist sound remarkably like the words of many shamans. Each in their own way these shaman-druids declare the same findings as Jean Charon, Fritjof Capra, and other scientists. They knew of their place within "the family of things" when they announced:

I have been in many shapes:
I have been a narrow blade of a sword.

4 Jean E. Charon, *L'Esprit, cet inconnu* (Paris: Albin Michel, 1977), p. 73.

I have been a drop in the air.
I have been a shining star.
I have been a word in a book.
I have been an eagle.
I have been a boat on the sea.
I have been a string on a harp.
I have been enchanted for a full year,
In the foam of the water.
There is nothing in which I have not been.

— TALIESIN, CYMRIC DRUID-SHAMAN[5]

Through the art of shape-shifting, and through various visionary and meditative techniques, we also begin to understand more fully the spiritual reality that every one of us has a reserved place within the great shape of things. This is an ancient consciousness shared by many tribal and shamanic people on the planet.

One of the ancient Celtic ideas about this process is rooted in the word *cruth,* which in Enlgish translates as "shape." The Scots Gaelic word for God is *Cruithear,* which means "creator" or "shaper." It is no accident that one of the ancient peoples in Scotland, the Picts, were referred to as the Cruithne. These tribes of old Caledonia were called the "people of the shapes" as well as "the painted people." Roman accounts, as well as Scottish oral tradition, tell us that the bodies of these ancient ones were covered in elaborate blue tattoos of various animals and other shapes. It was their way of honoring the sacred world that had shaped them.[6]

A whole psychology could be oriented toward this potent awareness of shaping and being shaped. This perennial insight

5 As quoted in Tom Cowan, *Fire in the Head* (San Francisco: HarperSanFrancisco, 1993), p. 29.

6 Caitlin Matthews and John Matthews, *The Encyclopaedia of Celtic Wisdom* (Rockport, Mass.: Element Books, 1994), p. 158.

could be formed into a third-millennium psychology, a third-millennium shamanism, that would assist us in shaping the world in holy ways rather than in ways that foster discord. All of us carry a quiver full of soul arrows, and our very lives are the bow with which we do the aiming.

PRACTICE: YOUR SKIN, MY SKIN, OUR ANCESTRAL BONES

The next time you find yourself in a crowded place, whether on a bus, in a bookstore, in a football stadium, or in a movie theater, do the following practice.

- Look at all the different people and then whisper or think to yourself: "Every man, my brother. Every woman, my sister. Every crying child, my child. Every old woman, my grandmother. Every old man, my grandfather. Every wounded soul, my soul."

Accessing such levels of insight is good power for the good road ahead. When we come into the holy tapestry of life's shapes at our birth, from a Celtic perspective, we are each born into what we might call "sacred standing" and "sacred relationship." From such a place we all have the same skin, the same ancestral bones. We are bound to one another through various means, not the least of which is our shared human experiences of breath, blood, hunger, thirst, and our need for both physical and emotional shelter. In the eyes of the Great Shaper and Shapers, we are sacred. Or, to use more neutral language, the fact that we have been born into the ancient stream of life means we have inherent value by virtue of our aliveness.

Yet how many of us live our lives as ambassadors of the sacred or perceive others as sacred? Many of us have not been taught to value or to care for ourselves. We have been conditioned to think that self-care is self-indulgence or selfish, and yet if we operate from the perspective that we are ambassadors of the sacred, we must take care of ourselves so that we can take care of the other sacred forms of life that we serve.

If we have not realized our sacred standing we can sometimes do or speak things that are not in alignment with our ambassadorship. Rather than fostering harmony and living in accordance with soul, we then find ourselves creating discord and destruction. This too is a teaching, however, for it is through the pain of discord that we realize our separation from the sacred. Through this realization come the desire and the longing to return to our sacred standing.

The Celtic path of returning to sacred standing is rooted in allowing ourselves to be shaped by the larger universe. In so doing we remember a beautiful strain of music flowing through all of life: the Great Song of Creation.

Chapter 7

The Great Song

The Celts of old believed that the world was upheld and sustained by a single all-embracing melody: Oran Mór, they called it, the Great Music, and all creation was part of it. Perhaps this is why Celtic music possesses the power to move us in unexpected ways — it touches that place deep in our hearts where legends still live, and we hear again the strains of the Ancient Song.

— Stephen Lawhead[1]

Indigenous peoples and religious traditions all over the world are oriented to a primal myth of creation, an original story that provides an understanding of origins. This story often provides an experience of spiritual container, an anchoring point of identity, and an explanation for the existence of life in the beauty of mythic terms. Stories of this kind are a cosmological declaration of how we all got here and who we are within the *prima materia.* From the Great Lakes Anishinabe (Ojibway) and the

1 Quoted in the liner notes of *The Bard & the Warrior* by Jeff Johnson and Brian Dunning (Windham Hill Records).

nomadic Sami of Lappland, to the great religions of Islam, Hinduism, Judaism, and Christianity, there are very few traditions that do not have such a story. It is a holy sourcing tale from which one can draw strength and assistance.

It has been suggested repeatedly that the ancient Celtic peoples did not have a creation story. Certainly the Christianized Celts oriented themselves to the "new faith" and its "new story" (the story of Creation in the biblical book of Genesis), but in looking into the primal Celtic traditions, before the influence of the desert tradition of Christian mysticism, we do not, in fact, find a clear-cut example of a unifying creation myth. Could it be that such an earth-revering people as the Celts would have had no cosmological vision, no mythic sense of the creation of earth and sky, land and sea?

Some of us in the Irish and Scottish spiritual traditions believe that such a story does exist. It isn't a story printed in an ancient text somewhere, nor is it a sacred tale that has been passed down from generation to generation orally. The reason we find no evidence of a Celtic creation story is because it is a living story — a story that waits for each of us to remember it. In other words, no matter how much we look, we will not find a story outside ourselves. We have all been woven into this story. It is our story, because we *are* the story, and it continues to unfold.

I think Scots-Irish myth bearer Frank Mills expresses quite well the nature of the enduring Creation story for the Irish and Scots. He states: "A Celtic Creation tale does in fact exist. Agreed, we will not find this tale in its full cohesive form anywhere in Celtic myth, but this does not mean that it does not exist. In fact, I think that it means just the opposite. The Celtic Creation tale is so primordial, so intrinsic to the Celtic mythos that the ancient Celts had no need to spell it out."[2]

The essence of the Oran Mór is that it is a story that cannot

2 From a brochure of the Oran Mór Institute, Frank Mills, Brigitsfst@aol.com.

be written, told, or fully articulated by human storytellers or mythmakers (though some mystics have alluded to it), but only by Creation herself. My sense of the reason why the Oran Mór has not become another written or oral story is precisely that the old Celtic Creation story is actually a song that is heard, felt, and experienced through holy remembrance and celebration. My own remembrance of the Great Song occurred for me while on pilgrimage in one of the Celtic motherlands of my family, Scotland.

A VISION OF ORAN MÓR

I saw more than I can tell and I understood more than I saw; for I was seeing in a sacred manner the shapes of all things in the spirit, and the shape of all shapes as they must live together like one being. And I saw that the sacred hoop of my people was one of many hoops that made one circle, wide as daylight and as starlight, and in the center grew one mighty flowering tree to shelter all the children of one mother and one father. And I saw it was holy.

— BLACK ELK, OGLALA LAKOTA SIOUX HOLY MAN[3]

In August (my birth month) 1997, I was on pilgrimage in Scotland, specifically in a region in the western Highlands known as Kilmartin. The Kilmartin Valley is a powerful place strewn with hundreds of ancient Pictish burial cairns, stone circles, and standing stones, all within a six-mile radius of the hamlet of Kilmartin. In this ancient valley one will find several sites that hold an undeniably numinous power.

---

3 John G. Neihardt, *Black Elk Speaks* (Lincoln, Nebr.: University of Nebraska Press, 1979), p. 33.

One night in Kilmartin I undertook a traditional Celtic vision-seeking practice. In the Celtic ancestral ways of seership and mysticism, sleeping on the side of an ancient grave, faery hill, or deep within a burial chamber is a way to commune with the spirits, the ancestors, or saints. It is a way to procure information and guidance. It is a way of becoming connected to the Great Shaper. Who is contacted and how is, of course, determined by the worldview of the practitioner.

When the in-between time of midnight arrived, I began my preparations for attuning to the spirit of the place. I walked out to the grave, which was concealed by a thick circle of trees. It was extremely dark, as the moon had not yet come up. What little light I had was cloaked by the incoming mist, which seemed to tiptoe silently from the upper reaches of the high hills down into the lower fields of the Kilmartin Valley, sometimes called the "valley of ghosts."

I circumambulated the large cairn three times, all the while lifting prayers quietly (also an old Celtic practice). I held my life and all the experiences that I brought to this ancient place in mind. I remembered the Sun Dance. I remembered my childhood. I contemplated my teacher, the mist, and its power to remind us in a deep cellular way of the process of creation. I have long imagined that at some point in the process of creation there must have come a point of stillness and silence after all the chaotic churning and gurgling of lava and rain. In my visioning eye I see this first moment of silence, almost as if I had been there, and the spirit of the mist is there, hovering.

The spirit of the mist hovered over me on this night too and looked on as I made votive offerings of various kinds (Drambuie, a liquor considered especially important to Highland Scots because of its association with Bonnie Prince Charlie and the battles for Scottish independence, juniper, tobacco, and heather). In keeping with traditional Irish and Scots ways, I purified my hands in the dew on the grass and lifted a prayer, while I practiced the old Scots custom of *saining* (blessing or purifying the space with juniper smoke, similar to smudging in the Native American tradition). I then began the process of sliding my body down into the dark cavern of the burial chamber. I had a thick sweater on, which I had to remove to fit my body through the narrow shaft into the chamber below the earth.

The grave was, of course, empty, since it had been excavated years before. The chamber was about three feet deep and five feet long, no doubt meant for the shorter but stouter Pictish chieftain it once housed. Flanked by two other chambers, and nestled deep within a larger cairn complex of hundreds of small loaf-shaped stones, even today the grave is known as *Ri Cruin,* the "round grave of the king." Although an enormous lid stone, pushed slightly aside, revealed that any bones or artifacts belonging to the chieftain have been taken, my experience is that the spirits remain connected to the ancient site. This is, after all, the way these sacred sites work. The power of such a place is rarely visible to the naked eye alone.

As I began sliding into the grave, I looked north a final time and noticed the northern lights shimmering green across the sky. The mist had finally settled in over a large portion of the grave site. Dogs in the distant hills began howling, and soon the cows and sheep joined in mooing and baaing from nearby farms. The whole valley seemed to be singing. I was not alone.

Then, very suddenly, it got frighteningly quiet. For a few moments I just leaned against the grave's top stone, paying attention to the surrounding area, when I became distinctly aware of movement in front of me, in a field on the other side of a barbed-wire fence. I heard clanking sounds, a cough, some talking, and the sound of feet kicking through the moist grass. It sounded like several individuals marching by, not the individual cow I originally assumed it was.

In the Gaelic, Manx, Orcadian, and Welsh traditions there is a deep and abiding belief in an ancient race of beings who live below the land. They sometimes come out in these in-between times and thin places. Some of these beings are mischievous, rather trickster-like. Others are more curious about us and, indeed, a great deal more familiar with us than we of them. Known by many names, and perceived of in different ways by non-Christian and Christian alike, their existence is rarely disputed, even by the most educated homeland Celt.

I sat for a moment longer, wondering if I might not be picking up on the good people, the shining ones of Gaelic cosmology, but I wasn't certain. I continued on into the grave. Once inside the burial chamber I tried to settle my mind. I was cold. I was nervous. I was shaking. To become calmer and more centered, I began to hum quietly. The sounds had nowhere to go and seemed to remain in the grave with me. Indeed, my chest resonated from the natural acoustics in the chamber and, after a while, the whole burial cairn seemed to be humming too. In time I was lulled by this sound and drifted off into a strange half-sleep, barely aware of my body or surroundings but continuing to hum almost involuntarily.

Then, a deeper, more potent sound began to develop inside the grave. It seemed to encompass my humming, yet it seemed to have its own source as well. Suddenly, I woke up, enveloped within the tones of an almost unearthly sound. What was it? To my utter astonishment I realized the sound was coming from me, yet it seemed to be connected to some greater sound, some greater source of energy than my own. I was performing a very powerful kind of throat singing or chant, *sgornan-ambranin* in the Gaelic. I was singing like thunder.

I eventually returned to a gentler humming chant, my quiet prayerful songs reverberating within the chamber, melding with the other sounds that were all around me. With this I entered easily into a deep trance within the grave. Again, somewhere between waking and sleeping, I began to receive one of the most beautiful visions ever bestowed on me. It set me on the formative path that I will walk the rest of my days. The vision, a combination of potent soundings blended with a cellular and fully embodied experience, has changed the way I experience music, voice, my senses, my body, and my understanding of the world around me.

A Gift from Ancestral Soil

The first image that presented itself to me seemed to be enveloped, almost encased, within the most beautiful sounds I have ever heard. The sounds emanated from the stars, from deep within the earth, and activated within me, yet again, deeper and deeper tones of the *sgornan-ambranin.* This initial image was of a spiral with four spokes radiating out into the four directions. It was made of stars, but I immediately thought that it looked like a Bridgid's Cross, or Bride's Cross, an ancient symbol in Ireland and Scotland. As I absorbed this vision, I could ascertain a low drone or humming sound beginning to vibrate again from within the cairn of stones. I then knew this sound to be the Great Song of the universe. I began to sense that it was the earthly emanation of the sounds of the stars in the spiral but felt within the earth.

In my vision the image of the spiraling stars was then superimposed by an actual Bride's Cross. Brighid (pronounced bree-jid), also known as Bride (pronounced breed, or even vree'jit on the Isle of Man), is a patron saint for many Celts. As a spiritual presence she is dear to the maternal side of my family. Another ancient Brighid figure in older Celtic lore occupies the role of a goddess of healing, sacred poetry, brewing, smithing, midwifery, inspiration, and maintenance of the hearth. So dear to the hearts of the Irish and Scots is Bride that the Catholic Church eventually formally acknowledged her as a saint.

Indeed, I felt a deep familiarity with this feminine presence while in the grave, as if she were midwifing me through a process of initiation, offering me a feast of heart and vision to carry back to my hearth and my life. Oddly enough, however, alongside the beautiful sensations of comfort I experienced, I also felt that I was being led through a death ritual of letting go of things that no longer served me. Naturally, as with any sacrifice, this aspect of my night vigil was emotionally intense and painful at times.

Glimmering above the other two images eventually came that of an ancient well. The sacred well is a common centerpiece in Scottish and Irish tradition, associated with primal goddesses and healing, later becoming consecrated as Celtic-Christian stopping places. Spilling forth from the well of my vision were four streams, which flowed into the four directions. Being familiar with some of the early Celtic stories, I wondered, "Is this the Well of Segais, Connla's Well?" I knew of one old story in which Manannan, an ancient sea god of the Irish, said that there are five streams pouring forth from Connla's Well. These five streams represent the five senses with which we take in knowledge. I studied and felt the image. The well in my vision seemed to point to something else.

In time I was shown that the four streams of my vision represent specific life-affirming streams of learning and spiritual experience, particular pathways of spiritual practice, but that an invisible, yet enduring, fifth stream exists that is beyond full comprehension. This fifth stream is the Oran Mór. It is the Source, the divine intelligence that masterminded the matrices and fractal structure of our universe.

Emerging again in the forefront of my vision were the spiral and spokes of the stars, and I was shown that all things emanate from these. All things emanate from this Great Song of power that is spinning vibrantly through all of life, from the microcosmic level of electrons, atoms, and cells to the giant swath of whole galaxies to the nautilus shell and hurricanes in between. To align oneself with the flow of this great music is to foster a life of wholeness, of healing and holism. It is a life of movement blended with stillness. It is a process of oscillation, outward, inward, outward, inward. Our breath. Our seasonal flow of activity. The Great Song is always present in all things and can be accessed at any time as a means of healing and realignment with the life-affirming powers that have created life.

In essence, my feeling is that this unifying power, this Great Song, is the Song of the Great Shaper. A felt knowing of this power does not, however, require a monotheistic approach to life. In fact, it does not even require a spiritual view. Scientists are now able to discern and articulate that the entire universe is made up of atoms moving at blinding speeds, occupying space in differing frequencies and vibrations not dissimilar to the frequencies of sound in music. The wondrous power of Creation has many faces, many expressions, all sharing an ancient source.

The Oran Mór can also be a deep spring that fills the sacred well of the human soul. This quenching power flows, moving majestically, beneath and within the world. Occasionally, and not often enough in my estimation, the Oran Mór emerges, like small pools in a desert. Then, "that which can be known but not spoken of" is felt as an undeniable presence, in places of power in the landscape and places of memory in the soulscape in the life of the individual and community.

Since I received this vision I have contemplated this information deeply. I have opened my soul to the Oran Mór and am continually brought to a particular feeling state. I believe that this primal energy of life, and the authentic experience of it, is known and understood by all the mystical, spiritual, and religious traditions. The activated expression of the Oran Mór, then, occurs in ways that are consistent and congruent with the cultures and ethos from which an experience of it occurs. In essence, if all of Creation can be likened to a great orchestra, different people, religions, and cultures hear different instruments and specific isolated strains of the great music in ways that are congruent with who they are.

The Oran Mór is part of my creation story. For me, it is undeniably connected to specific Celtic essences that exist in an eclipsed state waiting to restore and fuel the soul of modern people in an age of dynamic soul loss. The low droning sound and the holy rhythm of the Great Song continue for me. It resonates within my heart, and I know it to be the song of the universe. It is the song of life. It is the song of the shapers and the shapes. In certain ceremonies that I perform I recalibrate myself with the Great Song by performing the *sgornan-ambranin,* which has stayed with me since that night in the Kilmartin grave. Sometimes other forms of chant and song, reminiscent of Gregorian or medieval Christian music, will overtake me as the vehicle through which I experience a realignment with the source of life. At other times I use polyrhythmic trance drumming methods as a means of celebrating the ancient song and its life-shaping rhythms. This practice continually reminds me that the trees sing, the stones sing, the waters sing, the wind of the clouds sing, and the ancestors sing. Life is music. All things have their rhythm. The world is sound.

THE MANY DWELLING PLACES OF THE GREAT SONG

You did not come into this world, you came out of it.
You are not a stranger here.

— ALAN WATTS

The Oran Mór is an ancient rhythm, an ancient melody that one hears in the wind, in the waterfall, in the beautiful strains of sound in Celtic music, song, and chanting. It is a healing song, an enlivening song heard in the giggles of a grandmother, the whispers of a lover, the questions of a child.

Children understand the Oran Mór. They come here longing to hear the ancient melody again, and their fascination with "why the sky is blue" and "what makes a rainbow" is their attempt at remembering. All the religions would do well to foster in their followers the same kind of sensual innocence that we all had as children, the same kind of curiosity that leads us to ask, "How do you hear the Great Song in your culture? How do you hear the Great Song in your religion?" Therein lies our salvation.

I have heard the Oran Mór in the subway tunnels of the nation's capitol and whispered to me on a bus by a total stranger. I have heard the Oran Mór deep inside a grotto within the earth, high atop a windy hill in Scotland. I have heard it in my own heartbeat in the middle of the night and in the cries of a hawk that pierced the silent morning with her own thread of the ancient song.

At night I always close my eyes and sit in silence for a time before sleep. The great teacher, silence, in her many textured forms, embraces me. She is glad to see me slow down, to empty the mind, and to take a deep breath. While I commune with silence I concentrate on letting the day slide off of me like an old cloak, and in this gentle and pristine moment I sometimes hear a low drone of earthly yet ethereal sound. At times I merely listen; at other times I join in. At times, if I need to remember the Oran Mór, I will go into the forest to a nearby stream and listen to the sound of the water whispering over the stones. I know of two other people very dear to me who "source" themselves in this sound. I commune with their spirits while sitting at the river's edge.

The sun and moon rise and fall in song, the stars and sea tides ebb and flow in song. The cells within our body oscillate and breathe in song. Indeed, the first breath we take at birth and the last breath we take at the time of our death are part of the ancient melody. There is no place where the ancient song is not present.

Sometimes I even carry the Great Song with me. I put a

portable CD player in the bag I carry. I put in my earphones, and I listen to the deep soul-expanding soundscapes of Steve Roach's tribal music that, like none other, connects me to the many worlds. Steve, like David Darling, David Hykes, Robert Rich, Byron Metcalf, Vidna Obmana, Vir Unis, and others, has heard the power of the Oran Mór, the Great Song, in his unique way.

Sometimes the Oran Mór expresses itself in places we would not think to look. Perhaps this is part of the problem. We are an overly visual culture. When we learn of something we immediately turn our eyes to the matter to see it, but the Oran Mór invites us to rest our eyes and reawaken the skills of sacred listening and hearing. The visually impaired know the Oran Mór. They may not have thought in these particular terms, but their senses are profoundly attuned to the fact that the world is sound. They encounter a plethora of things that sighted people don't give a second thought to. The water splashing in your tub when running the bath or turning on the shower becomes the holy waters of the sea. The early-morning "caw, caw!" of the raven in the tree outside your window is an omen or living symbol reminding you of the dream you had last night. The frost cracking on a nearby fence is a spirit whispering gently of the turning of the seasons. Even our own breathing is sound and mirrors the coming and going of the ocean tides. In fact, one of the oldest forms of praying among the Scots involves the ocean tides, breath, and sound. As Alexander Carmichael recorded in the classic *Carmina Gadelica:*

> Sometimes prayers are intoned in low tremulous unmeasured cadences, like the moving and moaning, the soughing and the sighing, of the ever-murmuring sea on their wild shores. They generally retire to a closet, an outhouse, to the lee of a knoll, or to the shelter of a dell, that they may not be seen nor heard. I have known men and women of eighty,

> ninety and a hundred years of age continue the practice all of their lives, going from one to two miles to the seashore, to join their voices with the voicing of the waves and their praises with the praises of the ceaseless sea.[4]

This, then, is my own sense of the Celtic Creation story that originated in sound: *The beginning of all life as we know it was uttered long ago by an ancient sounding. The sounding moved outward from a center point of Being and continues hurling through space and time, manifesting as a complex matrix of interconnections. We are part of this Divine Unfolding. There is no one and nothing outside it. It is our collective lineage, our collective story.*

The Oran Mór remembered becomes a level of human consciousness that can help us accomplish great things. The macrocosmic dimension of this teaching is realized within the individual life as a microcosmic expression. As a Sufi mystic once said, "Music does not produce within the human heart that which was not already there." The Oran Mór is already within us waiting silently for the activation of our memory of her. The human soul enlivened with the Great Song becomes aware that it is a manifestation of the theophany of Creation, the divine manifestation of the Great Song that is all around us and within us.

This ancient view that our world is sound is not new, or indeed a purely Celtic experience. In the Hindu traditions of India (a culture believed to share common linguistic ties and spiritual ancestors with the Celts), for instance, there is an ancient phrase: *Nada Brahma,* which translates as "the world is sound." This phrase is a cosmological statement, as well as a mantra used in meditation by descendants of an ancient past. Even today there are those who pray humming or chanting *Nada Brahma.*[5]

---

4 Alexander Carmichael, *Carmina Gadelica: Hymns and Incantations* (Edinburgh: Floris Books, 1992), p. 575.

5 For more on this, see Joachim-Ernst Berendt, *The World Is Sound: Nada Brahma* (Rochester, Vt.: Destiny Books, 1991).

THE MATRIX OF CREATION

I find that simply talking about the Oran Mór excites people. Something just rings true for them when they hear me describe this vision of the creation and unfolding life of our universe. I remember one person who said, "Yes. This is beautiful. There has never been a time when I did not hear the music of which you speak." I am sometimes reminded of the film *City of Angels.* In this movie there is a particular scene in which a very large group of angels congregates on a beach at sunrise. They close their eyes and in a profoundly prayerful way they simply stand and listen to the Great Song of the morning.

Something that works so much better than simply espousing this teaching is to provide people with an actual experience of remembering the Oran Mór. Let us loosen our spirits to fly free for a moment and to travel on these words. Allow yourself to relax, to breathe, and to feel the Oran Mór wash over you. If you like, have a friend read these words to you, or record them into a recorder and play them back. Before beginning, I suggest putting on *Harmonic Meetings,* disk 2, track 1, "Kyrie Fragments," by David Hykes and the Harmonic Choir or *The Ambient Expanse* by S. Roach, P. O'Hearn, V. Obmana, S. Bacchus, and V. Unis.

PRACTICE: CONNECTING WITH THE GREAT SONG

- Close your eyes. Take three deep breaths, filling the cauldrons of your belly, your heart, and your head. Become aware of your beating heart. Notice the rhythm that your heart keeps.
- For a moment be aware of your body. It is comprised of a unique blending of the four elements: earth, air, fire, and water.

- The earth of your form is your skin, your bones. Clasp your hands together and be aware of the claylike nature of your skin.
- As you rub your hands together, become aware of the warmth in them. This ancient comfort of warmth is the fire of your form.
- Take three more deep breaths, allowing your lungs to fill with life-giving air. This is the air of your form. Be aware of how the air feels coming through your nose or mouth. Be aware that this ancient air is the basic essence of the winds, the four sacred spirit winds of the four directions.
- Move your awareness to your eyes. Note how freely they move to and fro within your eye sockets. Without moisture, you would not be able to move your eyes, you would not be able to swallow or to move your limbs. This fluidity of movement is the water of your form.
- Earth, fire, air and water: you are an expression of the four elements that have entered into a divine dialogue, a sacred dance with one another. Take just a few minutes to be aware of the four elements within you.
- Now allow your awareness to travel back in time and space, backward in time, backward in space to a dark void. This void was a fertile void. No qualities are known here, and yet all qualities are housed here. The fertile void is still; there is no sound, no light.
- Suddenly, a small quickening begins. It is subtle, almost imperceptible. It is a slight movement in a small seedlike place within the darkness. Very gradually this quickening gains in intensity, slowly forming a rhythmic wave. With this gradual increase in subtle motion come small pops and crackles, accompanied by small, almost imperceptible sparks of light.
- Slowly the small seedlike place in the darkness takes on even greater movement, cycles of motion beginning to swirl and

churn, gaining speed, the small pops and crackles turning into threads of brief soundings followed by flashes of brilliant light.

- Suddenly there is a pause in the quickening, a return to complete stillness and silence. As quickly as this pause occurs comes an explosion of sound and light, blowing into all directions from the center point of quickening.
- Ripples and waves of sound and light erupt outward, spinning, spiraling forth in grand array. All created matter begins taking form, each strand of Creation housing the divine melody of the original music: the Oran Mór.
- Use the words Oran Mór as a mantra and for the remainder of the time that the music is playing commune with the Oran Mór as a spiritual force within and around you. Know that you are cradled by the Great Song of Creation.

THE CELTIC-CHRISTIAN VISION OF THE GREAT SONG

Celtic Christianity is what we might call a "green" version of Christian mysticism. The Celtic people embraced Christianity rather easily, yet it is clear that, as a people intimately connected to the sacred world, they shaped the Christian tradition to suit their preexisting customs and inherent native mystical sensibilities.

Though some will suggest that Celtic-Christian versions of Christianity were not a unique tradition, that they did not differ from Roman expressions of the faith, this is clearly untrue. The early Celtic Church had a number of features that stood in direct contrast and opposition to the Roman Church, not the least of which was the tradition of maintaining the druidic tonsure, the inclusion of women in church leadership roles in Ireland, and the custom of allowing priests to marry. Some of the great Scottish Highland clans hail from ecclesiastical families who were originally involved in the druidic traditions but who later became leaders in the Celtic Church, such as the MacMillans ("son of the tonsured one"), the MacPhersons ("son of the parson") and the Colquhouns (spoken of as Celtic nature priests by the late Sir Iain Moncriffe).

The cosmology of Celtic Christianity says that all living things are sacred. For many people who have been wounded by patriarchal or politicized versions of the Christian faith, there is incredible healing to be had in realizing that there were and are earth-honoring versions of Christianity. In early Irish and Scottish communities there was a unique blending of the native spiritual inheritance (Celtic paganism, Druidism, faery traditions, and shamanism) with the vision of life as it was being taught by wise teachers of the desert fathers tradition of Christian mysticism. Both strands of the tradition, pagan and Celtic-Christian, heard and hear the ancient melody of the Great Song.

The essence of the Oran Mór is equally expressed in the words of Jesus' disciple, John, who tells us: "In the beginning was the Word." John is not referring to the words of the Bible, though some literalist Christian interpretations would suggest otherwise. Much to the contrary, the New Testament consists of written words of men who were attempting to interpret and express the beauty of the Word as they had remembered it and experienced it in Christ's presence. To limit one's understanding of the Word solely to the written words of the Bible is to vastly underestimate the power of what John is attempting to reveal to us through his mysticism.

Word in this context hails from the Greek word *Logos,* which is translated as "divine teaching," but it also translates as "utterance." As we read further in the Book of John, we are told that "the Word is God" and that with Creation there was light and that "all things created were filled with this light." The power of this sentiment in the Celtic imagination is that, like the druidic vision of an already blessed universe, the Logos (the Word) is the primal goodness that was already woven into Creation. Christ, in this fashion, is a god of light, who became enlightened and attempted to awaken others to their own luminosity with his presence.

For many Celts today, Jesus holds a potent place in their spirituality because he remembered his own ambassadorship, his own sacred standing in the world as a child of a loving and wakeful Shaping God. Learning of his own power to be a shaper in the world, his spiritual work in essence was to remind people of the "kingdom within," that holy place where we align with the Shape of Life and become shapers ourselves. His path was that of a revolutionist, actively calling into question the religious and political authority of his time, all the while seeking to teach people how to be their own catalysts for inner transformation. In a sense he blended, like the mist, with the inequities of his era and sought to change them through his own shaping influence as an ambassador of the Great Shaper. By his example we can see that the act of embodying our sacred ambassadorship and "standing in our sacred standing" is mist consciousness, Druid consciousness, and Christ consciousness.

Where modern Christianity has taken an unfortunate detour is that all too often the contemporary understanding of the Kingdom within does not also include our sacred connections to the living earth. As visionary ecotheologian Matthew Fox tells us,

> True to the theology of creation spirituality, [Meister] Eckhart does not consider the entrance of Jesus Christ into human and creation's history to have been primarily to redeem sinful humankind. Rather, he sees Christ's historical presence to be, first of all, a Reminder — Christ came to remind us of our blessed and divine origins as images and likenesses of God in a grace-filled universe. The purpose of his coming is more our divinization than our redemption from sin and guilt.[6]

---

6 Matthew Fox, *Western Spirituality* (Santa Fe: Bear & Company, 1991), p. 90.

Celtic-Christian tradition, as an ancestor of contemporary creation spirituality, also sees Christ as a reminder. Jesus, living the life of the Christ, remembered the Great Song of Creation and his own place within the shapes of things. As Fox says, Jesus — embodying the Christ energy — reminds us of "our blessed and divine origins as images and likenesses," namely, "shapes" of God.

When Jesus said, "I am the door" he was essentially inviting us all to walk through this door of a profound awareness, whatever our faith is, and become doors ourselves for others to walk through. We become what African shaman Malidoma Somé speaks of as a "threshold person," a person who is a living doorway of Spirit. Similarly, some Celtic linguists have conjectured that one of the root meanings of the word *druid* may have to do not only with "oak knowledge" or "far-seeing wisdom" but also with the root word for *door.*

In an era that has a tendency to demonize the druidic traditions, both in the media and in certain narrow religious movements of fundamentalism, I think it is high time that we revivify the ancient notion of the druid as a threshold person: one who is willing to walk through the doors of nature in pursuit of the divine knowledge of Creator and Creation. Similarly, in an era where there is also a tendency to romanticize the druids, I think it is important to introduce some common sense by looking at the druids and Druidism with a grounded, realistic view.

Some of the old Celtic monastics were also threshold people. These monks and nuns of the Celtic Church, including the *Celi De'* (pronounced kul-a-day, meaning "children of God," a group of especially austere monks among the Celtic-Christian monastics), took on a lifestyle in imitation of Jesus to manifest the Christ within themselves, to become sacred doorways, like their own druid ancestors. Although this is equally true of monks and nuns of other orders, such as the Franciscans, if we look deeply into the lives of certain Celtic saints, we see a particularly strong ambassadorship of the sacred world being embodied. In their view Jesus' every word and deed was a mirror reflecting back our own forgetfulness of the sacred. These dedicants sought to model their lives on Christ's example.

The Celtic monastic tradition (rooted in the desert monasticism of the pre-Roman Egyptian church) fit quite well with the Celtic soul's ancient legacy of "becoming one with the Great Song." Christ is, in effect, an ambassador of the Great Song, the Logos, and for many Celtic peoples this places him (and pure examples of creation spirituality) in alignment with the life-affirming teachings of the druids. This is mirrored in the old Outer Hebridean saying from Scotland, "Jesus was a good druid," or in the words of one Celtic saint, Columcille, who founded the monastery at Iona, "Christ is my druid."

John, one of the beloved saints of the Celtic people, remembered his own ambassadorship as well, his own sacred standing, because of Christ's presence. John then became an ambassador of the Great Song himself when he reminded us that "in the beginning was the Logos," in the beginning was the original utterance of the universe and of Creation, and woven in and throughout Creation is the divine wisdom. Our task is to listen for this divine wisdom, remember and realize it within ourselves and resume our "sacred standing" within the world as stewards of the Creation. Herein lies the environmental ethic of both the primal Celtic and Celtic-Christian traditions.

J. Philip Newell, author of *Listening for the Heartbeat of God: A Celtic Spirituality,* shares with us: "The Celtic mission [of the Celtic-Christian Church], inspired by John, remembered him as the beloved disciple who leaned against Jesus at the Last Supper. He had become an image of the practice of listening for the heartbeat of God. This spirituality lent itself to listening for the God at the heart of life."[7]

---

7 J. Philip Newell, *Listening for the Heartbeat of God: A Celtic Spirituality* (New York: Paulist Press, 1997), p. 1.

The Celtic soul is, in effect, "at one" with this ancient practice of listening for the heartbeat of the Creator within the created. In this way even the concept of sin becomes something very different.

Sin, from the Celtic perspective, isn't some sort of black mark against us with which we are born. The radical Celtic theologians Morgan of Wales (Pelagius) and John the Scot (John Scotus Eriugena) emphasized this point in their teachings of original blessing. Instead, sin is in essence forgetting the Great Song, forgetting the beauty of life, forgetting the holy thread running through our own lives, thereby forgetting the divine wisdom within the Creation and all the orders of Creation. Sin is what makes it possible for humans to destroy one another and the planet. Sin is what makes it possible for industrial plants to dump gallons of toxins into the water supply. Sin is what makes it possible for our government to be selective in exercising our humanitarianism, depending on whether or not it will affect gas prices.

ATONEMENT AS RENEWAL

Generally speaking, when a person has sinned in the Christian tradition, there is the necessary act called atonement. If you grew up in any Christian tradition, you probably heard a lot about "atoning for your sins." This is emphasized too much in modern Christianity. Atonement does not mean we need to wallow in self-pity, shame, or guilt. What good did this ever do anyone?

Atonement, if we really look at the word, means to return to a state of "at-one-ment": to remember what we have forgotten, to return to our sacred standing and sacred ambassadorship. It is to have our ancient citizenship in the sacred world restored. For some people at-one-ment is remembering to spend more quality time with their children. For others it may be coming back into a state of union with their spouse from whom they have grown distant.

For all of us it means remembering that our very survival depends on how we treat the earth and that what we do ecologically will affect the lives of our children's great-great-great grandchildren. When we forget that there is divine wisdom in every living thing, we cease to care for life. We begin living in such a way that the sanctity of life is no longer valued, and many living things are often destroyed as a result. Life, earth, woman, child, the whales, the wolf, prairie dogs, the ozone layer over Antarctica, the old-growth forests — all living things become profoundly threatened. Our forgetfulness is our sin. Practices that foster a state of at-one-ment with the Spirit of Life are our divine remembrance.

The emphasis of the Celtic-Christian vision, and its more ancient cousin, Druidism, is about renewal and restoration, not our past trials and tribulations. Certainly many disciplines, such as psychology, show us that we must understand the causes of our forgetfulness and pain to remedy our situation, but the Celtic vision seeks to restore the divine state. Recapitulation is often necessary as a way to understand where we have strayed from the path, but once we have realized we have strayed, it is time to step back onto the Mist-Filled Path and renew ourselves in our sacred standing with Creation.

Perhaps this is the difference within the Christian traditions themselves: Some people emphasize the Crucifixion and stay deeply entrenched within a contemplation of loss or one's own fall from grace, while others stress the Resurrection and therefore a renewal of sacred standing in Creation and how they can be of service to the deeper mission in life that we all have. These differences can even be seen in the different crosses used, with the Latin cross emphasizing the Crucifixion and the Celtic cross speaking to the state of the ever-renewing Creation.

In the Celtic-Christian cosmology there is more power in

contemplating the Resurrection of Jesu MàcMairi, as he is sometimes called. Jesus' trust in the Great Shaper of Life was gained through his practice of sacred listening. This, in turn, fostered an ancient lineage, with John and the many Celtic saints, of listening for the heartbeat of God in Creation. Some have stepped into this same ancient stream, realizing that their love of the trees and their love for Christ can be held together through the cosmology of Celtic-Christian spirituality. For them, there is no fall from grace, only an awareness of the forgetting followed by the all-important remembering through sacred listening.

Never at any point did Jesus shrink from the task of sacred listening. In this way we are shown that our renewal, our resurrection within our own lives, come through slowing down and surrendering ourselves to the act of sacred listening. It is through this practice of divine listening that we reconnect with the ancient melody of Creation, the divine wisdom of life, the presence of the Great Shaper.

Chapter 8

The Mothering Heart of God

Within the heart of God is the heart of a mother.

— Old Scottish Highland Saying

The process of reanimating the world with sacredness is rooted in opening ourselves to the energies of the divine feminine. The Celtic tradition is replete with expressions and examples of the divine feminine. As an archetype and a tangible energy, the holy feminine has deep roots in the Celtic psyche, and she wears many faces. Sometimes the sacred woman expresses herself as an initiatory power, as in the primal Scottish tradition of the goddess Scathach, who trained warriors, such as the great Irish warrior of Ulster, Cuchulain, how to fight. At other times the holy feminine is reflected in healing, midwifery, and poetic inspiration, such as with Brighid. Whether as initiator, healer, midwife, or guide, the Celtic spirit in both men and women openly embraces the feminine.

The archetype of the wise, nurturing, and powerful feminine

has a deep place in the Celtic soul. Unlike in many industrialized cultures, which have largely marginalized feminine power and have also victimized and objectified the feminine, the actualized Celtic relationship to the feminine is one of great reverence and protection. In the primal, pre-Christian customs and cosmologies of the Celtic world we find a rich and long-standing tradition of goddess worship. Various churches in Ireland even today show the influence of the goddess, as can be seen by the presence of various sculptures, such as the Sheila-na-Gig, a small goddess figure displaying her vulva, representing the womb of the earth and Creation. For others it is understood that certain rivers and waterfalls, certain wells and hills, are connected to holy feminine energy. Indeed, in the primal view of things, the entire landmass of Ireland is considered the body of a mother goddess.

This belief is eloquently expressed in contemporary language in a number of ways. A term used by Celtic mystic Tom Cowan openly refers to these sacred feminine energies as the "Celtic Mothers." I have come to call these life-protecting and life-sustaining forces the "Mothering Powers." Musician and renegade priestess Sinead O'Connor chimes in with a lyric that declares, "We used to worship God as a mother."

This ancient and nourishing image is the preeminent sacred woman. Once you feel her and see her, she is everywhere. I feel these Mothering Powers in the hills near my home, in the forest, and within certain trees, streams, and springs. The Celtic Mothers have been a healing force in my life as well as a source of wisdom. I sometimes meditate on a small sprig of heather standing upright in a transparent green vase on my writing desk. It reminds me that things of beauty are connected to the Mothering Powers.

Sometimes when I engage in visionary practices for entering the spirit world of Celtic primal tradition, I encounter the Celtic Mothers. When I have a backache, I will often slide into a steamy ritual bath, with sea salt, herbs, and essential oils dissolved into the water, each of my shoulders flanked by candles sitting on the ledge of the tub, and feel the healing touch of their powers. When I climb into a sweat lodge to lift prayers, also an ancient Celtic custom, I often feel that the Mothering Powers are with me. As you can see, the restorative energy of these powers can be drawn near in a number of ways, from meditating and sitting in a sweat lodge to appreciating things of beauty and even taking a simple evening bath.

REMEMBERING THE MOTHERING POWERS

To a large extent, modern society has forgotten the Mothering Powers, despite the fact that we all come into this world from our mothers. We celebrate Mother's Day. We may have good relations with our mothers, but in general the practice of viewing and relating to women as truly sacred beings has largely been expunged from modern culture. The expansive and far-reaching severance from the holy feminine has created deep wounds that we will be sorting out and healing from for millennia to come. Nonetheless, the undeniable value and holiness of the Mothers shine through in many circumstances that we take for granted.

Depicted in many war movies, for instance, and documented on the actual battlefield, many grown men call out for their mothers while dying from their injuries. They see their life flashing before their eyes, and the thing they yearn for most is the embrace of the one who brought them into life, just as they are about to leave it. It is as if at the gate of death these men receive the harsh reminder of the very underemphasized fact that our mothers are our source of life.

In a Celtic prayer-fasting program (a type of vision quest) in upstate New York, six people received a much more gentle reminder of the sacredness of the Mothering Powers. These individuals, over the course of three days and nights, had encountered the spine-tingling sights and eerie sounds of various singing, roaming spirits, in the haunted Ashokan Highland Range of the Catskills. They had experienced the effects of cold weather during the day and night. They had been visited by a whole host of animals, including bears, coyotes, and deer. On top of all of this, they had all abstained from food for three days and nights.

On ending their prayer fast, these brave souls returned to the central fire of our base camp and were met by three women, all of them mothers. These women had hiked in to prepare a breakfast (in the truest sense of the word). In addition to providing the vision questors with their first meal after three days, these three sacred women were also their first contact with the outside world since entering the domain of the mountains.

In a deep and compassionate manner, these mothers stepped into the role of the sacred Celtic Mothers and were impeccable models for bearing witness, hearing the experiences and the life-changing stories of the people. Like the sacred women in the Irish tales of Cuchulain who bore their breasts to him to route his war frenzy and remind him of his origins at the breast of his mother, these women embodied an ancient role of reminding people returning from the threshold of spirit and power that they were still in the land of the living. Even if not a word was said, their very presence alone whispered, "You are part of the great binding weave of life. You are now returning to the human community from your ordeal. Welcome home."

The Mothering Powers possess an undeniable energy. They are holy. They promote wholeness, integration, a sense of ease, a resolute knowing that we are within the fold of life. Their presence is ordinary, like a simple breakfast or cup of tea, yet they are also magical. Their presence is tangible, and their absence is undeniably felt. I often think that many people suffer from depression simply because they have not made time or room for the Mothering Powers to nurture them. We have to agree to, accept, and receive the nurturing and fostering of the Holy Mothers.

Reflection: The Mothering Powers Around You

- Take a moment to reflect on your life, the people in your life, the place in which you live. What role do the Mothering Powers play in your life? Do you feel their presence? Are you aware of an absence of the feminine, of the Mothering Powers? Perhaps there is someone who helps you to feel regenerated every time you are with them. Maybe it is not a person, but a time you make for yourself to remember your connection to life.
- The Mothering Powers have many faces and many energies. Reflect on what energies you need to surround yourself with. Some Mothering Powers are healing energies, like a Mother Theresa. Other Mothering Powers are female protector spirits, such as a Joan of Arc or a Julia Butterfly Hill. Other Mothering Powers are more cronelike, such as the wonderful Buddhist teacher Pema Chödrön. Attune yourself to the Mothering Powers, and make room for them in your life. Whether we are men or women, we need these powers.

The Denigration of the Divine Feminine

The patriarchal traditions of politicized Christianity, the surgical reasoning of certain Western philosophies, and the cosmology of society as a whole (science, government, and technology) have become shaping forces that do not value the feminine, the wild, or the sacred. The primal forces of feminine wisdom, of intuition, of wild earth spirits, and the "unexplainable ineffable" are obstacles, if not enemies, of what we might refer to here as the *Pater* Conspiracy. The Latin word *pater* (pronounced pah-tare) is the root word for *patriarchy* and *paternal*. In and of itself it is a neutral concept, in that it still holds a great deal of potential that could be channeled into life-affirming ways, rather than wielded for destruction, oppression, and power over others. In its actualized form, *pater* is the archetype of the Gentle Old Man, the Loving Father, the Wise Grandfather, the Life-Affirming Warrior, the Healer-Shaman, the Young or Old Male Druid, the Male Bard or Poet Enraptured with Life. These powerful masculine archetypes in the Celtic world, both ancient and modern, have long been known as protectors of the forests (the Green Man), keepers of sacred traditions (druids), egalitarian leaders (William Wallace or Rob Roy of Scotland), and lovers of the creative (warrior-poets). They are also, I should note, protectors of women.

More generally we can easily see glimmers of these archetypes that let us know the refined spirit of *pater* is still with us. Perhaps we see a picture of His Holiness the Dalai Lama on a magazine, or we read a book by Thomas Merton or Kent Nerburn and come to understand their level of devotion to the goodness of life. Perhaps we watch a Brother Cadfael *Mystery!* program on public television, and we remember some spark of the true gentleman, the refined but spontaneous, the gentle but powerful man who seems to be more at peace with himself and his world than most others.

What is it about these men that makes them different? What is it about their presence, their very way of being in the world that seems to slice through the illusions, so to speak? Part of the answer to this question lies in the fact that they have stepped out of the unconscious process of the *Pater* Conspiracy.

This conspiracy has profoundly limited the variety of positive male archetypes possible in this culture. It is as if young men today should only aspire to be a professional golfer, a "here-today, gone-tomorrow" rap musician, a cut-throat stockbroker, or a soldier. Many men of the sixties generation had an even tougher time plotting their course through manhood because of the tumultuous changes to the yardstick used to measure masculinity. They found themselves in a polarized world with no tolerance for ambiguity. You either had to be a "flower child" or a "leatherneck," a conformist or a communist, or so it seemed.

The *Pater* Conspiracy has ancient roots in certain brands of Christianity. Some forms of Christianity (what I call "Churchanity") have a long-standing tradition of despising women and have voraciously sought to "save the souls" of indigenous peoples and gain control of all that is spontaneous and wild. I refer to this influence as a conspiracy because, ultimately, it is an undercurrent that men are rarely supported in questioning. To openly assess the *Pater* Conspiracy, and the limited types of modern maleness it attempts to enforce, would be to call into question just about everything: our institutions, our government, our churches, indeed the very bedrock of our society. It would mean revivifying more enlightened examples of maleness in our ancient past as well as in our more recent past.

Calling into question the *Pater* Conspiracy is actually extremely powerful and liberating work for men. It puts us in an exciting position on the time line of history. This position is one of reclaiming our birthright for a refined sense of warriorship, based on gentleness and dynamic connection to the spirit powers of life, not rooted in unchecked aggression or bogus doctrines such as the Manifest Destiny, which was the guiding paradigm used by the U.S. government to justify its genocide of Native American civilization. Although we would hope that the days of such life-crippling, soul-thrashing cosmologies have been transformed, we have simply changed the appellations to such things as "globalization" and "petroleum exploration." Indigenous people and the wild places still face an onslaught of aggression.

Having an activated awareness of the *Pater* Conspiracy invites us into the extremely timely work of contemplating not only the senseless destruction that has taken place in the name of our religious and political institutions, but also of envisioning what an enlightened society might look like if our models of manhood and man-making were geared toward these aims.

The Healing Work of Men

My Father's God Beneath the Waves

Last night, among the blue dawning night,
I felt the tide coming in.
I left the warm, white-sheeted bed
and, barefoot, went down to the sea.
At the water's edge I stood,
with the cold water washing my feet.
I felt watched and watching.
The moon made shapes on the dark rippling waves,
and I imagined I saw in them
the face of my father, and his father,
and out to the horizon, all the fathers before me,
who mingled their blood with the sea
and who drank salt tears,
and danced when no one was looking.
And I whispered to the god beneath the waves,
"Make me something else,... and still man."

— Jathan Gurr

The *Pater* Conspiracy is a style of thinking and being that is unnatural for men, and yet most men are not conscious of this pattern of destructiveness within themselves, because we have not been shown another way. We cannot question or transform what we do not recognize as having a stranglehold on our true power as potential shapers of the world.

Thankfully some men have reached deep down with courage and have begun to examine the patterns and unquestioned models that have shaped us. Some men have reached, rather adventurously, into their souls, their warrior hearts, their shaman blood, their forest spirits, and they have had a vision. Unfortunately, these examples are the exception. The men still caught in unchecked patterns of limited identity suffer from a disease that all of us as men inherited in one way or another. The essence of it is the unconscious perception that we, as men, are somehow one rung on the ladder above women and at the veritable apex of God's Creation.

Warriorship in its present form in Western society is an outgrowth of this perception. Warriorship is thought to consist of brute strength, the ability to kill, and the power to overcome any other forces that might threaten. From this vantage point, strength is seen as the ability to prevent oneself from becoming vulnerable. The irony is, as we see from the life of Gandhi or of the founder of Aikido, Morihei Ueshiba, true strength and power come from dynamic vulnerability and openness, not from guardedness or the ability to kill and maim. Indeed, in the true warrior cultures of the world it has always been considered dangerous for a man to learn anything of the way of the warrior before having a firm understanding of the feminine energies within. This is reflected in the old Celtic axiom, "Never give a man a sword until he knows how to dance."

The *Pater* Conspiracy is anti-*mater, mater* being the Latin word for "mother." This undercurrent of opposition to the feminine is a disease in the soul of man, a cosmological cancer. It runs counter to indigenous models of leadership and power, such as the

Haudenosaunee, or Iroquois, whose elected male chiefs are chosen specifically by the clan grandmothers. These women are the wise women, who have a deep, piercing knowledge of the "good mind" that is a prerequisite for Iroquois leadership, even today. The women have even more status in the culture than the chiefs themselves.

This style of governance and leadership is known in the primal Celtic cultures as well. Many of the Celtic tribes were under the leadership or instruction of female chieftains and warriors, such as Boudiccea among the Gauls, Scathach on the Isle of Skye (where the island gets its name), and Lady Anne Farquharson in the Battle of Culloden in 1746, who led her husband's clan, the MacKintoshes, against the Hanoverian and English forces, despite her husband's wishes, I might add.

When contemplating the clan grandmothers of the Iroquois, as well as these revered women in the Celtic past, I find myself looking into the face of such glaring questions as:

- When will the male-dominated religions welcome the wise women back?
- Why, even today, are women not recognized as possible candidates for the presidency of the United States, while Ireland has already known the unparalleled grace of handing over the reins to a wise woman to serve as leader?
- Of course the questions run deeper. Why will three out of four American women be sexually abused in their lifetime, while women in some countries who have been raped are then murdered by their own families in sanctioned "honor killings" because of the "shame it will bring upon the father's name?"

These imbalances exist because of a fundamental flaw in our cosmology and an experiential disconnection from the sacred feminine, including the feminine face of our own masculine divinity.

Essentially, the male soul has been given the sword before learning to truly dance with the feminine.

This kind of thinking is essentially an external manifestation of an internal war going on in the soul of many men. All phenomena, in this vein of thought, are laid out very neatly into either/or consciousness, a process that for our purposes we might refer to as "enemization": making created matter the enemy (matter as the expression of *mater*). Created matter — earth, animals, people of other religions and cultures — become the enemy. Women become the enemy. The wildness of Creation becomes something simply to manhandle.

Indeed, in the first book of the Bible we read the words, "have dominion o'er all the earth." Undoubtedly many "green" Christians have revamped this line of the Scriptures to reflect a Christian vision of earth stewardship and ecological ethics, but by and large if we look at the current treatment of the planet, of women, and of people of color, we will see quite clearly that the "dominion myth" is in full swing. It feeds religion, science, and government, and it is shaping the world our children's children will live in.

Albert Einstein formed a perennial question for us all when he asked, "Is the universe a friendly place?" It is difficult to know how to answer this question. We can survey our brief history and see that the track record is not so great, with Inquisitions and the Burning Times, with aberrations of human belief and behavior (such as religious fundamentalism and white supremacy). We can also see, unfolding right before our eyes, special interest petroleum agendas dangerously complicating geopolitics and the health of the environment and destroying native cultures and ecosystems, while cutting-edge scientist after scientist is denied patents for technologies that have been proven to be more sustainable, removing our dependence on foreign energy sources.

What is the cure to this rampant disease of making an enemy of created matter and the feminine, of constantly seeing the other as the enemy? We have gotten off course. How do we restore ourselves?

TERTON-MAMA

A poem for Maya Angelou

I once heard instructions from a wisewoman.
An eyebrow raised like a druid's sickle,
she whispered magic.

"Words stick to walls," she said.
"They are alive and must be revered,
and softened,
for they dwell wherever they land,
wherever they travel.
Even in stone and in flesh."

She was one who lost her speech, once.
Now, she is a many-streamed *terton;*[1]
A revealer.
She knows the shaping power of words
taken to air like a many-feathered dream;
power to do, and undo.
She leans toward silence, away from the vexations
of loud and rootless laughter.
In her gleaming eyes she sees a different world.
Holy words, pillars of faith,
in place of bars that divide us.
A river;

---

1 A *terton* is a Buddhist teacher who is a revealer of lost treasures and the dharma.

the power of the river flowing
through our eyes.
Holding hands to the arc of the sky
I blow forth a wordless prayer.
Words before words.
May her world be.
May Woman be invited home.

— FRANK MACEOWEN[2]

It is time for the paradigm of enemization to be overturned. It is time for our society to do away with this toxic worldview, to cross-examine the cosmologies and archetypes that are driving our reality, and to inaugurate new ones — or old ones — of a more life-affirming nature. Even more important, it is time to weep and weep before the keening altars of grief and invite the Mothering Powers back into our lives.

We all have to be willing to take these diseased parts of ourselves and our cultures and, like in an old Celtic fire ritual, place them carefully into the flames of transmutation to birth a new way of being that integrates the best of *pater* and *mater.* It is only through a process of befriending created matter and befriending the feminine that life on this planet will survive. This is not some warm and fuzzy New Age notion. It is a fact. The pendulum has swung too far now. It is time for a reconnection with the sacred feminine within man and woman and within life. It is time to return to right relationship with Creation.

We must be able to look on one another, on our planet, and within ourselves with the eyes of the mother that is within the heart of God. Men must start, first and foremost, by inviting the banished Mothering Powers back into our souls.

---

2 From Frank MacEowen, *Building Fences in High Wind: Poems of Longing.*

ANIMA: THE MOTHERING POWERS WITHIN

Carl Jung, the Swiss psychiatrist, was the first to formulate a working, life-affirming psychology regarding the feminine aspect of man's psyche. A term he put forth, drawn from Latin, is central to our work here: anima.

On an individual level the anima is at the heart of the healing work of men. Men have been just as wounded by the *Pater* Conspiracy as women, but in different ways. On a grander scale, befriending the feminine, welcoming the Mothering Powers back, are also at the heart of healing the matrix of Creation, of the planet, of humanity. Unless this healing takes place, the epidemic rate of sexual assault will continue, and the rape of the planet will continue.

If we look closely at the word *anima* we see that it has word cousins related to our discussion. *Anima* is related to *animism,* and also to *animal* and *animation.* In the Celtic mystical view, there exists a deep and empowered understanding of the relationship among animism, sacred animals, the animating powers of life, and the Mothering Powers. For men to heal, and for our planet to heal, we must rediscover this thread in our lives. Men must openly reclaim a stance of "empowered vulnerability," which involves developing a strong relationship with the anima. This is the way to "invite Woman home."

Jung defines the anima in this manner:

> Every man carries within him the eternal image of the woman, not the image of this or that particular woman, but a definite feminine image. This image is fundamentally unconscious, an hereditary factor of primordial origin engraved in the living organic system of the man, an imprint or archetype of all the ancestral experiences of the female, a deposit, as it were, of all the impressions ever made by woman.... Since this image is unconscious, it is always unconsciously projected.[3]

---

3 Carl Jung, "The Development of Personality," *The Collected Works of C. G. Jung,* vol. 17 (Princeton, N.J.: Princeton University Press, 1973), p. 198.

A more simplistic way of putting it is that each of us has an outward face that we project to the world. We also possess an inward face, so to speak, that rests within our psyches as an unconscious expression of the energies of the opposite gender. For women, the masculine dwells within as the animus, while for men the inner feminine is the anima. This has less to do with actual gender and more to do with those styles of being we tend to associate with each gender.

However, this does not mean that only women are nurturing or that men are the only ones with the potential for violence. Some of the most tender and feeling people I have known are men, great but quiet warrior-poets who love women, men, children, and the earth. On the other hand, some of the most energetically violent people I have known in my life are women, who have adopted rather *pater* approaches to life (and business) to further their aims and ventures. These attributes are universal, not gender based. It is possible for each gender to adopt, embody, and live from the actualized expressions of both the masculine and feminine energies, be this strength or nurturing, but we must each seek to transform the shadow dimensions of each of these energies in ourselves for this to occur.

Calvin Hall and Vernon Nordby, authors of *A Primer of Jungian Psychology,* state:

> Every person has qualities of the opposite sex, not only in the biological sense that man and woman both secrete both male and female sex hormones, but also in a psychological sense of attitudes and feelings.... If the personality is to be well adjusted and harmoniously balanced, the feminine side of a man's personality and the masculine side of the woman's personality must be allowed to express themselves in consciousness and behavior.[4]

---

4 Calvin Hall and Vernon Nordby, *The Primer of Jungian Psychology* (New York: Penguin Books, 1973), p. 46.

It is precisely through men rediscovering their animas that the necessary remembrance takes place. We remember our childhood love of the forest, the mist, the stars, and rainbows. When man embraces the Mothering Powers within he becomes whole. He becomes the warrior who, in the primal Celtic way, knows how to dance and handles a sword with the care of life rather than the carelessness of hate. It is, after all, no accident that the old Irish and Scottish kings were symbolically married to the goddess of the land, or that Excalibur, the unbreakable sword of sovereignty and power, was given to King Arthur (in Welsh, Arth Vawr, or Great Bear) by the Lady of the Lake. The true power of the warrior comes from the watery depths guarded by the feminine face of earth.

Embracing the anima, for men, and the animus, for women, is an invitation to a kind of rebirth. In such an embrace not only are we met with an embrace, but we are also met with the embracing force of animism, which sees the world as filled with soul. The animated soul seeks relationship and dialogue — holy encounter. The reanimated soul follows the Spirit of Longing. It seeks to restore harmony to situations of discord and to celebrate its place along the wider path of life.

GOING OUT TO MEET THE MOTHER

One of the first steps of restoring right relationship with the Mothering Powers of Creation is to truly grasp the reality that we would not be here without these primal feminine powers. One of the most effective processes I know to facilitate this deep knowing is to remove ourselves from the illusionary structure of the modern world (the "man-made world") that deludes us into thinking we have everything under control. In many indigenous traditions, as well as in the Celtic ways, one of the customs that drives this point home quite well is the prayer fast, sometimes called the vision quest, such as the one I embarked on in preparation for the Sun Dance among the Lakota.

No one culture has the monopoly on this ancient ritual. Going into the natural world, fasting, and seeking a vision are practices known to most earth peoples. The Celtic tribes, the Taoists of China, ancient Christian orders such as the Essenes, certain Buddhist sects, some practitioners of Shinto, and shamanistic peoples the world over have all employed fasting as a means of receiving guidance and returning to harmony, both in spirit and in body.

When we have gone out into the wilderness and fasted for an extended period, suddenly the priorities of life are arranged for us very clearly. For practitioners of shamanism, the vision quest is also a method for building power. For practitioners of contemplative spirituality, it can be a poignant process of prayer. Everyone, regardless of spiritual tradition, is granted a deep sense of the holy presence of the Great Shaper of Life and the sanctity of the earth on a prayer fast.

With our tails tucked between our legs, we see clearly that we are such small, fragile, and finite beings. A blessed level of awareness is often cultivated. We come to realize that the Mothering Powers and the presence of the divine feminine are in all things. As if in a sudden flash of enlightenment, many people are returned to a primal remembrance of the Great Mother when on a vision quest. We "get it" on a very deep level that each and every one of us was born of mother, both our biological mothers and this earth, our Mother.

Each of us is meant to be suckled at the breast of our biological mother, but on a wider scale we are all suckled at the breast of the earth. On a prayer fast we begin to see with astonishing clarity that we are all dependent on the life-giving energies of the Mother as planet. No technology can replace or alter this dependency or relationship. From an ecopsychological standpoint, anyone who believes they are outside the fold of this reality sufers from a form of mental illness. Currently ecopsychology is an embryonic field, but it is a discipline that examines the psychological causes and the spiritual and ecological ramifications of global soul loss that result from our individual and societal disconnection from a life-affirming relationship with nature. In essence, the newly evolving path of ecopsychology and the ancient Celtic spirit have a great many things in common, not the least of which is the search for ways to foster a connection between humans with the sacred earth.

The prayer fast is one potent method for working to reclaim a renewed sense of connection to the healing and life-giving powers of earth. In the Celtic tradition many of us fast from food, but not from water. Some tribal people, such as the Lakota, require abstinence from both food and water in their ceremonies. For myself I have discovered that continuing to drink water during a prayer fast not only accelerates the process of flushing toxins from the body, but it is also an excellent way to stimulate sacred dreaming while engaged in the work.

Before attempting a Celtic prayer fast, I recommend performing a night vigil. A night vigil also consists of fasting from food, but the practice lasts for twenty-four hours rather than three days and nights. Before attempting any of the following practices, please consult a physician to assess your physical capabilities of fasting from food.

Celtic Prayer Fast

- Find a place in the natural world where you can sit undisturbed for the full turning of the night. You may want to work with an *anamchara* (an ancient Irish word for soul friend, which was a druidic and a Celtic-Christian role of spiritual support) who can hold a base camp for you while you undertake your vigil. They will be the person who greets you in the morning when you are done.

- In a night vigil it is best to stay awake for the entire night. Having a soul friend who can give you a ride in the morning is not only a safety measure (since you may not be physically able to drive) but it also gives you the opportunity to process your experiences with someone you trust.
- When I do a night vigil, I usually enter the green realm of nature, but a great many insights can also be gained from performing a night vigil in a darkened room. The old Celtic vision poets would seal themselves into dark earth chambers, or within beehive cells, with a stone on their bellies, and receive inspiration. Try doing the night vigil in a room that you set aside in your home.
- To engage in an actual three-day vision fast, I wholeheartedly recommend soliciting the support and guidance of a shaman, seer, or trained vision-quest guide or wilderness rites-of-passage instructors. Unless you are a seasoned practitioner with full access to your land, it is advisable to participate in a vision-quest program, such as those offered by the School of Lost Borders (www.schooloflostborders.com), the Center for Ecopsychology at Naropa University in Boulder, Colorado (www.naropa.edu), or through the individual offerings of a trusted teacher. A number of spirit and health issues must be taken into account in a traditional prayer fast, and for the sake of your ritual work, it is best to have these issues monitored and addressed by someone else.

We can learn a great deal from the deeper spiritual leanings of the Celtic soul in relation to the feminine. There is an impassioned sense within the Celtic vision to seek and commune with our primal origins. Ultimately, however, this search for primal origins is rooted in a longing to know that we belong, that we have permission to be here in this body, on this planet, that we are loved. The true teachers of this love are the Mothering Powers.

As men we must learn to befriend the feminine, truly, before we are worthy of the sword. As Celtic descendants, both men and women, we must actively seek to restore the woman's place of honor in our lives, our families, and in our society, recognizing that it may very well be at a woman's hand that the problems of our era are to be solved. As people, regardless of ancestry, regardless of culture, it is time to welcome the Mothering Powers home.

Chapter 9

The Body as Holy

People say that what we're all seeking is a meaning for life.
I don't think that's what we're really seeking. I think that
what we're really seeking is an experience of being alive,
so that our life experiences on the purely physical plane
will have resonances within our innermost being and reality,
so that we actually feel the rapture of being alive.

— Joseph Campbell, *The Power of Myth*[1]

Celtic spirituality is an embodied spirituality that not only includes the holiness of the body but also extends from it. It is a spirituality that trusts the senses, trusts the inner stirrings and intuitive prompts that the body offers us each moment of our day. It is a spirituality of motion and emotion, flowing with the tides of the human heart like white foam on the ocean wave. In essence, Celtic spirituality supports us in feeling the "rapture of being alive."

1 Joseph Campbell, *The Power of Myth* (New York: Dell, 1998), p. 1.

Embodied spirituality is not some grandiose philosophy made up of ethereal ideas that are never brought to fruition in outward ways. It is not a path of becoming bogged down in notions that cannot support the harvesting of its fruit. Spiritual concepts must be like seeds that take root in the soil of our life. All too often, however, our hungry spirits, shaped by the spirit of these times, eat the seeds themselves and do not tend or nurture growth that will truly feed us or the generations to come.

Embodied spirituality should foster an integration of the inner and outer, the body and the spirit, the inner sanctum of the home and the outer world. Think of it as climbing up the side of a great mountain using a rope. We must not let go of the rope. We must maintain a proper creative tension between the wisdom of the body and the wisdom of the soul within the Soul of the World. This creative tension is another way of thinking about spiritual practice. Spiritual practice that includes and employs the wisdom seat of the body is a rope that gets us to the top of the mountain. It is the thread that ties the inner life to an outer life of action.

As John Scotus Eriugena, the great ninth-century renegade Celtic theologian has said: "The human being consists of a body and a soul. Binding together the body of this world and the soul of the other world, the human being, humanity, creates a single cosmos. For the body possesses all bodily nature and the soul all spiritual nature, and these fitting together into a single harmony make up the cosmic world of the human being."[2]

Celtic spirituality is what we might call an integrative spirituality because it fosters this sacred weaving of body and soul. It is an embodied path because it is a spirituality of the soulful body. In both the primal druidic and the Celtic-Christian vision of life, spirituality is about our bodies engaged and enlivened with a soul directed toward peace. There is an understanding that divinity

---

2 C. Bamford, *The Voice of the Eagle: The Heart of Celtic Christianity* (Hudson, N.Y.: Lindisfarne Books, 1990).

permeates all things, including the body. Spirit, or divinity, is the force that fills out matter.

Celtic spirituality as an embodied path clearly celebrates the body rather than demonizing it. The body is perceived as a vehicle, a sacred friend, to assist us in sensing and participating in the dynamism of life. The Celtic tradition recognizes that the body has an innate intelligence that is trustworthy. The body, in effect, is one of the places through which we can feel the influence of the Creator, the Lightener of the Stars. Like John the Scot instructs, we become a living, breathing spiritual cosmos through the unification of body and soul. We cannot, like those in some religious traditions do, disregard the body in our pursuit of spirit, soul, and enlightenment. Body and soul are related, interfused, mirrors. They are one. What is done to one is reflected in the other. In the Celtic view of our soul's journey, our enlightenment occurred the moment we were conceived and born. We are born already blessed, privileged guests with a lifetime membership in the great binding weave of shapes.

We cannot afford to misuse, abuse, or mistrust the body. In some religious traditions, however, an unfortunate process of eschatological warping has occurred. Some shame-based traditions propagate the idea that the only reality with any true value is that of the afterlife, instantly making it possible for discord to rule in the earthly domain of the body (including the body of the earth). In this kind of paradigm the body and earthly life are often perceived of as a prison that keeps us locked up, preventing us from experiencing union with the divine. Whether in the form of a twisted, self-deprecating, and martyred emulation of Jesus' earthly pains in one's own life or in the blatant disregard for life shown by some Islamic extremists willing to cast away their bodies in terrorist acts "to join Allah," any personal or cultural theology that abuses the body is on a treacherous road far from the awareness of a wakeful and loving universe.

On the Celtic road of life we are invited back into a loving embrace. Within this embrace the body is experienced as a reliable barometer. We reclaim what is rightfully ours: awe at the majesty and grandeur of life, a quality of joyfulness, even in the midst of pain or difficulty. We suddenly realize that we are not human beings having a spiritual experience, but in the words of Angeles Arrien, "Spiritual beings having a human experience."

On the Celtic path of bodily befriendment, more is possible. The seership of the mystic or the healing work on the shaman's path, for instance, are made possible precisely through maximizing the resources offered by this spiritual cosmos formed by body and soul. The work of the shaman or mystic is not only a matter of soul or spirit. Without a body, the shaman is simply a ghost. The body is the sacred temple through which the shaman, mystic, or healer receives certain prompts and guidance. We all have access to this soulful bodily wisdom, but we must open ourselves to its richness and not cut ourselves off from our own earthiness. Our earthiness is holy. In the words of the Rhineland mystic Hildegard of Bingen, "Holy persons draw to themselves all that is earthy."

Embracing Our Earthiness

An alive and activated body, with heart and senses open, is able to feel the profound influences and unseen ties of holy relationship. This is not just a concept. It is an experience that can be felt throughout the body. In this way the soulful body, our own body, becomes a most important teacher. It offers us the knowledge that we can, and must, open ourselves to the soul of the earth and come to understand that we have come from her, that the earth and our body are profoundly related. Our bodies are but a microcosmic expression of the body of the planet. We are her, and everything that is has been set into motion by an intelligence that is tied to her intelligence. The earth is not just some random boat we are all on. It is our home, much like the body we inhabit. Although it might appear that we exist as individuals, separated from one another, living in our own universes, the reality is that we share the same body, the same earth, the same breath.

Learning to love our earthly home, learning to love what the "soft animal of our body loves," as poet Mary Oliver puts it, is the bedrock of Celtic spirituality and the unique Celtic approaches to ecopsychology, shamanism, and animistic spirituality. There is no one who is not woven into this holy tapestry. Our ancestors, the animals and trees, the quality of our time here: all these can serve as reminders of our earthiness.

An embodied approach to spirituality, of welcoming the spirit powers into the body, is a path of sacred remembrance. It is an open invitation made by the many life-affirming forces to the soul-body complex of the person. To accept this invitation, as opposed to the invitation from the land of the sleepwalkers, is to have the spiritual cosmos of Eriugena's teaching awakened and activated within us. A spiritual intelligence within our cells, cells that already know and understand their tie to the holy tapestry of earth and spirit, then become our guides on such a path.

Cells hold memory and wisdom, and perhaps songs as well. On this path we turn our attention to these vibrant strands of wisdom. We come to listen, more and more, for the Oran Mór, or for what ambient musician Vir Unis calls the "drift inside." We listen, again, to the wisdom cells within us to see what they have to say.

PRACTICE: CELLULAR KNOWING

- Put on *The Serpent's Lair,* disk 1, by Steve Roach and Byron Metcalf. (NOTE: Unlike in some of our other exercises, I recommend using all the tracks on this CD in performing this journey. Steve and Byron have cocreated a masterful recording of soundscapes for vision seeking and working with the inner landscapes.)

- Take three breaths, filling the cauldrons of your belly, your heart, and head. Allow this sacred music to carry you into a deep state of relaxation in which you are also aware of the deeper flow of energy within your soul body. Allow yourself to feel how your body responds to the dynamic rhythms and the flowing sounds of this music.
- Now breathe in through your nose slowly to the count of four. Then breathe out through your nose to the count of four. As much as possible, maintain this style of breathing, allowing your breathing to be supported by the music. Let the music be almost like a "spirit horse" that carries you. Give yourself over to its intelligence and rhythm. If it assists you, allow your body to move to the music.
- Now prepare to take a journey into your body. Your intention is to search your body for a cell that contains a kernel of wisdom or knowledge. Cells hold memory and energy. Some cells hold the electrons that have known other existences. Some cells hold untapped resources of knowledge. Open yourself to the many images and sensations that may arise, but focus on the task at hand: to locate a cell of wisdom that will benefit you in your life at this time. Repeat this intention to yourself. Perhaps it is a word, an image, a phrase, a color, or even a set of instructions, but whatever this information is, it is stored within your own cells.
- When you embark on this journey into the body, perhaps you will enter the inner recesses of your body through your navel, as some shamans have reported doing. Perhaps you will suddenly find yourself in your bloodstream, or swimming along in

your lymph system. In any case, do not judge or analyze. Simply allow the music to take you deeper and deeper into the strands and fibers of life that make up your body. Search for a cell of wisdom. When the music comes to rest into silence again, sit up, take three deep breaths, and record in your journal what you encountered.

In a sense, an animistic cosmology suggests that the path of spirituality in our "ancient future," to use Seminole-Oneida shaman Leslie Gray's term, will be akin to the spirituality of our ancient past. We might call it a microscopic spirituality. It suggests that the macrocosm that is our world is, and will be, a direct reflection of the inner world of the individual and the spiritscape of the human community. One way that we can come to understand how we shape the outer world into a place more aligned with harmony is through exploring this cellular dimension for our own inherent source-seeds of wisdom. To work with "technologies of the sacred," be it an entheogenic path (using sacred plant medicines or hallucinogens, such as *ayahuasca,* mushrooms, or peyote), a shamanic path, or a contemplative path of prayer, is to invite the Great Shaper(s) of Life to "set up camp" within us.

In this way individual soul loss and individual soul retrieval become dynamically connected to cultural soul loss and cultural soul retrieval. Consider for a moment the existence of a sacred culture. Perhaps it is Celtic, Peruvian, African, or Siberian. In any case, an ancient energy source exists that guides the culture and the inhabitants of the culture. It has always been there, this ancient spirit, the soul of the culture. However, there are also political, social, and cultural upheavals, such as the encroachment of the Romans on the Celtic world, the Irish Famine, the Scottish

Highland Clearances, the African diaspora, the coming of the Spanish Conquistadors to Peru, the Soviet murder of various shamans in Tuva and Outer Mongolia, to name but a few examples. Like the example of the individual whose soul hides a portion of itself until conditions are ripe for a return, parts of a culture's soul can go underground when faced with such culturewide traumas.

Then, at a later juncture, an individual descendant of the culture whose soul has been eclipsed (or whole cross-sections of the remnant culture) plugs back in with the ancient energy source via their own cellular awakening and ushers in the return of the missing soul parts. From this precious ground of awareness we come to realize an insight long held by indigenous peoples around the world. They have always known that the same energy complex of body and soul that formed the spiritual cosmos for a shaman or mystic hundreds of years ago is equally available through the body, sacred senses, and gateways to spirit and nature that we have now. The same thresholds that informed them then can form and inform us now.

Some literalists would suggest that spiritual continuity or recovery of this sort is not possible. This belief negates the reality of the transpersonal. It negates the potent cellular process that can occur when modern people interface with ancient traditions and the technologies of the sacred found therein. It also negates Eriugena's view of each human being as a holy spiritual cosmos. When this spiritual cosmos (and its associated visions) thrives in our lives, it connects us to other times, places, and people who were also deeply nourished by the spirit of the path, the soul of ancient cultures. It does not make us special, or "holier than thou," or part of an elite class. Much to the contrary, the activated spiritual cosmos in our lives makes us true beginners, aware that we are now lifetime students, filled with "radical unknowing," as renowned scholar and transpersonal theorist Ken Wilber puts it.

This vision of human life as an inherent spiritual cosmos is the ancient beating heart of who we are and can be. In an age of exhaustive domestication of the wild spirit of the earth, it is time to be earthy again. Perhaps this earthiness is the biggest soul fragment that we must "set up a squawk" over to have it return. It is our earth soul, our earth body, and the undeniable expression of this soul part when it enlivens our limbs.

When we provide for this opening to occur within ourselves, we are changed. Suddenly we are aligned with something much greater and fuller than the individual ego or personality. Our providence lies in providing for this opening for radical unknowing to occur. We can be opened by a raw, unexpected, unrehearsed, and undiluted experience of the mystery. On the Mist-Filled Path we soon experience the simple yet profound reality that the same doorways to holiness that our ancestors passed through become our own gateways to a fully lived and loving life. Our reclaimed primal and earthly senses are, in fact, the very mother root that feeds and quenches the ancient stream of spirituality of the Mist-Filled Path, a path of opening the soul to rekindling ancient wisdom.

THE MISTWALKER

In or around the year 600 C.E., after the Christian teachings had been introduced into Ireland, a man named Senchan, the chief poet of Ireland (known as the *ollamh,* pronounced o-lav, in Irish), called a council of the many *seanachie* and *filidh,* vision poets and tribal historians on the island. The purpose of the meeting was to determine if anyone could remember one of the great epic poems of the Irish, namely the *Tain Bo Cuailgne,* or *The Cattle Raid of Cooley.*

After much discussion and debate it became clear that, despite the gathering of many of Ireland's best, the ancient tale had fallen from common memory. Only fragments remained, but not enough to put together the complete story. So the chief poet sent three young men on a journey to look for a wizened old man living somewhere near present-day Roscommon who was believed to know a great many things.

The three young men arrived at the grave site of an ancient poet named Fergus MacRoich. Two of them made their way down a path to a homestead to see if they could find accommodations for the night, while the third young bard remained at the grave. This bard is said to have recited a poem of his own creation to the grave in memory and honor of the great spirit of Fergus MacRoich. Suddenly, the young poet became thoroughly enveloped in a thick mist. His companions looked all over the hill, through the mist and down into the surrounding wood, but to no avail. They could not find their companion. Meanwhile, much to his surprise, the young poet found himself in the presence of the spirit of Fergus MacRoich, who proceeded to recite the entire epic of the *Tain.*

Although there are different versions of this story, all agree on a few major points. In one, in keeping with the ancient Celtic practice of sleeping on or meditating atop graves and ancestral hills, the young poet places himself in a "thin place," a threshold of history and wisdom. Second, all accounts suggest that the young poet communed with the spirit of Fergus MacRoich for three days and nights, three being a sacred number to the Celts and the number of days employed today by many Celtic practitioners who practice the vision fast. Finally, it was precisely through the act of honoring the ancestor with an offering (a poem) that the ancient spirit of MacRoich was stirred and called forth.

Here we are provided with some of the formulaic stepping stones of one expression of Celtic mystical practice. Three days and nights, beseeching the spirits for knowledge and assistance, approaching the spirits with an offering, and being offered knowledge while in the threshold of the mist. But the most poignant point of all in this story is that ancient knowledge, wisdom, and sacred information that had become lost was regained by a young man sitting on the side of an ancestral hill. Such a simple practice, a simple gesture, this leaning toward the powers of life for assistance, but the ramifications of opening ourselves to the ancient energies are endless.

On the Mist-Filled Path of Celtic spirituality the simplest of things becomes a gateway for us to enrich our lives and to celebrate the sacred world — even sitting on the side of an ancient hill. These profound moments of vision and opening to the universe become priceless stopping places for the soul to turn away from the addictive distractions of modern life, distractions that would have us forget the important stories of our lives like the *Tain.*

The animism of the Celtic spirit beckons us to reenvision how we spend our days. This is a crucial process. It is a timely study of the soul, not rooted in lofty esoteric ponderings but in the rich and earthy ground of our own bodily experience, with senses alive and awake.

Celtic spirituality is a kind of somatic archaeology, a study of unearthing the deep resources of spirit within ourselves by accessing the wisdom, power, and inherent knowledge of the body. We have largely been taught to ignore the body and the deep resources of spirit within ourselves. Celtic spirituality stands in direct opposition to the fragmentation that lulls us into a state of sleepy neglect. It asks us to go forth into the dewy grass of the morn, wash our faces in the nectar of a new awakening earth, and reclaim our place within the flow of its unconditional love for us. It is time to reclaim, once and for all, the sacredness of the house of memory we live in — our body.

Chapter 10

The Hearth Way

When we have a combination of spiritual practices that have withstood the test of time and a practitioner who is able to approach the practice with a soft mind, a chemistry results that opens new gates of awareness.

— Rabbi David Cooper, *Silence, Simplicity and Solitude*[1]

Authentic spiritual practice requires a practical spiritual framework. By this I do not mean some kind of self-help program designed to "fix" us. Spiritual frameworks that are based on fostering an empowered spiritual cosmos within the human being, what I have called the body-soul complex, do not attempt to fix us but, instead, seek to support the emergent spiritual reality that is dormant within each of us.

By *framework* I also do not mean a spiritual formula that is part of some esoteric or occultist high-magical rite or ritual. If you are into this kind of thing, more power to you, but all too often I have found that these human structures are exclusive, elitist, and

1 David Cooper, *Silence, Simplicity, and Solitude* (New York: Bell Tower, 1992), p. 173.

hierarchical to a fault and that they foster a quality of spiritual codependency. This quality is not what the world needs now and will produce few results in a seeker whose mind is not in the right place. Anything, including the spiritual, can be employed to reify the distortions of the ego that, left unchecked, seeks to deify itself.

A true spiritual framework, rooted in a practical embodied spirituality, brings people together authentically, not in ways that foster exclusivity. It fosters community, or as I sometimes say, "communion with the spirit in unity." In this way a Celtic spiritual framework is extremely inclusive and accessible. Forever steeped in the awareness that we are all bound together in this holy tapestry of living shapes, a Celtic spiritual framework for practice merely acts as a general map, a basic pathway with guideposts to direct us. A spiritual path, worked with animistically (that is, in a way that acknowledges soul in the world), is opened to the beating heart of life within and around us. A map such as this can go a long way in providing guidance for our spiritual needs.

These days our spiritual needs may vary, and in rather complex ways. Perhaps we have a need to be in greater connection to nature or to experience greater aliveness in our bodies. Others of us may feel a poignant need for a deeper awareness of our place in the Soul of the World as a shaper, one who is effecting change through service or creativity. Some seek to belong within a greater community. Still others may prefer solitude, hermitage, and a desire to use spiritual practice as a means of doing inner work and personal refinement. In any case, in addressing these varying needs, a spiritual framework can often provide an effective path for producing the kinds of authentic changes we seek in our lives. I personally see such a framework as a sacred method for reactivating our citizenship in the sacred world, a way of restoring our sacred standing and sacred ambassadorship of peace.

Until we reconfigure our lives so that they lean toward holiness, meaning will always be cast haphazardly outside of ourselves onto the closest and shiniest thing. What is spawned from this reality is a culture in which the modern person's reference point for meaning and identity is consistently placed onto external authority, the media, and ever-changing fads rather than grown from within. People whose identity, source of meaning, and experience of life are relegated to societal reference points outside themselves become caught in a glimmering, shimmering, isolated world. The media begin to cut, splice, and graft together what is supposed to be our "common experience." This pulse of overly directed life experience sometimes fosters what we think is fellowship and communion, but this monoscape of experience does not constitute a true interaction with the sacred world.

I would like to explore with you a spiritual framework that has become an effective way of orienting myself to the sacred world. These are time-tested orientations that offer the promise of renewal and sacred experience. These orientations to the sacred world have been gleaned from the ancient wellsprings of the Celtic spirit. I invite you to try actively orienting your life to these three "stations of the soul": hearth, heart, and earth. I refer to these orientations as the Hearth Way, the first of which I discuss in this chapter and the other two in the chapters that follow.

THE HEARTH WAY

All religions, all spiritual traditions, have sacred orientations. Some involve a set sequence of times for prayer each day, while others entail working very closely with sacred texts. We see this practice in traditional Islam, Sufism, and some types of Catholicism, in the Christian monastic tradition of *lectio divina,* in the sacred Jewish tradition of reading Torah, and in the Buddhist tradition of reading sutras. In the Celtic spiritual tradition, a triune orientation available to all of us, of Celtic descent or not, can be gleaned from a reanimated view of the hearth.

The hearth is the heart of the Celtic home. There is a very old tradition of burning turf, or dried earth, for warmth and cooking in the hearth. The hearth also serves as a gathering place for community, family, and friends, a fact that may hint at a link between two Gaelic words: *teallach* ("hearth") and *teallagh* ("family").

The hearth is a place where stories are told. It is a place where the family traditionally gathers before the start of a day and at the day's conclusion. From the sound of the fiddle to the giggles of children listening to old family stories, from the hot water of a boiling teakettle splattering on stones to a fresh loaf of bannock bread being pulled from the fire: the hearth is a hub of activity in the Celtic world, ancient and modern.

In the Celtic tradition the hearth is the heart of the family, both biological and spiritual. Traditionally, the hearth is a site where the Celtic family gathers for both physical nourishment (for cooking and eating) and for spiritual nourishment (in the form of storytelling, spiritual teaching, prayer, and healing). It is widely understood in the Celtic world that the hearth is a sacred place. It is a practical, yet spiritual, epicenter of Celtic culture. In essence, with the nourishment of the body through food cooked at the hearth and nourishment of the soul through spiritual practice at the hearth, we see very clearly Eriugena's notion of the spiritual cosmos of the human being in the Celtic hearth tradition. Heaven and earth are enjoined in this single place within the home. Nourishment of the body and nourishment of the soul become interconnected; a spiritual cosmos is born and sustained.

KEEPING THE HEARTH

It was in winter that the islanders gathered round
the hearth fire to listen to stories. Harvest was gathered in.
The ears that had listened only to necessary farming and fishing
words all the year of toil and ripening were ready
for more ancient images and rhythms.

A tongue here and there was touched to enchantment
by starlight and peat flame.

— GEORGE MACKAY BROWN, *WINTER TALES*[2]

In Celtic spiritual practices the hearth may be an actual hearth or fireplace in the home, spoken of by some as an *altair teallach* ("hearth altar" or "hearth shrine"), or it may be a traveling bundle of sacred objects connected to the hearth that are used to create a hearth away from home, not unlike the *mesas* (shaman altars) of the *altomesayoq* shamans of the Inca of Peru. In the Celtic traditions it is a sacred role to maintain the hearth in the home. This holy role has been generally reserved for women. I feel that it is through reclaiming the sacredness of the hearth in our homes and honoring once again the role of the hearth keeper that the sacred standing of women can be restored in our culture. Likewise, it is in the practical and spiritual usage of the hearth that we restore a place of holiness within our homes and families.

To work with the hearth in the Celtic way of being is to invite very ancient energies, sacred energies, back into our homes and into the rhythms of our lives. An ancient spirit of nourishment begins to dwell at the hearth when it is invited in and worked with daily. It is, to use Tom Cowan's term, a "sheltering spirit." In the maternal side of the family, the sheltering spirit of the hearth and hearth altars that we work with is Brighid. We feel her and know her as one of the many sheltering spirits of the human soul and the soul of the land.

In her introduction to Noragh Jones's *Power of Raven, Wisdom of Serpent: Celtic Women's Spirituality,* Caitlin Matthews reminds us:

> The hearth is the first altar, sacred both to St. Brighid as well as her forerunner, the goddess Brighid. Neither is a lady who would tolerate the peevish modern term "housewife," with all its disempowering connotations. A woman can be a

2 George Mackay Brown, *Winter Tales* (London: John Murray Publishers, 1995).

> hearth keeper, as well as a wage-earner, vigorous, able and hospitable: a true keeper of the flame of life itself who rekindles enthusiasm in the discouraged, who strengthens the despairing, who counsels the undecided, who inflames the hearts to act justly and effectively.[3]

This perception of the hearth and the hearth keeper is a most ancient and holy one. It isn't "playing house" but an empowered role often centered in the home. In any case, many hearth keepers today are living ambassadors of a fire they associate with Brighid's hearth, making them soothers of the heart and keepers of the earth.

The loss of the wise woman tradition is unfortunate. This important figure in the tribe was a keeper of ancient lore that sustained life and fostered healing. Part midwife, part herbalist, part counselor of the heart, the wise woman hails from a long lineage of *ban-draoi* (female druids) who, in many cases, slowly became transferred into ecclesiastical roles.

Druid priestesses, foster mothers of warriors and poets, eventually became priestesses of the "new faith," such as the nuns on the Isle of Iona or the nineteen priestesses of Saint Brighid at Kildare who maintained the ancient fires there. However, not all women took to the cloister. Some retained their herbal knowledge and maintained their own healing practices. In later eras, these practices sometimes led to women being labeled as "witches" by the Church patriarchy and being burned at the stake. The last wise woman labeled a witch and burned at the stake in Scotland was one Elspeth MacEwen. It is in her memory, and the memory of women like her, that I sometimes sit at the hearth and pray for the rebirth of a culture that can respect the energy, healing wisdom, and power of the feminine.

---

3 Noragh Jones, *Power of Raven, Wisdom of Serpent: Celtic Women's Spirituality* (Edinburgh: Floris Books, 1994), p. 12.

THE HEARTH AS THE HEARTBEAT OF THE HOME

There is something profoundly unifying about the hearth. It is a center point of consciousness and activity. The feminine, the Mothering Powers, are woven like luminous strands to the hearth in Celtic tradition. As I have shared, Brighid is an undeniable presence at the hearth for many, but perhaps when you open your soul to the memory of "hearth times" that you have experienced, other Mothering Powers — a clownish aunt, a storyteller grandmother, or perhaps a rather animated uncle who sipped Guinness and told jokes — come to your mind.

In the old days the hearth fire was in the direct center of the home. Some of the early Irish, pre-Christian Picts, and other Caledonian tribes of Scotland lived in crannogs, small, protected island villages that were made in various Irish and Scottish lochs (lakes). In Scotland the ancient Caledonians lived in round homes with thatched roofs that were built on posts out over the water of the loch. In the center of the crannog was the hearth fire, the flaming heartbeat of the life of the family and community. The floors of these ancient homes were covered in bracken fern and heather, plant materials that would fall through the slats of the floor of the crannogs. Over time the build up of sediment from these materials would become packed soil beneath the living structure. This sediment would eventually become a small earthen island, the same small islands seen today in many Scottish and Irish lochs. Often, today, the word *crannog* is used to refer to the small islands, as well as to the thatched dwellings.[4]

Central fires have always played an important role in Celtic society. In ancient Ireland sacred fires were lit to initiate the new phases of the year. One tradition involved the observances of Bealtinne (pronounced bee'el'tin'a, roughly April 29 to May 1) and

---

4 This summary is based on information from the Scottish Crannog Centre at Loch Tay, Kenmore (www.crannog.co.uk/).

Samhuinn (pronounced sow'en, October 31 to November 1). During these times the *ard-righ* (high kings) of Ireland would order all hearth fires throughout the land to be extinguished. Kindling of the sacred fire at Tara (considered one of the spiritual epicenters of Éire) would usher in the new phase of the year, and people would then relight their hearth fires at home to mimetically align their hearths with the central sacred fire of the island.

These observances were almost like a national holiday or celebration, not unlike the Olympics, when the entire world gathers for a brief moment to light the fires of the Greek Olympiad tradition. Although the hearth no longer plays such a grand role as it did in the days of the Tara fires, it is still a personal experience and practice for many. The hearth is a simple, quiet, and rustic doorway to spiritual practice that has its roots as much in utilitarian function as it does in spiritual practices or prayer. This is true of everything in Celtic spirituality, if it is practiced authentically. It is not a matter of grandiosity but of simplicity. There is no separation between the Celtic spiritual path and one's daily life. One's life becomes a brightly woven cord of mindfulness that weaves through the ordinarily mundane dimension of living and imbues it with a sacred dimension. In sweeping ashes we discover sacred world.

VISUALIZATION: LIVING AROUND THE HEARTH

We live in an era where imagining such a numinous place as the hearth within the home may be difficult. Living in small apartments or in homes without fireplaces, for instance, many people have not even seen a hearth. For a moment allow your mind to wander with me as we take a brief trip to another time, another place, where the hearth was a center point of activity.

See a one-room cottage. Allow it to present itself to you in your mind's eye. To one side in this cottage is a sitting area and a dining area. Around the periphery of the room, against the far wall, are three bed boxes (bunklike beds built into the wall). You are a child asleep, blankets pulled up around your chin. There is a slight chill in the air this morning.

Suddenly you become aware of heat in the room, accompanied by a bit of smoke and the sound of crackling fire. You sit up to find a female figure in front of the hearth, stoking the embers, breathing life to the flames. You notice that you can see your breath, and you are glad that the fire is relit and burning. It is a much needed and necessary part of the morning. Your family gets dressed by it, cooks and eats by it, and talks of the day beside it.

You hear the woman speak of the fire as the need-fire and of how it is by God's solar graces that the fire has come to be inside this hearth this morning.

It is this way every morning.

Moving forward in time, an entire day has passed. Like a cell that contracts and expands, moves inward and then outward, the family left the morning hearth to attend to different things but has now returned to the home to find the fire of the hearth still aflame. The heart of the home is still beating, not in full blaze but throwing just enough warmth to the room for comfort. The "gloaming," the time of twilight as it is spoken of in Scots tradition, brings a chill to the night air. You know it will soon be cold.

The female figure is there again beside the hearth. She stokes the flame a bit, throwing another brick of peat onto the embers. This is a Gaelic fire. It does not burn wood, but rather hardened turf.

Soon the fire is ablaze, and the family gathers around for a meal. Stories from the day are told while the meal is prepared. Hot water splatters from an iron kettle, and it is announced that tea is nearly ready. There is laughter and more stories.

Suddenly the woman raises two hands in the direction of the flames and says, "Keeper of the Elements, King of the sun, stars, and moon, we thank you for this meal, this daily bread."

As the family eats the meal that the hearth keeper has prepared, there comes a knock on the door. The door opens, and in walks a beloved figure in the Celtic world: the *seannachie.* The *seannachie* is a bard, a storyteller, and tribal historian. In the old days he or she would travel all over the island on foot, a small *clarsach* (harp) slung over the shoulder.

The bard is heartily welcomed into the house, handed a bowl of soup, and given a seat immediately to the side of the hearth: the seat of honor in the Gaelic home. In exchange for a warm meal and a bit of ale, the storyteller begins to recount ancient tales of the ancestors and important events in the history of the clan. Stories of the Otherworld, of the faery people, of strange shape-shifting animals fill the air. Everyone's eyes are glued to the storyteller's gestures. Everyone hangs on every word uttered by the *seannachie.* It is a Celtic pastime to allow one's consciousness to flow freely when a story is told. The hearth is the site of story. The story is otherworldly and the hearth becomes a doorway, a threshold to the ways of the spirits.

In time the old bard bows in appreciation and makes his or her way into the night. With this there is cleanup from the meal, and the family prepares themselves for bedding down.

The fire is stoked to a full flame again to create lasting warmth inside the small cottage. Everyone except the hearth keeper slides into bed, beneath the heavy blankets of tartan wool, and prepares himself or herself to hear the final prayers of the evening. Several minutes pass as the final blast of heat from the hearth fills the room and the woman slowly lowers herself down onto bended knee and faces the flames, hands raised upward, palms facing the fire.

O Gleaming Grace of the Evening.
O Great Spark of the Sun.
May all within this house be blessed
And protected,...
by the hand of Brighid, on this night.

The wing of Saint Michael,
The salt kiss of Manannan,
Keeper of the Sea.
I smoor this fire, this night.
In the name of Brighid,
Foster-mother of Christ.
In the name of Christ,
In the name of Lugh,
I *sain* this heart, this hearth.

The woman pitches a sprig of dried juniper onto the fire and waves the smoke over her heart and then waves the smoke into the room with a goose feather. This practice, known as *saining* (pronounced sahn-ing, meaning "to purify" or "to cleanse") is similar to the Native American practice of smudging. She then divides the embers of the fire into three distinct piles inside the hearth and slowly and gently covers these piles over with ash from the burnt turf, as if the embers themselves were being put to rest or tucked in for the night, like the children of the home.

In the morning the woman will be there again, in front of the hearth, and she will begin the process all over again, as she has done every day since her mother, who learned it from her mother, taught her. She will rekindle a living flame from the sleeping embers, adding new turf, blowing new life into the embers that have been covered over.

THE NEED-FIRE

The scenario portrayed above is imaginary. Though there are pockets where such customs are maintained, most Celtic people today live in more modern homes. It is becoming increasingly rare for the hearth to play such a central role, but there are certainly still families in Ireland, Scotland, Wales, Cornwall, Brittany,

Orkney, Shetland, and the Isle of Man whose mornings and evenings are oriented to hearth time.

The practice of covering over the embers for the night is called *smooring* in Gaelic, and the fire that is rekindled in the morning from the same embers is called the need-fire. Celtic culture and our associated spiritual traditions are like this ancient fire. In time the traditions and the fullness of culture were eclipsed by institutionalized religion and the political agendas of imperialist governments. In post–Culloden era Scotland (1746–1782), for instance, cultural elements such as tartan, the bagpipes, and Gaelic would be officially outlawed by the British Crown in a final attempt at genocide. Even earlier earth-honoring practices and customs would have to go into hiding. Visiting certain holy wells, faery trees, and groves was actively discouraged by the Church. With these elements of the cultural and spiritual soul under attack, the result was inevitable.

The Celtic Way was *smoored.* In one expression of cultural soul loss, the embers of our ancient fires were slowly but surely forced to be covered over, with many families continuing the earth-honoring practices of their ancestors in secret, consciously concealing these things from the watchful eye of the Church.

Now we find ourselves in the time of the need-fire. The very principles that the primal Celtic path fosters — of loving the earth — are what we as a human community now need collectively — principles that serve both the human soul and the natural world. It may be that our very survival depends on whether the fires of these ancient earth-honoring practices and principles can be stoked again in our lives. Presently we have a great need for these practices to return in fully empowered, life-affirming, and authentic ways that foster a change in our paradigm and in the ways we approach our relationship with the planet. Now is the time for us to rekindle our spiritual fires, for our lives to be fanned into flame from the ancient spark of the traditions that were *smoored* and concealed until such time as they could return.

THE HEARTH AS OTHERWORLDLY DOORWAY

Another powerful aspect of the hearth in the Celtic tradition is its presence as an otherworldly doorway. Similar to how some *altomesayoq* shamans of the Inca tradition "source their souls" in their altars or perform a soul flight through them, so too can we use the *teallach,* the hearth, as such a doorway. The hearth, as an altar, is a threshold in the home. Physically the fireplace is a passageway that leads from the interior of the home to the outside. It is a place of mixing elements as well: fire, water in the kettle, air in the form of smoke, earth placed on the embers in the form of turf. The entire universe is right there, in the hearth.

The hearth represents the in-between within the home, similar to how other thin places exist in nature. As Elizabeth Sutherland writes in her excellent book *Ravens and Black Rain: The Story of the Highland Second Sight:* "Celtic mysteries occurred in twi-states between night and day, in dew that was neither rain nor river, in mistletoe that was not a plant or a tree, in the trance state that was neither sleep nor waking." Sometimes people travel from "this side" to "that side" using the hearth. At other times people on this side receive visitations. This happened for my maternal grandmother.

My maternal grandmother, Nonnie, was a woman who had involuntary moments of the two sights, or second sight, known as *an da shealladh* (pronounced an-da-hoo-lah). Even many people in her own family did not know that she had this gift, since she chose to be very quiet about her experiences. During my childhood I remember hearing stories about how she had dreamt of things before they happened or about how she would sometimes sense and see things. One night in particular my grandmother had an experience of *an da shealladh* that involved her *teallach,* her hearth. At that point in her life she had reconnected with an old boyfriend. My grandpa had long since passed away back in the 1960s, and Nonnie had not had any sustained or significant male companionship since then. She welcomed the chance to spend time with this man, as he was a dear old friend with whom she shared a great many memories and interests. They enjoyed each other's company.

Over the course of several months, Nonnie and her friend — I will call him Robert — spoke at length on the phone and had dinners together. As a gesture of her fondness for him, my grandmother gave him a particular sweater. Toward the end of one evening around the Christmas season, known as *Nollaig* in the Scots-Gaelic tongue, the phone rang. It was Robert's son calling Nonnie to inform her that his father had died. This came as quite a shock to my grandmother, especially since she had just reconnected with Robert. Her sadness was great.

The very next evening, as she was sitting in her living room, her attention was suddenly drawn to the hearth. According to her, the entire area in front of the fireplace "went black." She could no longer see the bricks or the burning fire. Suddenly, my grandmother saw Robert, who had passed on the night before, wearing the sweater that she had just given him for Christmas. He had come to say good-bye to her. After saying a few brief words to her, he turned around and stepped through the hearth again. Nonnie's vision was gone as quickly as it had arrived.

This account reads like one of the many stories of these occurrences of seership recorded in Irish and Scottish lore. It has all the components that ethnographers and folklorists have found in many of the rural areas of the Celtic world: a *taibhsear* (a vision seer, one who sees the spirits), a *tannasg* (the apparition of someone who has already passed on), and the ability to see such an apparition, known as *an da shealladh* (the second sight).

Although undoubtedly sharing all the features of seership in the Gaelic world, and of the Celtic world in general, this account involved a Scots-Irish descendant of the Celtic diaspora living in the United States. It is but one of hundreds of stories sharing nearly identical features in which *an da shealladh* becomes activated in someone, despite the fact that he or she does not live in the land of their ancestors.

THE HEARTH AS HOLY STOPPING PLACE

Any time we take time out of our routine to sit in silence we invite the holy. If you are a musician or poet, the *imbas* or *awen* (divine inspiration) comes. If you are a druid, a whole host of impressions, memories, and teachings from the spirits, as well as the presence of ancestors, may draw near. If you are a contemplative Christian, sitting in silence is to open the door to an authentic connection with God. If you are a worn-out human being who has experienced fifty-two straight weeks of rushing to work so that you can pay the bills, sitting in silence can sometimes be akin to an internal massage. Sitting heals. Silence heals.

Consider the hearth a sitting place. Consider it a holy stopping place in the wide arc of your travels. Start your morning at the hearth. End your day at the hearth. Sit with your wife or husband beside the hearth and reaffirm your love for her or him every night. Sit by yourself and pay attention to your body, the movement of your soul. Allow the hearth to be a spot that reenlivens and reintegrates you. Call relatives and talk to them at length while sitting at your hearth. Ask for the numinous spirits of good ideas to come dance at your hearth. Bake some cookies and have some tea with a friend by the hearth. Allow your hearth to become holy ground and a sacred shrine to the love of life. Below are some further ideas for working with the hearth.

PRACTICE IDEAS: THE HEARTH ALTAR

- Set aside a time around twilight to activate and consecrate the hearth as a working altar that you will engage with regularly. An altar is a bit like a houseplant. If you water the plant and make sure it has enough sunlight, it will thrive as a beautiful expression of life. Similarly, if you consecrate an altar and feed it with your attention, the same will occur. However, if you neglect a plant and fail to nourish it with your attention, it will simply wither. Think of your hearth altar, whether it is a fixed altar in the home or a traveling hearth bundle, as a living being you must nourish with your attention and energy. The hearth is a living thing, a living presence.
- Place pictures of ancestors around the hearth to remember them. In the manner of the Celtic fire observances or the feast days of the saints in the Catholic and Celtic-Christian traditions, honor the birthday or death day of a relative who has passed on by setting up a picture of her and preparing an ancestor meal of her favorite foods and drink. Hold your ancestor in your heart and lift prayers for her. If others are with you, tell stories about the person. In many Irish wakes the stories often turn to humorous tales involving the deceased, accompanied by a celebration, clearly pointing to the ancient Celtic comfort with death and a belief in the afterlife.
- If you are a pagan, place images of your gods and goddesses around your hearth altar as a way to welcome their influences and energies intimately to your home. Some fine statues can be found of old Celtic deities, such as with a company called Sacred Source/JBL Statues.
- If you are not of Celtic background, weave in your own ancestors and traditions at the hearth. Perhaps you are African

American, Slavic, Romanian, Japanese, or Mexican. Whoever you are, make your hearth a centering place.

- If you are a Catholic or Celtic-Christian, honor the feast days of your saints by praying at your hearth. Weave the hearth into your Christian practices. View the hearth as a sheltering spirit, which is at the heart of any form of Christianity not plagued by wrathful notions of life. Welcome the sheltering spirit of Christ to your hearth.
- If you are a shamanist by faith, or a shamanic practitioner, try using your hearth as an entryway or portal. You might be rather surprised by where you find yourself taken on your spirit flight. Explore the important process of inviting your ancestors, both recent and ancient, into your shamanic practice. Remember the saying, "Just because they are dead doesn't mean they are wise." Welcome only those ancestral presences that are life affirming, but avoid those that feel burdened with anger, rage, jealousy, or addictions. In time, you can facilitate a healing on those ancestor spirits that are still caught in hard places. Very often our personal transformation involves a transmutation of things still held within the energies of our ancestral lines.
- Once you have established a regular hearth altar that will remain in your home, create a hearth bundle that you can take with you when traveling. Take one object or a small sampling of objects with you to link you to your home and to loved ones while you are away. If you are so inclined, set up an altar based on the Four Airts, four sacred winds or directions of Irish and Scottish lore. Have representations of the four elements present. In the primal Irish and Scottish ways, fire is in the east, air is in the south, water is in the west, and earth is in the north. This ancient template appears in different ways for different people. Some Gaelic-descended families still remember and work with the old fivefold division of Ireland, with west being the place of vision, north being the place of

battle, east being the place of prosperity, south being the place of song, and the center being the place of sovereignty or the ability to rule one's own life in balance. If you hail from other cultural backgrounds, learn of your ancestral cosmologies or evolve ones that feel relevant to who you are and where you live.

- In time, you may feel drawn to trade hearth objects with various *anamchara* (soul friends) in your shamanic or spiritual community who are also working with a hearth altar, as a way of connecting your family hearths. Some advanced practitioners are able to communicate with one another long distance through these methods, known in Scots lore as *kything.*
- The hearth can also be a rather potent and effective place for conflict resolution. When two people are in conflict they can sit in front of the hearth altar to explore a resolution. Call in the spirit of the hearth, the ancestors, or any other life-affirming energies, and have an unbiased third person to sit as a witness of the process, to act as hearth keeper. The people in conflict then voice their issues and make a commitment to the hearth to move away from either/or thinking and closer to a way that is imbued with a sense of "hearthness," which I would describe as a basic sense of respect, sanity, and goodwill.

Work with your hearth often enough that the energies do not become stagnant or stuck. Working with altars and shrines is an ancient way of being, both in global shamanist traditions and in Christian, Druid, and Buddhist ways. Shrine work, and shrine work specifically at the home hearth, is a way of working tangibly with sacred energies. It can almost be a kind of "Celtic feng shui," in the sense that our homes can be set up according to the template of our hearth altar.

CHAPTER 11

THE WAY OF THE HEART

Come now to the secret places of the soul.
Let us each inspect ourselves with care,
looking at the emotions which stir our
hearts and the thoughts which run through
our minds. Let us learn the essential goodness
of the heart from the heart itself.

— MORGAN OF WALES (PELAGIUS)[1]

One of the abiding cultural traits in my upbringing was the spirit of hospitality. I never gave it much thought when I was growing up. It was simply a part of life. Hospitality was an unspoken code that governed all human interactions in my extended family and in my immediate culture. I remember the spirit of hospitality during the holidays, and I remember it during tragedy. Just as we have discussed the way of the hearth in Celtic tradition, now I would like to turn our

1 Robert Van de Weyer, *The Letters of Pelagius* (Worcestershire: Arthur James, Ltd., 1995), p. 9.

attention to the second facet of the Hearth Way: the way of the heart.

During the great Easter flood of 1979 in Jackson, Mississippi, the Ross Barnett Reservoir swelled and jumped its dam. The Pearl River swelled, flooding huge swaths of the city of Jackson. It was a treacherous time. Children drowned. Houses, schools, churches, and automobiles were engulfed in the floodwaters. Venomous snakes and alligators from the nearby swamps, carried along by the swelling currents, began to appear in people's homes, which everyone was wading through to salvage whatever property they could.

At this time I witnessed firsthand the spirit of hospitality in action. My father hit the streets, served hot coffee and doughnuts to the National Guard, who had been aiding people displaced from their homes. At another point, from inside a canoe, he paddled his way up familiar streets, now unrecognizable, owing to twelve feet of standing water. He helped people he did not even know to hoist soaking-wet furniture onto their roofs, and he chased enormous snakes from waterlogged living rooms and garages. In the end our home became a stopping place for people who needed a hot meal, a place to rest their head, a place to renew and recuperate.

I marvel now that I did not truly comprehend the power of this hospitality in my early years in Mississippi, yet I think we rarely contemplate the nature of such things until we have experienced a stretch of our life path without them. I had no idea, growing up, that I hailed from such brave and heartful people. I look back now and see that at every moment, at every turn, my relatives on both sides of the family were people steeped in the spirit of hospitality.

Hospitality, Southern and Celtic Style

Southern hospitality is well known. Celtic hospitality, however, from which so much Southern hospitality springs, is legendary. I can look back to my childhood and recognize, now, something of a distinctive Southern, Celtic spirit of hospitality that was always present. There was an ever-present love and openness to people, all sorts of people. No doubt there are a number of ways in which homeland Celtic cultures have shaped and formed much of American Southern, Appalachian, Ozarkian, and Canadian Nova Scotian culture. Hospitality is one of these shaping forces. Hospitality is, we might say, the first face revealed by the Celtic spirit. Even ghosts, angels, and faeries are traditionally extended hospitality in Celtic tradition. As one old Irish proverb says, "Never turn any stranger away; it could be an angel in disguise."

Anne Ross, the preeminent Scottish folklorist and Celtic scholar, says this about Celtic hospitality:

> Travelers have always been astonished at the unquestioning generosity of the Highlander to the stranger; the custom of always leaving a portion "for the man on the hill," i.e., the chance guest, is widely observed. The stranger had only to arrive at even the poorest dwelling, to be given a portion of whatever happened to be available.... Such was the sacredness of the stranger and the traveler in the eyes of the Highlanders to whom hospitality was almost a religion.[2]

Certainly Southern hospitality as a cultural sensibility stands on its own, but for many families this abiding spirit was, no doubt, shaped by and patterned on Celtic ancestors who came to these shores and who modeled this way of being on their own ways. It is a way of living from the heart and extending the heart to the stranger. On the Celtic road of life, there are no strangers, at least not for very long.

For this reason, and many others, it is so disheartening to see some white supremacists co-opt the beautiful ideals of the Celtic culture, and our associated symbols and mythic images, to express their intolerance and hate. What an astonishing aberration, especially given the fact that many of these Celtic descendants hail

---

2 Anne Ross, *The Folklore of the Scottish Highlands* (New York: Barnes & Noble, 1976), p. 101.

from ancestors who were also recipients of oppression, genocide, and racism. Although there are glorious examples of Celtic people (both in Ireland and in the American South) supporting African Americans and Native Americans in their fight for freedom and civil rights, there are also deplorable expressions of Celtic descendants who have become racists and oppressors themselves. The Celtic spirit of hospitality has left their hearths and their hearts.

Other Faces of the Spirit of Hospitality

The spirit of hospitality expressed itself in other ways in my family as well. Both of my parents are ordained clergy, liberal ministers in the United Methodist tradition. As I think back on this unique spiritual environment in which I was raised, I now see that the "method" of their Methodism was a sense of localized numinous spirituality that knew no limits to hospitality. Theirs is a path of extending a profound "color-blind" and ecumenical love to all people, lacking all the phobias of the current era.

One Sunday morning stands out in my memory as an example of when the spirit of hospitality blew in like a holy wind. It was a Sunday morning like any other. My father, the associate minister, was reading the liturgy, and the all-white congregation was preparing to take Holy Communion. On this particular Sunday something out of the ordinary occurred, however. Right when the senior minister and my father were about to offer Communion, a poor disheveled African American man wandered in off the city street, complete with a McDonald's hamburger in his hand. He made his way down to the very first row and sat down. The man was a street person.

I looked around. I could tell that his presence made many of the parishioners uncomfortable. The presence of the man, we might say, put us all into nonordinary reality. He was, by some standards, out of place. Yet I thought his presence was beautiful.

It put everyone on call that morning, putting to the test the notion so many have come to associate with the United Methodist tradition: all are welcome.

Women in fur coats shifted uneasily in the pews, men squirmed in their Sunday best and fiddled with their beards. A thick tension hung in the room, as if a common mind held a common question, "How are the ministers going to handle this one?" To my glee, the ministers did not handle anything.

When it came time for the front row to make its way up to the front of the church for Communion, the gentleman carefully placed his hamburger down on the railing in front of him and stood up. The row of people shuffled, a bit awkwardly, to another railing where one kneels to receive the unleavened bread and grape juice. What happened in that moment, to some eyes, was nothing special. Yet in the Mississippi of my childhood, it felt like a historic event. Without hesitation the street person was given Holy Communion, just like anyone else. He was not passed over. He was not asked whether he had "lost his way." He was given the blood of Christ from Rev. Jack Loflin, another Scots-Irish-American Southerner, and, when my father came to the man's place in the line of kneeling parishioners, he simply smiled, nodded, and uttered the words, "The body of Christ given to you."

The Spirit of Hospitality stood off to the side and wept at the beauty of it all, wept with joy that hospitality had been granted where it had been needed most.

I think back on the presence of my parents' spiritual tradition in my life and know that their faith, though different from mine in outer form, has shaped me. Now, as a shaper of the world and a participant in the Soul of the World, I cannot ignore this influence on my life and soul. I value the power of the heart reflected by the spirit of hospitality that they taught me by example. This was just one of many things I learned from them.

Another formative experience came around the age of ten, when I was in a particularly inquisitive time. It was a curious phase in my childhood years, when I began to explore the many world religions. It was a time of exploring the labels of religion rather than practicing spirituality beyond labels, as I do now. I read everything I could get my hands on about Taoism, Confucianism, Buddhism, and Islam. In between Jung and Black Elk, I even read a bit from the Book of John, which has so profoundly shaped the Celtic-Christians.

All the religions made sense to my childhood heart. They all had a valuable way of looking at the landscape of life and offering a possible map for us as a human community to use. Elements of each seemed foreign to me as well, but I learned to look past that which seemed strange or esoteric and embraced all that resonated in my soul. The deep seeds of an ecumenical ethic vibrated in my soul and, no doubt, formed my spiritual sensibilities today. It is a sensibility that holds within it a central assumption: that peace on our planet is directly related to not only interfaith tolerance but also shared exploration. It is just good hospitality, after all.

One day, during this time, I asked my father, "Why are we Methodists? Why not Buddhists? Why not Muslims?" By this point in my childhood, I had had a number of experiences that could not be swiftly explained by the modern church in which I was absorbed. My father's response has stayed with me to this day. He said: "The Methodist tradition had its start as a social activist tradition, of challenging the conditions of poverty they saw around them, but in the beginning it all started out very simple. They would meet in small circles, either out in the forest or in each other's homes beside the hearth, and they would ask one another one of the all-important questions: 'How is it with your soul?' "

I now read over this description of my familial religious tradition, and my mind is a swarm of different memories. I remember my mother as a chaplain, over and over again offering comfort to families who had lost a loved one in the hospital (the word *hospital* sharing a root with the words *hospice* and *hospitality*). I remember her sitting beside people who were dying, holding their hand, talking to them, telling them stories, meeting them in spirit, whatever their religion, faith, or tradition. For her, a central unwavering tenet of her profession as chaplain is to meet the dying in a spirit of interfaith embrace and to walk with them, like in the old Celtic tradition of soul leading, right up to the gate of passing over. Having almost passed over herself, she knows what a holy moment the dying person is encountering.

I also remember when my father led a church service out in the forest, with a smaller contingent of parishioners. It occurred over the course of a weekend camping trip, with only a small group from the church. The weekend trip consisted of a Friday evening and a Saturday of hiking and fishing and culminated in a Sunday morning worship service, among the trees. It was a small circle of people "taking the bread" and drinking from a chalice. For me it stirred memories of the mist of my childhood and even more ancient memories of people praying in the trees.

Meeting in the forest, or by the hearth. Providing hospice and hospitality. Asking the question, "How is it with your soul?" All these things bring to mind a strange quote from a Welsh minister named Rev. S. Baring-Gould, who wrote, "Under the name Methodism, we have the old Druidic religion still alive, energetic and possibly more vigorous than it was when it exercised a spiritual supremacy over the whole of Britain."[3] While questionable in its historical accuracy, this sentiment does seem to express the deeper spirit reflected in the practices shared by the two traditions: sitting in circles, turning no one away, providing food, communing

3 Lewis Spence, *The Magic Arts of Celtic Britain* (Van Nuys, Calif.: Newcastle Publishing, 1996), p. 51.

with the holy, asking the perennial question, "How is it with your soul?" These customs seem rooted in the ancient spirit of hospitality that has shaped the Celtic spirit.

In looking at an embodied and animistic spirituality, we must naturally see hospitality as an extension of it. On this path we are perpetually aware of how we are connected to all of life around us. We are stewards, caretakers, guardians, and protectors of life. What we do to others and the earth, we do to ourselves. On the Mist-Filled Path of Celtic spirituality we see all people as equal, all people as unique and sacred expressions of the Great Song. Like the mist, which slowly moves and blends with all that it encounters, so too are we beckoned to move through the Soul of the World and blend in ways that foster the hospitality of the heart.

Listening for the Heartbeat of God: Part One

Although I have shared some of the beautiful flowing words in J. Philip Newell's book *Listening for the Heartbeat of God: A Celtic Spirituality,* I have not shared with you how the essence and title of this little book changed my life. *Listening for the Heartbeat of God* is a small, compact book in which the reader is taken on a wonderful journey through the history of Celtic Christianity, from the time of the nature-honoring druids to the thriving Iona Community today, an ecumenical organization on the Isle of Iona, off the coast of the Isle of Mull, Scotland.

Reverend Newell, a Church of Scotland minister and Warden of Spirituality for the Anglican diocese of Portsmouth, offers us the "inside track" on a bit of a conspiracy that has taken place, a quiet pushing down of something extremely sacred and extremely important. The conspiracy of which he speaks is centered on a meeting that took place in the year 664 C.E. in Northumbria. At this meeting a clash of two cultures — Celtic and Roman — occurred, as well as a profound clash of theologies. Before this meeting the Celtic Church had evolved independently of the papacy and the Roman Church, evolving its own unique form of spirituality that was, like the mist, a weave of localized nature-based traditions (the water) and the contemplative mysticism that hailed from the desert mystics of Egypt (the air). With the two combined, the Celtic people of Ireland, Wales, Cornwall, and Scotland danced with the mist.

Honoring nature was and is a profound part of Celtic Church practice. Priests and monks maintained the custom of wearing their hair in the old druidic tonsure (hair shaved from ear to ear with the hair worn very long, as opposed to the Roman style with the crown of the head shaved in a circle). Women were considered sacred, and therefore representatives of the Creation, with many women occupying important roles in the leadership of the Church. Priests could marry. A sense of the sacredness of all life, all matter, permeated the practices and teachings of the Celtic-Christian tradition. The mystery of the divine was considered just as accessible in the wild places of nature as they were in a chapel. In other words, for the Celtic-Christian, God was as much written in the book of nature as in a book of scripture.

Many *filidh* (vision poets), seers, and druids slid very easily into the newly forming institution of the Celtic Church, not perceiving the original Christian mysticism they encountered as a destroyer of the native traditions but rather as a creative spirit that rounded out the druidic vision they had always known. It is almost as if, where for other Christians Judaism was the faith of their Old Testament, for the Celts Druidism was their Old Testament and Christianity their New Testament, their covenant, or completion of the older druidic vision.

The assumption for most of the Celts, or so it would seem from looking at history, was that the Christian teachings were not, in effect, an antagonistic message. The teachings seemed to align in some way with the indigenous wisdom of the Celtic tribes. It was not, in their minds, a replacement but rather an opportunity for an augmentation of their own inherent sensibilities that comprised the native Celtic way. There were exceptions to the rule, of course, but all in all history suggests that the adoption of a "green" form of Christian mysticism occurred rather easily in the Celtic world.

However, something was severed at the meeting in Northumbria, where the two theologies collided. The theological split between the Celtic and Roman traditions, as Newell so eloquently reminds us, was that the Celtic people felt more of an affiliation with John, who had leaned against Jesus at the Last Supper. For them he was a teacher of a very Celtic-feeling approach to spirituality, of seeking communion and communication with the divine through all Creation, which included nature and the earth, as well as the human heart. It was a kind of "leaning toward life" that we have discussed. The Roman Church, however, stressed the unassailable authority of Peter, suggesting that Scripture had declared that Peter "was the rock on which Jesus had promised to build the Church."

Known as the Synod of Whitby, this official meeting of the Catholic Church declared, in the end, that all expressions of the old Celtic Church must come under the sway of the Roman Church. Fundamentally, the Celtic spiritual road of listening for the heartbeat of God in all Creation was to be overtaken by the Roman way, which stressed only the structure, institution, and ordained teaching of the Church. The same would occur in later years with Augustine's assertion of the doctrine of original sin, with the renegade Celtic theologians, such as Pelagius and John the Scot espousing a more druidic spirit in the doctrine of original blessing. The official Church politic would later align against the Celts again, with a full excommunication of Pelagius and many of his followers.

With the Synod of Whitby, the druidic tonsure was banned. Women would eventually lose the right to occupy leadership roles within the church on the same level as men. People in the Celtic countryside would eventually be admonished for maintaining certain customs, such as visiting the holy wells, or tying prayer flags on certain holy faery trees, though this did not prevent them from doing these things, even to the present day. In short, the Celtic tradition was forced to live, as it has ever since, under the strictures of the Roman Church and, in time, under the veneer of Calvinism and other forms of Protestantism. A truly heart-centered and ancient people was forced into exile by a politicized Roman institution that had been oppressing Christians just a few hundred years before.

Nonetheless, listening for the heartbeat of life within all Creation is so integral to the Celtic Way — Druid and Christian — that, of course, it never fell out of practice. It exists today and is still accessible as a living path of spirituality. Upon reading Newell's book and learning of this particular synod and its ramifications to the old Celtic sensibility of loving Creation, some very deep part of my childhood self reared up in anger. I knew in my soul that it was the truth, not only from other historical research I was doing at the time but also from unprocessed visionary "information" I experienced at the Sun Dance. At a later point I also encountered past-life material, as well as composite ancestral memory that was "dredged up" through potent sessions with a master of such work.

Strangely enough, these events were a second wave of Roman genocide against the Celts, the first being a military assault against the druids in Gaul and then on the Isle of Mona (Anglesey) by Suetonius Paulinus in 61 C.E. Yet the dynamics of these politics of spirituality seemed to mirror something equally as traumatic that I remember from within this life. Suddenly, I remembered my own struggle for the right of determining my own soul's course. I remembered, more fully than ever, my deep wound associated with Christianity. When I went back in time I realized that this wound was made by a Sunday school teacher I had when I was young, whom I will call Mrs. S.

The wound, and the ensuing negative reaction to all things Christian, came from this woman's extremely rigid interpretation of God and the particular ferociousness with which she asserted this perspective every Sunday. I shiver when I think back on this formative time of my childhood. I still see Mrs. S.'s face, as if she were the horrid Washer at the Ford of Celtic myth, washing blood-soaked shirts in the river at night, a portent of impending death. The potential death was, in fact, my open and innocent childhood spirituality.

As I read Newell's account of the smothering of the bright green spirit of the Celtic vision of life, I realized that I had tasted something of my own Synod of Whitby as a child in Mississippi. Newell's book caused me to think back to the event that originally caused me to leave the church, formally, to forever "wander through the wilderness," as I do today.

A week after the Communion service my father led out in the forest, we returned to the normal routine of the church in Jackson. It was "up and at 'em," bright and early, for coffee and sweet rolls; then we would scuffle over to the church. My father would go on about his business, and I would make my way to Sunday school. When I walked into the small room where Mrs. S. led our Sunday school class, I could sense that something was in the air. I did not know exactly what it was, but to my childhood self it felt like thick brown cords were floating all around me. I sized up the situation and instantly and intuitively knew that Mrs. S. did not approve of the camping trip the weekend before, nor did she have much love in her heart for those who had gone on the trip. I knew this included me. I assumed my seat, as usual, and kept quiet.

Suddenly, Mrs. S. looked in my direction and asked, in front of the whole class, "So, Frank, why don't you tell us what happened last Sunday when you were camping instead of attending Sunday school?"

I took a deep breath and responded honestly, knowing full well that I was pulling the rope on my own guillotine. "Well, it was fine, just fine. We fished. I did a lot of exploring in the woods. We ate lots of food, including marshmallows around the fire. We sang some songs and heard some stories. Then, on Sunday morning we had Holy Communion right there beside the lake, right there in the woods. It was grand. And, you know, I remembered something on Sunday morning. I remembered how much I love mist. And, I remembered how much I used to talk to God in the trees when we lived in Georgia. And, you know, I really..."

Before I could finish my thought, the woman had launched into a fiery tirade about how the "grace of God can only be found in His house." She pounded her fist on the table and yelled. I bristled and cowered. Her condemnation of the camping trip and of the church service in the forest was not only an attack on a whole group within the congregation but also a formal calling into question of the sensibilities and integrity of my father as a minister. Furthermore, she denigrated a very precious childhood mystical experience, in which I remembered both my experiences with the mist when I was younger as well as even more ancient experiences of people praying in the trees.

I stood up. Without so much as a word, I turned and left the room. I walked out of the building and found a small, concealed cavelike nook beneath a huge holly tree in which to hide myself. I wept. I wept for the woman and her closed heart. I wept for myself, for I knew I was now in exile, no longer welcome in a tradition that did not understand me or the strange winding gyre that my soul seemed to travel. I would have to wander now.

An hour later the church service began. I was not a part of it. I could hear the organ crank up from under my holly tree. I could hear the congregation singing. There were long stretches of silence when the liturgy or the sermon itself was being said, muffled by the brick and stone of the church walls. More singing and organ music would rumble forth. I heard the cackle of a nearby raven up in the oaks.

In that moment the raven's call was a healer. It reminded me that the presence of the sacred flows through all things, even the raven, even the holly tree, even the very turf beneath me. I was suddenly content to be the "outsider," the "pagan," the "heathen" (all words that simply mean "one who lives in the country, the outlying areas or the woods"). I knew at this moment, beneath the holly (one of the sacred trees in Celtic tradition) that it would always be my way to live in the outlying areas of spirituality. I would have to find my God out beyond the bricks and mortar, as I had done earlier in my childhood, in the mist and the trees of the in-between.

Suddenly, I had a strange compulsion. I wanted to see the face of my father. I wanted to have one last look at him in his robes, in one of the elements I had grown accustomed to seeing him in. I entered the church through the foyer and silently tiptoed over to one of the three back doors. I was so used to the flow of the order of worship that I knew the service was but moments from being completed. I knew if I was going to see my father that I needed to catch my glance quickly. I slowly opened the door. There stood my father, near the very spot where he had given Holy Communion to the homeless man a few years before. The service was over and my father stood with his arms upright, palms open, fingers pointed toward the heavens, praying the last prayer of the service.

I look back and realize that he was standing in a sacred posture. I would learn, years later, that this sacred posture was one used by the druids and Celtic monks alike, for both prayer and invoking protection. This image of my father, captured like a Polaroid in my visioning eye, an imprint on my soul body, stays with me even today. I remember now that there were many times that he and my mother stood in this posture when praying over people. Now when I pray in this posture myself, like my druid ancestors, like the old Irish monks before me who observed the Rule of Tallaght,[4] like my parents, I say a prayer for them all, all shapers of my path.

Listening for the Heartbeat of God: Part Two

Soon after I encountered *Listening for the Heartbeat of God,* I was asked to present at a conference in San Francisco, specifically the Kinship Conference, sponsored by the San Francisco Society for the Prevention of Cruelty to Animals. As I thought about what I wanted to do at the conference, I immediately knew that one of the presentations should be about the ancient Celtic notion of sacred relationship to animals. The primal tradition, as well as the Celtic-Christian tradition in the era of the saints, is replete with stories, customs, and traditions surrounding the sacredness of animals. This topic would certainly be enough to chew on and work with for my daylong intensive. However, I had another presentation to give on Sunday morning.

As I kicked the topic around a while longer, the notion hit me that I could explore the Celtic notion of listening for the heartbeat of the Creator in Creation. This would allow me to develop a more experiential approach to this concept by putting the concept (*gnosis*) into practice (*praxis*). Little did I know to what degree I

---

4 The Rule of Tallaght is an ancient practice of praying to the four quarters or four directions used by the Irish Celtic monks. Because of the overwhelming evidence that druids prayed in such a posture, Philip Sheldrake, author of *Living Between the Worlds,* believes that the Rule of Tallaght is of pre-Christian origin.

would be putting it into practice. I facilitated my daylong intensive on Celtic totemic explorations, answered a few questions, and then shoved off for the night onto the streets of San Francisco. Somewhere between a slice of cheese pizza and a pint of Guinness, I turned my awareness again to this notion of listening for the heartbeat. "What does this really mean?" I asked myself. "Can everyone do it? Can it be done when we aren't clear? Can it be done in the city, a city like this one, a city like San Francisco?" These were just some of my questions that night.

I decided to perform an experiment. I would hurl myself into the city. I would simply walk and wander and listen for the heartbeat of God in the Celtic way of approaching life. I would listen for the heartbeat of God in the city.

Listen I did. I also opened myself to the "signs" and found that the city is equally a part of the sacred world, though it is a world layered in problems. I wandered through ritzy parts of town and "bad" parts of town. I walked by strip clubs and taverns. I walked by coffee shops and record stores. I walked by greasy spoon restaurants and bookstores. I walked by drug deals going down, and even a few fights. I walked by prostitutes, who hit on me for business. I walked by innumerable homeless people, who asked me for loose change and whom I would respond to with, "I'll give you a bit of change in exchange for a story." I heard some interesting tales, to say the least, yet all the while I listened, listened deeply for the heartbeat of God in all Creation.

Sometime near midnight I rounded the corner onto a busy thoroughfare that I had seen earlier in the day. During the daytime, Market Street is a bustling stretch of road. Limos and buses rumble by. People walk by in all the latest fashions. The activity is at a high pitch. By night, however, Market Street — like any number of streets in any number of cities — looks like a bomb shelter without a roof. People are crammed into store fronts, sleeping under cardboard, grocery carts turned on their sides to provide some sense of shelter, some sense of safety.

While I had seen homeless people in my time, and most recently in a move to the nation's capitol, nothing prepared me for sections of San Francisco. It is not that the city has any more homeless than any other city. It was that I was listening for the heartbeat of God and heard it beating among the homeless. In my *experiment,* a word that instantly speaks to the reality of my white privilege and affluence, I had every conceptualization about myself as a free spiritual being shattered. Somewhere along Market Street and Third Street my ego spilled forth from my body and trickled down a street drain. On the streets of San Francisco I met three people who have altered, irrevocably, my sense of self, my sense of the path ahead and just exactly what it means to be spiritual in the world today.

MR. RAVIT: TOASTING THE MOON

The first person I met I will call Mr. Ravit. The minute I laid eyes on him I knew he was a holy man of some kind, someone who had encountered some kind of sacred tradition and had refined himself within it. Even from halfway down the block, I knew that although he was a "street person" he was also filled with glee. He was laughing at something someone had said just about the time I was walking by him. Then I heard the unmistakable shake and jingle of a cup partially filled with coins.

"Change?" he muttered.

"Why, thank you, sir. I could really use some change!" I replied, reaching into his cup, as if *he* were the one offering me money. He beamed with a sudden smile, like a person who had no worries. I smiled back and dropped a few spare quarters into his San Francisco Giants cup.

"I knew you were funnin' me. Thank you kindly."

"You are most welcome, sir, but I must insist, now I want to hear a story from you."

His eyebrows collided in the center of his forehead.

"A story?"

"Yes, who are you? Where do you come from?"

I listened as Mr. Ravit told me how he had come to this country from Pakistan. He was, in essence, chasing the American Dream. I deduced from his long winding exposé that he had moved here during some period of social unrest in Pakistan. He was able to come to the States with the assistance of his wife's family. With a kind of dowry, or so I gathered, he was able to secure a taxi with which he could make a living. He described how proud he was the day he first got the cab. "It was nice, very nice. Better than mine back home."

I learned that, in time, things did not go so well for Mr. Ravit and his family. He described how it had become nearly impossible to make a secure living in northern California as a cabbie. After the high monthly rent for the actual car, along with the percentage cut of all earnings that the cab company takes off the top, there is little left with which to feed a family of four.

Mr. Ravit wept for a moment and then touched his chest over his heart, and then his forehead, as if paying homage to the memory of something. Then he continued this story: Ravit's wife and three children left when he could no longer support them. They had, for all he knew, returned to their home country. Now he lives on the street, panhandling for change, unskilled in anything but driving. He told me that he usually makes enough for one meal a day, and one small bottle of brandy per week.

"I'm not a drunk," he announced. "Some out here on the street are not in their heads. Not me. It is my treat. I drink brandy, watch people. I watch the moon. Sometimes I walk to the water to watch the lovers, to remember what it is like. I miss my wife, but I have the moon."

"The Lady of the Night," I chimed in.

"Yes. The Lady of the Night."

Deep inside I wept. Who among us has not known this profound feeling of utter aloneness in the universe? Yet Mr. Ravit knew he was not alone. We clasped hands in brotherhood. Mr. Ravit was obviously a refined gentleman, with a bit of poetic spirit. Three bean-and-cheese burritos later, and a vanilla milk shake to top it off, I handed Mr. Ravit a ten-dollar bill, knowing full well that he would warm his gullet that evening with a small bottle of brandy. Sometimes when we are exiles, wanderers, and seekers we have to warm ourselves from the inside out. Though I was invited to toast the moon with him, I moved onward, listening for the heartbeat.

JAY: PROTEST AND HOSPITALITY

Next I met Jay, a Vietnam vet in an old wheelchair. An extremely bitter man, Jay spat his words at me like bullets. He described how he had been drafted into the war. Like so many veterans of the Vietnam War, he returned with his reality shredded. The woman he had left behind married another. His mind had been utterly and thoroughly "jacked up from the heroin," as he put it, when he became hooked on it in the trenches. His knee, but a shrunken stub now, had been blown apart by a piece of flying shrapnel, which eventually led to his leg being amputated from the knee down.

Jay sang songs of anger as a way to move the strong emotions that coursed through him. "I'm half the man, half the man, half the man I used to be...." He laughed maniacally in between his various tunes, playing a perpetual card game of solitaire on his blanketed lap.

Jay cursed "Uncle Sam" for taking his life as he had known it away from him. He cursed Lyndon Johnson and Richard Nixon.

"F— 'em all! None of them want to do right by the world. None of 'em want to do right by me! Look at the Persian Gulf War. The babies of Gulf War soldiers are being born left and right with birth defects. Is the U.S. going to treat the Desert Stormers like they did us Ho Chi Minh Troopers?"

Jay bit his lip, almost making it bleed. "All of the U.S. presidents have been corrupt, 'cept Jimmy Carter and J.F.K." Oddly enough, we found ourselves laughing together. His bitterness had a strange ironic twist of humor to it. The wounded do not lie. Yet in the midst of his nearly demonic laughter, he screamed, "I wish there was some way to force the government to wake up!"

I was moved by this sudden declaration. It felt like a blade of sanity piercing his ordinarily frazzled thought process. I decided to tell him some stories, about druids and Celtic warriors. It felt like one of the only ways at my disposal to support his soul — a soul that had been abandoned by the world around him.

I told Jay about the old Irish tradition of the *troscad*. The *troscad* is an ancient practice of protest fasting that hails from the primal era of Irish culture and has survived to the present day in the form of the various "death fasts" performed as protests by I.R.A. prisoners of war. Believed to come straight from the druidic era, the *troscad* has always been considered a powerful pathway for drawing attention to and affecting an energetic shift in situations of injustice. In effect, the *troscad* is a way of shaping the Soul of the World.

In the old days the Brehon laws (the sacred spiritual laws that governed the early Irish people) stated that an individual with a grievance had a right to perform the *troscad* as a means of seeking reparations for an injustice or wrongdoing. Brehon law required that all leaders make space for this kind of protest, providing a place for the *troscad* to take place. The old druidic view of this act is that the power of fasting affects the shamanic reality of things, as if the soul energy of a person begins to influence the shape of the world. This may seem far-fetched to modern people, yet many people undoubtedly believe that the peaceful revolution of the great Mahatma Gandhi of India was no less a mystical, magical act.

Until we can recognize protest as the spiritual act that it is, our society will only continue to demonize and marginalize the protestor. Bad idea. This paradigm only serves to ignite fires of violence that could otherwise be hearth fires of peaceful, meditative, earth-centered protest, as it was always done in the Celtic tradition. To continue to silence the spirit of protest with pepper spray and steel-toed boots only adds more energy to our national shadow. These actions to silence protest are attempts to prevent a change in consciousness from taking place, yet the force of the human soul and the consciousness of the planet are far more powerful than any human structure that has been created. Besides, the spirit of protest, the living spirit of the *troscad,* is nothing more than the spirit of hospitality wearing an activist face. In the coming years, we may see more expressions of the *troscad* tradition being practiced to raise awareness about human rights and environmental issues.

Jay's demeanor softened a bit when he heard of this powerful Irish tradition.

"Well, I'll be damned. Little did I know that I've been sitting on a *troscad* bench, complete with a set of wheels!" he barked loudly. I gave Jay a small amount of money to have a meal that night. Without so much as a good-bye, thank-you, or "good talking to you," Jay rolled off away from me and straight into a McDonald's.

I wondered, for a brief moment, what the vegetarians at the Kinship Conference would think about my putting hamburgers into the hands of a hungry homeless man.

LORETTA: THE FACE OF MY UNBORN DAUGHTER

Finally I sat for a time with Loretta, a mixed-race African American and Caucasian woman, around my age. A former office worker in a prestigious company, she, like so many others, had been laid off from work in a massive corporate downsizing. While many others are able to experience a quick turnaround of luck in finding employment, Loretta found herself evicted from her apartment. With no family to support her and no friends to stay with, she began her life on the streets.

Sexually abused more times than she cared to remember, Loretta wept at what she "had allowed herself to become," as she described it, as if her dismissal from employment and the following experiences had been her fault. When you live on the street, you learn quickly where it is safe to be at night and where it is not, she told me. I shivered as she told me how she had been robbed at knife point. Her face, which earlier had held an expression of sadness, was blank. It was an expression I knew quite well: the expression of soul loss. She recounted the details as though she had seen them in a movie rather than having experienced them firsthand.

At one point Loretta remarked, "Things are looking up for me, though. I've got a way now outta this mess. I'll be on my way next week." She had enrolled in an urban assistance program, which was part of a Catholic Charities organization. Her face lit up as she contemplated the future, of being employed again, of having a roof over her head, of having a few extra coins to buy fruit at the store.

Suddenly I was filled with a deep grief for Loretta. I studied her face in the light of the street lamp. I imagined Loretta as my daughter. The thought was almost too much to bear. I handed her $25. She shot me a suspicious glance, as if I "wanted something" for the twenty and the five. I just shook my head and waved my hand, as if to say, "No." I bowed and received a bow in return.

As I walked away from Loretta, I began to sob. Mr. Ravit, Jay, and Loretta. Normal people. Exiles. Wanderers. Seekers. Every man, my brother. Every woman, my sister. Every old man, my grandfather. Every old woman, my grandmother. Every crying child, my child. Every wounded soul, my soul.

My ego, my self-contrived notions of myself as "spiritual

teacher" or "counselor" or "shamanist" flaked off like old skin. I realized in a few short hours that if my spiritual pathways, and the practices I engage in, are not aimed at the Soul of the World in some fashion, then I simply dwell in a false, disconnected world of my own design.

I listened for the heartbeat of God and found it beating among those who are often overlooked, unseen by the rushing world around them. They are rarely extended the spirit of hospitality. For days after, including the remaining days of the conference, I was disoriented, shaken, "beside myself." Angeles Arrien sometimes speaks about the notion of "just showing up." For the next few days about all I could accomplish was just showing up, speaking a bit about finding the heartbeat of God in the city, sharing my newfound notion of kinship with all life.

PRACTICES: EXTENDING HOSPITALITY

- Consider volunteering at a homeless shelter.
- I have adopted a custom in Washington, D.C. I sometimes go to a breakfast buffet. For $2.20 I can stack up a to-go carton with French toast, eggs, fruit, biscuits, and gravy. For $2.20, a person who is struggling on the street gets a breakfast. I cannot solve their problems. I cannot get them a job. I cannot provide them with an explanation of why life has thrown them a curve ball, but for a mere $2.20 a day, I can slay the dragon of hunger in the belly so they can feel the spirit of hospitality. Consider putting some food into the hands of someone who needs it.
- In the foyer of your home create a space that will hold an altar to the spirit of hospitality. When people enter your home, welcome them with a deep and open heart.

- I have actually visited the homes of people who fail to ask, "Would you like some tea? Would you like an ale?" This would be considered poor manners in the traditional Southern and Celtic home. Make sure to offer liquid nourishment to your guests as a way of extending the spirit of hospitality.
- Give someone your seat on the bus, even someone who does not need it.
- If you see someone struggling with a heavy box in your office building, or someone who has dropped something, offer to help. I have been very surprised to see people in the city walk right on by when someone has dropped a number of items at their feet. Why are we in such a rush?
- Help someone. Maybe someone is loading a truck or is moving. Perhaps someone is behind on a number of projects in their home. Spend your time enriching this person's sense that they are loved and held in true hospitality.

When we approach every moment and every human interaction in the spirit of hospitality, something ancient and holy begins to dwell within us. Welcome this presence into your life and know that with it you can shape the Soul of the World.

CHAPTER 12

THE WAY OF EARTH

One of the shaman's main tasks is to gain access to the dreaming process during the day.

— ARNOLD MINDELL, *THE SHAMAN'S BODY*

This land, like a mirror, turns you inward.

— GWENDOLYN MACEWEN, *THE SHADOW-MAKERS*

We have explored the first two facets of the Hearth Way, the way of the hearth and the way of the heart. Now we turn our pilgrimage to the final domain of this spiritual framework: the way of earth. The way of earth also involves living deeply within our senses, befriending and embodying the sacred world, but here we explore a way that interfaces with the green realms of nature, experiencing deeper layers of our relatedness to life, inviting us into a communion with the holy earth.

As we have discussed, the notion of the world as sacred in the Celtic spiritual traditions is rooted in experience, not just conceptualization. We all live in a psychologically savvy culture. We can conceptualize our way to the moon and back, often without experience, and often without any sense of having been made the better for all our theoretical posturing. An empowered spirituality of the senses, in the Celtic way of being, uses the fullest range of our abilities as humans. Our souls are expanded. Our spirits are open. Our hearts have become a doorway through which we travel, sojourn, go on pilgrimage.

Conceptualization is fine if it helps us understand something or get our heads around it, so to speak. But if conceptualization is where the road stops, it is hardly worth the effort of the journey. Carrying our ideas into the realm of experience is what the Celtic mystical traditions teach us: the experience of the moon, with or without the brandy. The experience of the roundness of your lover's eyes upon you. The experience of gratitude when feeling the warmth of the sun on a cold day. These experiences are the marrow of it all.

An even deeper level to work with is exploring our sacred world as a divinely imbued mirror that not only conspires on behalf of our soul but also faithfully presents to us a stream of teachings and knowledge, every moment of every day. This knowledge is not some esoteric gnosis that takes fifty years to experience or apprehend. It is true that some of the druids felt that it takes ten to twenty years to truly master this level of awareness, but all of us have access to it. As children we knew when the sacred world was mirroring back to us, and we can feel this again, day after day, as humans continuing the journey from infancy to elderhood.

Part of the work has to do with relaxing our monkey mind. Monkey mind is that incessant chatter of scientific rationalism in our noggins that deplores the unknown, seeks to explain away the ineffable as "superstition" simply because it is the one domain remaining that cannot be codified and strip-searched by people in white coats. However, the Great Mirror is so vast and far-reaching that even the people in the white coats are part of the mirror and they, too, mirror something about all of us.

When we slow down, as I have said over and over in this book, we are providing for an opening to happen. It is an opening that is much needed at this time in our history, for it is an opening to the heart of the Great Shaper (or Shapers) of Life. We can learn from the great shapes, through a most holy dialogue between our senses and the outer world, and, finally, from processing the nature of this dialogue in both the conscious and unconscious mind.

THE LANDSCAPE AS MIRROR

The landscape is a mirror. It is a splendid revealer of things not often seen with the eyes of everyday life. When walking out on the land, it is good to invite the "eyes of the seer" and the "eyes of the poet" to be present. These are eyes that see the true shape of things. Poets and seers see things differently. When we relax the literal thinking mind and enter a landscape with more fluid perceptions (a soft gaze), we soon find that we become changed. We are then able to connect with our primal, preliterate selves. This preliterate, or perhaps postliterate, state of consciousness opens us to the Great Mirror of Nature.

The Celtic tradition of divination and seership is rooted in an understanding that clarity of thought and vision can be found in nature. It is no accident, for instance, that so many Celtic seers, ancient and modern, have been shepherds, drovers, and crofters. These individuals are often out on the land hillwalking. Their souls are customarily deep in the consciousness required to receive vision, spiritual insight, and prophecy. This thread of the Celtic tradition understands well William Butler Yeats's notion of "the condition of quiet that is the condition of vision."

These shepherds and seers are not some elite caste of human

beings. With practice and refinement, these skills of vision and seership are accessible to everyone. The difference is that modernity fosters an atrophy of the senses, while the natural, rustic, and rural spirit facilitates a healing of the senses. Family bloodlines genetically predisposed to seership, or living the entirety of our lives in a rural setting, are not requirements for cultivating these abilities. Removing ourselves, with some frequency, from an urban setting and communing with the Great Mirror of Nature is.

The Great Mirror, as I call it, is that striking feature of Creation that soulfully reflects back to us our own soul when we slow our rhythm and our daily pace down long enough to be recipients of its wisdom. Through the Celtic practice of merging the human soul with the soul of nature and the soul of place, a deep healing occurs. A profoundly sacred education awaits us all. But, as Quaker educator and philosopher Parker Palmer has said, "Education isn't necessarily a learning, but very often an unlearning of false perceptions or a remembering of what we've forgotten."

The Celtic path of working with the beauty of Creation is one of dialogue. It is not a one-way conversation. This work is about allowing ourselves to become one-third of the sacred dialogue. We open ourselves to the inherent intelligence of the earth, the earth leans toward us in response, and a third thing is created: a true human being.

Those who follow the Celtic mystical paths have always perceived nature as sacred. There is an unspoken understanding that nature acts as a reflective mirror, shining back our own soul's essence and sometimes even prophetic information. The Great Mirror reminds us of our truest self. For this reason any spiritual work with the natural world, whether prayer, pilgrimage, hillwalking, fasting, or purification practices, is an invitation to return to the primal (meaning "original") essence of who we really are.

The Hindu tradition has a beautiful image that expresses quite eloquently the notion of the Great Mirror. It speaks of it as Indra's Net. Indra's Net is a metaphor for the phenomenon of reality. Any particular thing within Creation is a juncture point in the great net of reality. At a juncture point various strands of the net move off and are connected and bound to other objects in the net that occupy other juncture points. Several strands flow from each created thing to several other created things. At each juncture point there is also a jewel or multifaceted diamond that reflects the essence of every other created thing within the net of reality or Creation.

This is a very Celtic image, as can be so easily seen in all the Celtic knot work on various stone crosses, in jewelry, and in the ancient manuscripts, such as the *Book of Kells.* The ancient knot work does not exist merely for adornment or ornamentation. Knot work is essentially a cosmological statement about the interrelatedness of all things within the divine Creation.

Moving through the Landscape

Hillwalking is an ancient practice among Celtic peoples. You might say that the spirit of pilgrimage is what drives us, but hillwalking is what truly gets us there. In the Scottish and Irish sensibility, walking is never just a form of exercise. It is a poetic and sensual experience. It is a spiritual act. Walking is an art form, a dynamic communion with the landscape where one dwells. It is also a special time to connect with another person, should the walk involve a companion.

In some circles the term *hillwalking* denotes technical climbing or mountaineering. Yet hillwalking, in the truest sense of the word, does not require technical know-how. Celtic hillwalking requires nothing but our two feet and a willingness to engage the natural world with fresh senses. Hillwalking is neutral. It is just what it sounds like: walking in the hills, in the forest, along a stream. Yet hillwalking often serves a deeper purpose for the person undertaking a jaunt. It may be a way to visit with a friend who lives in town or a solitary act to clear one's head of thoughts. Hillwalking may also be an important facet of working with the soul, as in a kind of walking purification or walking meditation.

The degree of spiritual depth infused in one's hillwalking will, of course, depend on the hillwalker. In some cases the purpose of hillwalking is simply to enjoy natural sights and sounds. The Celtic spirit is in love with the natural world, and hillwalking can be a way of nurturing this love. For someone else hillwalking may involve a pilgrimage to an ancestral site, such as a formal walk to a clan cairn. Perhaps the person is undertaking a religious observance of some kind, such as the stations of the cross, or as they do in Ireland, a pilgrimage up Crough Padric, a sacred mountain to the druids that was eventually adopted as a prayer site by Saint Patrick. Sometimes hillwalking can even feel a bit like a form of autopsychotherapy.

I am reminded of the words of the great Danish philosopher Sören Kierkegaard, a great hillwalker who said, "Above all, do not lose your desire to walk. Every day I walk myself into a state of well-being and walk away from every illness that would have me; I have walked myself into my best thoughts, and I know of no thought so burdensome that one cannot 'walk' away from it."

The Spirit and Practice of Hillwalking

The Celtic people have always been a people of voyages, and hillwalking is a natural outgrowth of this voyaging spirit. It is, in some sense, a way to step into the flow of voyaging and participate in the dynamism of ancestral memory. Hillwalking is a practice and custom rooted in the celebration of movement: the movement of the tides, the movement of the ancestors, and the movement of our own feet across the sacred landscape. Hillwalking is, in effect, a way of assuming our place among the cycles of movement of stars, ocean waves, and rain clouds. Hillwalking, in this light, becomes a sourcing exercise, an experience of recalibrating our spirits to the mystery that is all around us, a meditation of movement.

There are, of course, as many ways to approach hillwalking as there are people. I have been on some hillwalks that were storytelling events. Our hillwalking was like stepping into the "Dindsenchas," the Irish "place stories," where every hill, cave, well, and stream has a name and an ancient genealogy. I often learn a great deal when I am a guest at someone's home and we go hillwalking. Every person has a story, and every person has his or her own way of seeing things that offers me a lesson about his or her love for the land. At other times hillwalking has become a healing event. As we walk my companion reveals a heavy heart, and the spirit of the land herself beckons for a purification of these "burdensome thoughts," as Kierkegaard has put it.

Sometimes when someone comes to me with a problem, I will get the sense that hillwalking is what is needed. The lack of movement around an issue receives an almost sacrosanct momentum when the troubled person gives voice to his or her trouble while we are hillwalking. Some of the best healing that can occur, I think, takes place out on the land, walking. And sometimes, as will be demonstrated in the last chapter, hillwalking can become a conduit for divination within the natural world.

Revisiting Soul As Tangible Energy

The body is in the soul.

— John O'Donohue

The primal perception of the human soul among the Celtic peoples is that the soul envelops the body, not the other way around. The soul is a field of energy that surrounds the body and has the potential of expanding outward in varying distances. Practitioners of Reiki, Qigong, and Therapeutic Touch, or students of advanced shamanic energy medicine, will recognize this description of the soul's energy.

EXERCISE: IMAGINING A WALK

- Think for a moment about walking in nature. Imagine that you are walking on a path on a cool autumn day. The sun is shining down through the trees. The path is covered with crisp leaves that crackle and crunch beneath your feet as you walk.
- See yourself raising your arms for a moment and take three deep breaths. If you were to attune to your soul's energy, what would you notice?
- Now imagine that you are standing in a crowded elevator or on a packed bus or subway. There are people on either side of you and a row of people in front of and behind you. The elevator, bus, or subway is hot and stuffy. Allow yourself to tune in with your soul's energy again. What do you notice?
- Return to the forest path and the cool, sunny autumn day with the trees all around. Lift your arms again and take three deep breaths. What do you notice now?

If you did not experience a tangible sense of your soul energy contracting and expanding, then I recommend performing the practice again by going into a crowded store, elevator, or subway and observing through your senses what happens with your soul's energy when you are in these crowded conditions.

Most people report that they feel their "spirit has expanded" or that their "soul energy has moved out several feet" from their body when they are contemplating being in nature. In turn, many people report that they notice that their soul energy has been "pulled in" very close to their body when they are in cramped conditions. The energy mechanics of the soul are real. The soul is not merely an idea, but an energy that we can experience. Traditions all over the world have articulated different concepts and definitions for this soul energy. The words *qi* from China, *ki* from Japan, *prana* from India, as well as concepts such as the "aura," have slowly infiltrated Western culture as ways to express the felt and perceived reality of the soul.

A Few Words about Divination

Divination is a cornerstone of the old Celtic spiritual traditions, both primal and Celtic-Christian. Many newcomers to the Celtic traditions are astonished to hear that many of the Celtic saints were also impeccable seers, as in the case of Crimthann of Gartan, Ireland, who later came to be known as Columcille (pronounced ca-lum-keel-ya) of Iona. Columcille's life is recorded in *The Life of St. Columba* by Adomnan of Iona, and his life is filled with example after example of his skill with both the second sight and divination.

Hailing from a thirty-thousand-year-old Indo-European shamanic tradition and flowing forward to the present day, divination has always played a part in the Celtic traditions. From the *neladoracht* (druidic divination by clouds) to the Augury of Mary in the folk Celtic-Christian tradition, the Celtic soul has always sought to know the mysterious flow of spiritual reality as it manifests in material reality.

There is nothing particularly magical about divination. I remember hearing one shaman from the Huichol tradition say,

"Divination is not supernatural. It is commonsense." Divination certainly is not supernatural, yet it is truly a numinous process to attune to the rhythms and tides of synchronicity in this way. As master dreamer Arnold Mindell says, "We are always dreaming, even when awake." Divination and seership are a way of attuning to the living dream.

A great many people interested in divination get lost in the paraphernalia of tarot cards, runes, bones, and so on, yet it is much more important to cultivate the proper kind of consciousness in divination work than to focus on the tools. The power is not in the physical objects but in the consciousness of the user. In essence, a successful divination can be performed using any objects or no objects at all. I once performed a divination for a woman using a set of Guinness coasters. An hour later, after having established what each of the coasters represented, it was clear to the woman which path she needed to choose for her life. I did not tell her what to do. She explained to me what was happening. We assigned a certain meaning to the coasters, and any amount of insight or direction that was gained from the process came from the "waking dream" and from the Great Mirror, not from me, not from the coasters.

Paying attention to the signs that are all around us is where the true art lies. I have always referred to this particular flow of consciousness as "soul watching," for soul is everywhere around us. We ourselves have soul energy, and the process I am about to outline is merely a way to "follow the soul" and "watch the soul" within and without. One of the ancient methods of divination in the Celtic tradition relates directly to hillwalking. I sometimes say, "I'm going hillwalking," and I really mean that I am going out onto the land to perform a divination. This can be confusing, so another name I have come to use that I rather like for this practice comes from kinsman, author, and teacher Tom Cowan. He simply calls this practice the Scottish Omen Hunt.

Conclusion
Working with the Great Mirror

The Scottish Omen Hunt

The primal Celtic tradition experiences the soul as existing outside the body, hence the ability to send the soul energy out on soul flight, as is often done in shamanist ritual and shamanic practice. When we work with the Great Mirror of Nature, it is important to approach this realm with a sense of dynamic openness in our soul energy, so that we can pick up information from the soul of a place. We cannot gain anything from the spirit of nature, including an appreciation of her, if we enter in a closed or rigid state.

All too often people go into nature for a hike or to camp and in a short time they return home untouched by the power of the natural world because they did not open themselves to it. We must have humility to surrender long enough to let the sacred into us, but all too often the humility required (the word *humility* is related to the word *humus,* meaning earth) never appears.

I feel that it is best to perform the practice of working with the mirror during the daytime so that you can truly see the signs and omens in nature. As you deepen with this practice, you will also find that sunny days (what I call "bright days") and gray days (what I call "mist days") will have a different bearing on your results. A completely different experience is available when you move through the natural world at night.

PRACTICE: WORKING WITH THE MIRROR

- To begin one must first perform a process I call "loosening the soul." This is nothing more than going into nature, closing one's eyes, taking some deep breaths, and allowing one's soul energy to expand outward from the body. With this energetic state of openness achieved, one is truly in the correct mind-set to receive the guiding wisdom of the natural world as it is reflected back to us.
- The second step is to attune oneself to a deeper question you are grappling with or to some situation in life with which you need guidance. Perhaps you have some hard decisions to make. You may have talked to a few people about it, yet you still feel profoundly unclear about what to do. Perhaps as you have struggled with this decision you have found that you are falling prey to a variety of self-deprecating messages you inherited from your younger years. Perhaps fear is gripping you. With particularly important questions or decisions, many people find that they get ensnared in the trappings of self-doubt. The solution to this habitual pattern is to "get out of the head," "get into the heart," and "get out onto the land."
- The third step is to pose one's question to the Great Mirror of Nature. See or feel the situation or decision that you are working with as dwelling in your chest, specifically around the

area of your heart. It may appear to you as an object or a symbol, or it may simply be felt as a sensation. If you are visually oriented, the question or situation may appear to you in your visioning eye. Once you have really anchored yourself in the feeling of the situation, question, or decision you must make, beseech the Great Mirror of Nature, asking that its healing and guiding powers reflect back to your heart the deep knowing needed to address the situation. You might choose to crystallize everything you are holding into a "seed question" (a very simple and brief question that captures what you're working with). Pose the seed question from your heart to the spirits of nature three times.

- Your task now is simply to maintain your soul's energy in a state of energetic openness while walking through nature. This also means allowing your vision to remain relaxed. If your vision becomes extremely focused on an object, stop, take a few breaths, return your "seeing" to a relaxed state, and proceed walking.
- In many ways the success of an omen hunt depends on your ability to surrender to a shifting consciousness that may move around quite a bit. Your attention may be brought to something. You focus on it for a moment, making a mental note, and then return to a soft gaze.
- Remember, the type of focused precision required in analytical thinking is not what is called for here. A flowing intuitive way of sensing that is rather slow in rhythm is best for working with the Great Mirror. After all, the Great Mirror of Nature *is* nature. To access the wisdom and healing of nature, you must slow your personal rhythm down to match the soul energy of the spirit of nature.
- Be open to images that may present themselves to you in the clouds, in the intersecting branches or the bark of trees, in the shadows of stones, and in the land. Be open to sounds and

smells. Try to see the natural world around you as one field of vision, rather than as hundreds of distinct objects. Allow yourself to take in the landscape in such a way that the edge of a stone might blend with a tree root that may also be blended with a pool of water. Rather than seeing a stone, a tree root, and a pool, see these things blended as a perfect whole.

It is unlikely that every miniscule detail you encounter is of import, yet while you are engaged in this practice, do not dismiss anything, for it may have meaning once you have contemplated it further. Usually when people encounter signs and omens that are directly related to their situation, a powerful surge of recognition and understanding washes over them, something Carl Jung and others would recognize as synchronicity.

Like the flock of geese that flew by my window the morning my illness broke, the soul energy of the person encountering the sacred signs of the Great Mirror will often react viscerally and powerfully the first time she or he perceives a sacred reflection from the spirit of nature. Actually, I have found that the feelings associated with numinous recognition never go away. It is a powerful "ah-ha" experience any time our soul is reflected back to us by the Great Mirror of Nature.

As always, I recommend keeping a journal of the images or sensations you encounter in nature in relation to your question. If you treat these images like waking dream images and keep a faithful record, you will slowly discover that you will begin to see with your own unique symbol system. What is taking place is the cultivation of the same propensities as those of the seers in Highland tradition, who have developed a unique local symbol system for decoding the omens that come from the Great Mirror of Nature. Trust in your visions.

An Omen Hunt with Mary

Your grief for what you've lost lifts a mirror
up to where you're bravely working.
Expecting the worst, you look, and instead,
here's the joyful face you've been waiting to see.

— Jala-ud-din Rumi[1]

A few years ago a client sought me out for some counseling. She was a middle-aged woman (I will call her Mary) who was experiencing a great deal of crisis and turmoil. Mary reported that she had come to an impasse. She didn't know what she was supposed to do with her life. All sources of meaning for her were now inaccessible. It was familiar territory to me.

She shared with me how all her children had moved out and had gone to college. She also described that the summer before her oldest child had been killed in a car accident. On the heels of this tragedy, her husband of twenty-three years had moved out and had secured an apartment in a neighboring town.

When I first met with Mary, one overarching word summed up her appearance to me: *numb.* In our first session, a session I use as both assessment and an opportunity to lay down the ground rules of the work, I had to repeat myself a few times with each point I had relayed to her. As is often the case with people who have experienced soul loss, there is usually a sense of struggle, paralysis, or a quality of being "checked out." All were true of Mary.

After Mary described to me in detail the events of the previous year, it was obvious that it was of paramount importance to address her state of soul loss, first and foremost. Her outward circumstances screamed of abandonment: empty-nest syndrome, the

---

1 From "Birdwings" in Coleman Barks, trans., *The Essential Rumi* (San Francisco: HarperSanFrancisco, 1995), p. 174.

death of a child, and the severed ties of a trusted marriage, but the most serious case of abandonment facing her were parts of her own soul energy to which she no longer had access. She would need these soul parts to engage the healing process that was ahead of her.

I set up my accustomed ritual space for soul flight and soul retrieval, explaining briefly the mechanics of shamanism to her. Even if a person does not understand or believe in an animistic worldview, I have had very good results in sharing my orientation with people. Just hearing of my desire to assist them often engenders the necessary component of trust for true healing to occur. After activating the space, which involves calling in certain ancestor spirits from both sides of my family, I performed an initial soul flight (shamanic journey) as a matter of assessment. I always do this. This enables me to see the many angles to a situation, to consult with certain advisers, and to discern if I will be able to assist a person or not.

I crossed paths with old Eoin, an ancestor, who always meets me by a large round boulder near a wooded hill. Eoin and I walked up and over another nearby hill. We approached an outcropping of rocks, beside which stood a couple of large oak trees. In one of the trees was a nest, the dwelling place of a large sea eagle roost.

Eoin and I watched as an eaglet took flight from the nest. The small bird landed on a nearby stone. Suddenly a large fox lunged from the undergrowth, grabbing the eaglet and killing it. With the sight of this the mother sea eagle began to screech. Her distress signals filled the air. Three other small eagles shivering from fear, obviously not understanding what was happening, also walked to the edge of the nest and took flight. These eagles stayed in the air and flew in different directions.

Suddenly, we looked to the south and saw another large sea eagle flying toward the nest. It was the male sea eagle, the father. It landed on the edge of the eagle roost, the mother eagle continuing to screech. To my astonishment the mother eagle suddenly turned on the male sea eagle and began scratching him with her razor-sharp claws and pecking at his head around his eyes. The male sea eagle took flight from the nest and began flying in a wide arc. The mother sea eagle continued to screech, the blood of the male sea eagle dripping from her beak.

After another moment the male sea eagle returned to the nest. Just as before the mother sea eagle attacked him instantly, tearing at his wing with her claws. Once again the father sea eagle took flight, this time continuing to fly away, back to the south from where he had come.

Old Eoin turned and looked at me, as if to say, "got it?"

"I believe I have it," I responded.

From this vivid imagery I saw some of the internal dynamics that may have occurred between Mary and her husband at the death of their child. I also saw there that something may have happened between her and her other children, but I did not know for sure.

I intentionally use the words *may have,* because doing shamanic work on behalf of someone else is a way of being offered general impressions but it is the rare occasion when I am shown the exact details with no omissions. It is only after communicating my vision to the client that I know more of the truth of the matter. I cannot speak for everyone, but this is the way that the Great Mirror and the Soul of the World reflect information to me.

Old Eoin and I walked back down the hill, past the large boulder he sometimes sits on, and we continued down to a small path along a stream. In this stream I saw a mound of frog eggs, new tadpoles slowly emerging from some of them. I took this as a good sign that I might be able to assist the woman. It was a sign of new life, resiliency, healing, and renewal.

I returned to the room.

Mary and I sat in silence for a few moments. I then explained to her that sometimes the images I see are dynamically "on" and sometimes they are "off." I asked her permission to share what I had seen and asked that she be truthful in responding to me about what I had to say.

She agreed.

I translated the vision into a pragmatic interpretation: "What I saw was that when your child was killed in the car accident something may have happened to you. I saw that you may have turned on your husband, perhaps unconsciously blaming him for the death of your child, and that some kind of pattern may have been set up with him coming to offer you comfort and you attacking him each time. I also saw that something may have happened between you and your other children as well. Eventually, it seems, your husband left you because it was too painful for him to stay in connection to you."

The look in her eyes and the tears on her face were all that I needed to discern that what I had seen was correct. She began to sob and nodded her head in affirmation.

"I chased them all away. Now I have no one. They were my life, and I am lost without them. I don't know who I am anymore."

I worked with Mary for several more sessions. We addressed certain deeply held beliefs that she had about herself as a woman. We were also able to do some very good work on restoring the level of her soul energy, retrieving an animal spirit guide for her protection, as well as establishing a rhythm of things she could do daily to provide centering and healing. With each session more and more of Mary became present to her again.

We eventually addressed a central question: How could Mary find her path, her identity, her purpose in life, that stood outside her habitual roles? The night before my last session with Mary I had a dream that offered me instructions about how to provide closure. I sometimes receive dream instructions surrounding my work with a particular client. I have learned to heed these instructions when they come. Sometimes I will intentionally take a client's issue and try to "dream on it." Other times I will receive rather spontaneous and involuntary precognitive dreams of things the client will be bringing into the session.

In this dream I was shown that I needed to take Mary on an omen hunt. I also knew that the crux of what she would be bringing into the session for our closing was how to go about reestablishing contact with her family.

We sat down for this last session, and I asked her point-blank, "So, you're kicking around the idea of how to make peace with your family?"

Mary smiled, her face gleaming.

I told her of my dream and also proposed the omen hunt, describing it and the potential power it has for guidance. This work seemed very good to her and, in her words, "especially appropriate for our last session."

We traveled to a pristine wilderness area very near my home at the time. In keeping with custom I handed her a hillwalking stick and gave her very specific instructions about how to go about doing an omen hunt. I included the disclaimer that the omen hunt is not a replacement for therapy when dealing with particularly volatile emotions but that it is a reliable way to receive clear reflection and guidance about a situation. Mary acknowledged this and we began, with me assuming a position out of sight some thirty yards away, drumming lightly and requesting help from the spirit of the forest.

After an hour Mary returned with tears streaming down her face and a big smile. She shared with me the following account of her omen hunt, which I have attempted to retell true to Mary's spirit:

> I started walking down the path away from where you were sitting. As I walked on the path I started to get annoyed, even frustrated. Something about staying on the

"defined" walking trail felt constricting to me. I started thinking about how I have always felt some resentment that I have not known any other part of myself other than Mary as mother, Mary as wife, Mary as daughter, Mary as the person who always stays on the defined walking trail.

As I entertained these thoughts I softened my gaze and continued walking. I stopped for a moment, and right beside me was an interesting sight.

There was a large boulder, part of which had sort of a cavelike overhang to it. Under the overhang two trees have grown up from the ground. One tree met the stone of the overhang and grew downward, back toward the ground. The other tree met the stone of the overhang and literally grew sideways to a point where it was free from the restriction of the overhang. At that point the tree started growing straight up again, still in connection to the stone but no longer defined by it. I realize that I am at that point in my life.

I continued to walk a little further. I started to think of my husband. I remembered some of the things I said to him after our eldest child was killed. He was out of town on a business trip when it happened. I blamed him.

As I was walking I found a small branch that had broken off from a pine tree. I studied it. It had six little branches coming off of the main branch. This reminded me of my family when we were all together. I named each little branch after each one of us, even one for my son who died.

I returned to the question you asked me to hold in my heart. My question was, "How can I restore the love in our family the way it was before I became so hard-hearted?" Suddenly, it occurred to me: place the branch broken from the tree back where it belongs.

> The funniest thing happened. I was able to fit the broken branch, "my family," back onto the part of the branch it had fallen from. The pieces fit together perfectly. It looked like it had never broken.

I asked Mary what she thought this meant in terms of her question and her own evolving Great Mirror of Nature symbolism. She explained that at no point had she asked her husband to come back. They had simply separated, and that was that. Her own hard-heartedness and hard headedness had prevented any movement. She also explained that, while her kids would call occasionally from college, she herself had done a very poor job of extending to them and was rarely fully present for them when they reached her. She was like the tree that met the stone and ceased to extend.

She exclaimed, "I realize now that I am the one who 'broke the branch,' and I am the only one who can 'put the branch back together.' My mistake was in lashing out and not seeking the necessary support I needed back then for my grief process. But I couldn't see this then. I just thought everyone was leaving me."

I shared with Mary the numinous imagery associated with my Clan MacEwen: the wounded stump growing green saplings again, and the associated motto of *reviresco* (we grow green again). Mary felt a deep sense of inspiration from this image, as so many do upon hearing it. I told her that I firmly believed that no matter how broken something has become, new life, new beauty, and new connection can be grown from it. A few weeks later I received a phone message from Mary. She had arrived at a brilliant idea. She purchased plane tickets for her three children and her husband, and enclosed them in an invitation that she mailed to each of them.

The invitation was for a rendezvous as a family, on the anniversary of her son's death in late summer, at a seaside location that was a longtime favorite of the child who had been killed.

In the letter to her family she shared a bit of her process of healing and deeper self-exploration with them, as well as her insights into some of her inappropriate behaviors and mismanaged rage. She openly apologized for any wounds she had caused and asked for forgiveness, as well as the opportunity to heal their connection. She requested that each of them come for an all-expenses-paid weeklong vacation in what she described as "putting the branch of our family tree back together again."

In late September of that same year, I received a postcard from St. Croix, Virgin Islands. It was inscribed simply, "Reviresco! We are all growing green again. Blessings, Tears, and Smiles, Mary."

Mary's experience on that heavily wooded hillside, of encountering the topography of her own soul in the topography of the landscape around her, may seem random or contrived to readers who have not experienced this dimension of spiritual work. As the saying goes, I guess you had to be there. For me there was no doubt at all that Mary had been led to the very places where she could experience a powerful sense of healing from the natural world. We called on the spirit of the mountain, the spirit of the trees; Mary leaned toward them, and they leaned back and embraced her. In the realm where mountains and trees become standing prayers, transformation awaits.

Mary had, from a druidic perspective, found her *fidnemed* (an ancient Irish word for forest shrine) — a place of spiritual communion with the natural world, a place to remember who she really is. She had, from a Celtic-Christian mystical perspective, discovered her resurrection place; a holy juncture point discovered through hillwalking out on the land — a place where her new life could begin. From the vantage point of ecopsychology, she had come to understand the tender experience of what is sometimes called "place-bonding," a word that describes how the earth and our own hearts mirror each other in certain locations. And, through the lens of Celtic seership, she had received glimmers of a hopeful future through the form of an omen.

In essence, Mary had found her soul parts again, along with a new resolve for living, and the initial waves of understanding what Scottish mystic and faery-seer William Sharp called "The Green Life" (a term used for the deep abiding flow of primal earth wisdom inherent in the natural world).

This book has not been about providing you with a destination or a point of arrival. No book can do that. Indeed, it is not even a complete map of the vast domain of the Celtic spirit or the mysticism that springs from it. My hope, however, is that these pages have inspired you, in the same way that the spirit of this work inspired Mary, to seek the impassioned green life of becoming your own mapmaker on the Mist-Filled Path of your life.

May you find your resurrection place, your own forest shrines, and trust that what you discover there is good. May you come to embrace the wisdom that the mist can teach us about blending, about making compromises in our fixed and solidified states of mind, and may you learn to trust and rely on the holiness of the longing in your soul. May you and the life of your soul grow green again. *Reviresco.*

Glossary

Altomesayoq (all-toe´me-say-yok): a particular class of Incan shaman who works specifically with an empowered altar that is linked to a variety of power places and landscapes through sacred objects.

Anamchara (ah-naam´kara): literally "soul friend," the *anamchara* is akin to a spiritual adviser, known in both the druidic and Celtic-Christian traditions.

Ancestral transmission: a term I coined to denote the very specific process in which ancestor spirits wake up the shamanic potential within the living descendant through the introduction of imagery and energy, as opposed to the specific instruction of living shamans to a student, which is often called hereditary transmission.

An da shealladh (ahn´daa´haa-loo): literally "the two sights," the phenomenon of the second sight or spiritual seeing, long considered a feature particularly prevalent among the Scottish Highlanders. Examples of contemporary seers are Swein MacDonald, Henderson Lynn, R. J. Stewart, and the late Eliadh Watt.

An nela dubh (ahn´nella´doov): the black cloud; my own nickname for spiritual emergency or crisis where the body and the inner states of consciousness of the person mirror one another.

An sith (ahn-shee): the peace; a qualitative state of consciousness achieved through deep meditation whereby one is utterly merged with the harmonious pattern of the universe.

Awen (ah-win): a word from the Welsh for divine inspiration.

Baisteadh geinnleidh (bye´stee, guyn´lee): the rain wedge of protection; believed to be an ancient druidic rite of water blessing.

Ban-draoi (ban-dree): female druid.

Bodhran (bo-rawn): the distinctive Celtic drum, sometimes played with the hand and other times played with a small wooden double-headed mallet called a tipper.

Broken clan: a clan whose chieftaincy lies dormant and who have lost their lands.

Cailleach (kyle-yuk): a crone or hag; eventually fell into use as a derogatory term for an old woman, but originally was an honorable term for an old priestess of the old religion.

Cairn (care-n): a collection of stones, usually on a hilltop or along a shore line, that commemorates something of importance, such as an ancestor, a clan, or some historical event such as a battle.

Caoineadh (keen-ee): Anglicized into the word "keening," this is the custom and practice of fully embodied grieving long known in the Celtic traditions. The keening women were a group of women who attended wakes and funerary proceedings for the purpose of keening for the souls of the dead.

Celi de (kul-a-day): a particularly stoical and austere group of Celtic-Christian monks who followed very closely the imitation of Jesus while maintaining ties to the natural world.

Children of the Mist: a term originally used by historians to refer to those Scottish clans and families who were forced into hiding due to various conditions.

Churchanity: religious expressions in the Christian tradition that have forgotten any sense of the mysticism, love, and tolerance that Jesus taught.

Clooties (kloo´teez): strips of natural cloth tied to branches about springs and holy wells, or on special faery trees.

Crannog (kran´og): wooden homes, usually with conical huts with thatched roofs, that were traditionally situated out over the water. Over time sediment and debris from inside the crannog would sift through the floor planks and create small earthen islands, many of which still exist today in Irish and Scottish lochs. The word crannog is used for the wooden houses and the earthen islands interchangeably.

Cruithear (coo´tea-r): creator, a Scots Gaelic term for God, the Great Shaper.

Deiseil (jee-shil): clockwise, or sunwise; anciently considered a holy direction of movement, employed even today in practices such as circumambulation, walking around ancestral cairns, and sacred trees.

Drala / dralas (dra´la): an exceedingly difficult term to define in English, *dralas* are primal energies as perceived in Bön shamanic lore and the Shambhala traditions of Chögyam Trungpa Rinpoche.

Druids: the spiritual elders, medicine people, philosophers, wisemen and wisewomen, mystics, and shamans of the Celtic people until the introduction of institutionalized Christianity.

Entheogen (en-the´o-gin): a word being used today in place of hallucinogen or psychedelic; the word denotes having God revealed within; entheogens are plants, herbs, or mushrooms that facilitate healing and access to divine states of consciousness; entheogenic shamanism is the use of entheogens to obtain sacred knowledge, ancestral guidance, or healing power.

Eolas (e-oh-lass): knowledge.

Fey (fay): denotes the faery people and/or places that are known to be inhabited by faery energies; other worldly, visionary.

Filidh (feel´ah): vision poet in the Irish and Scottish Gaelic traditions.

Green Martyrdom: the self-imposed exile from human contact to wander for God in the natural world.

Hiraeth (he´ry-the): an ancient Welsh word for longing.

Imbas (em-baas): a word from the Gaelic for divine inspiration.

Imbolg/Imbolc (em-olk): an ancient Celtic observance, also known as *Oimealg* in Scottish Gaelic, occurring roughly around the first of February; associated with the quickening energies of spring, the lactating of the ewes, and the goddess Brighid.

Immrama (em-raam-a): one component of the ancient Irish tradition of mythopoetic sourcing tales, involving long voyages over the sea to a series of islands.

Lectio divina: meditations on the Scriptures, deriving from the ancient mystical strands of the desert tradition of Christian mysticism.

Mesa: the altars of a particular kind of Inca shaman.

Mothering Powers, The: the feminine powers that teach, protect, guide, heal, and soothe.

Neladoracht (neela´dor-ock): a divination performed through the use of clouds in the sky.

Ollamh (o-lav): chief poet.

Primal earth: a central concept in the Celtic Underworld tradition, deeply rooted in traditional cosmologies of a spiritual realm beneath the ground inhabited by ancestors and faery people.

Reviresco (riv-va´resk-o): a word or phrase of Latin origin used as the motto of two Scottish clans, the Highland MacEwens and the Lowland Maxwells; in both cases the term has various translations, usually "we grow again" or "we grow green."

Sain/saining (sahn, sahn-ing): to cleanse, purify; similar to the Native American custom of burning sage and smudging sacred objects or a room to prepare them for ceremony or to purify them of heavy energies; in the Scottish Highland customs juniper has long been used for the same purpose; one can also *sain* with salt, water, or saltwater.

Samhuinn (sow-en): originally a purely Gaelic Irish and Scottish custom or fire festival honoring the ancestors and the new year, the term has been employed by a number of non-Gaelic traditions.

Scottish Omen Hunt: a practice combining divination and seership with hillwalking, using the landscape as a mirror of revelation.

Seannachie (sha-na´key): a sacred storyteller and tribal historian among the Irish and Highland Scots.

Seid (say): to blow; can simply mean to blow as in blowing out a candle, but also in a manner to mean a sacred breath as in shamanic work.

Selkie (sell-key): a race of beings in traditional Irish and Scottish lore believed to be part human and part seal.

Shamanist: a term I first heard from Buryat shaman Sarangeral; it is a functional term in that it delineates one who follows a shamanic faith or religion, as opposed to someone who may practice shamanic techniques with no religious affiliation.

Sitchain (shee´con): an alternate word used for contemplative peace.

Sith (shee): peace; also a word used to refer to the faery people, who are sometimes known as the people of peace, the good people, the shining ones.

Smooring (smoor´ing): the sacred custom in Gaelic lands of bedding down the fire for the night by embanking the ashes to blanket the embers.

Soul flight (shamanic journey): the practice of sending out one's spirit into the Otherworld, or into one of three dimensions often perceived by shamans, the Lowerworld, Middleworld, and Upperworld.

SSC (shamanic state of consciousness): a term coined by anthropologist, author, and shamanic teacher Michael Harner to denote the state of consciousness in which a shaman, shamanist, or shamanic practitioner has achieved the ability to move in nonordinary reality.

Taghairm (ta´rum): literally "echo," this is a word for a variety of different practices that originally hailed from the primal shamanic lore of the Gaelic people and that involve attunement to the spirits of the ancestors or the spirits of nature to receive guidance and direction; often involved wrapping a seer in a hide and placing this person in a mist-filled place, such as near a waterfall or on a hill.

Taibhs (tai´shh): sometimes used simply to mean a spirit, this is the image or spectre a *taibhsear* sees.

Taibhsear (tah´shar): vision seer, one who sees the apparitions of the departed, or the fetch or double of a person still living.

Tannasg (tann´ask): an apparition of someone already dead.

Teallach (tee´all-uk): literally "hearth;" also used here in reference to the altars people used that are situated at the hearth.

Tir nan Sinnisir Mbeo (tear-naan sin-i-sear, m-be-yo): Land of the Living Ancestors.

Troscad (tro´skaad): an ancient form of protest-fasting in the Irish tradition.

Twi-state: in-between state, such as twilight, where it is believed that the veils that separate ordinary reality and nonordinary reality, the land of everyday reality from spiritual reality, are removed.

Walking between the worlds: one phrase used to refer to the practice of shamanic soul flight and/or the literal physical transmigration from ordinary reality to the realm of faery in the Celtic faery lore.

Resources

Wilderness Rites of Passage (Vision Quest Programs)

The School of Lost Borders
Steven Foster and Meredith Little, Directors
Box 55
Big Pine, CA 93513
www.schooloflostborders.com

The Naropa Center for Ecopsychology
Naropa University
2130 Arapahoe Avenue
Boulder, CO 80302
303-444-0202
www.naropa.edu

Sacred Journeys, Shamanic Pilgrimage Programs, and Soul Retrieval Work

Tom Cowan
Riverdrum Institute
17 South Chodikee Lake Road
Highland, NY 12528
www.riverdrum.com

Larry Peters
1212 Old Topanga Canyon Road
Topanga, CA 90290
www.tibetanshaman.com

Oscar Miro-Quesada
Mesaworks/Heart of the Healer Foundation
525 South Flagler Drive #27C
West Palm Beach, FL 33401
www.mesaworks.com

Dream Change Coalition
P.O. Box 31357
Palm Beach Gardens, Florida 33420-1357
www.dreamchange.org

For a listing of other visionary organizations, shamans from other traditions, and/or visionary teachers in the Celtic traditions, visit: www.celticwisdom.org and visit the section called "The Binding Weave: Links."

Ancient Scottish Studies, Celtic Studies, and Celtic Mysticism

Dalriada Celtic Heritage Trust
Taigh Arrain
Brodick, Isle of Arran, KA27 8BX
www.dalriada.co.uk
Dalriada@dalriada.co.uk

Kilmartin House Trust
Kilmartin, Argyll, Scotland, PA31 8RQ
www.kilmartin.org
museum@kilmartin.org

Frank Mills
The Oran Mór Institute
Oran Mór Conferences & Seminars
20050 Eldora Rd.
Rocky River, OH 44116
440-331-2398
OranMorConf@aol.com

Index

A

alone, not having to do it, 120–21
altomesayoq, 191, 199
American Indian Freedom of Religion Act, 98
an da shealladh, 104, 199–201
an nela dubh, 68
an sith, 14
anamchara, 204
ancestral transmission, xxxi, 104–11
anima, 168–70; defined, 168
animism, 21, 76, 114, 123, 168, 185
animistic and nonanimistic cosmologies, 117, 181
animistic spirituality, 212
animus, 169, 170
"as above, so below," 85–88
atonement, as renewal, 151–53
awen, 201

B

ban-draoi, 192
baptism, Celtic form of, 39
Baring-Gould, Reverend S., 211
Ben Cruachan, 38, 39
big drum, 100–101, 107
bodhran, 101, 107
body: embracing the, 177–78; innate intelligence of, 177, 179. *See also* embodied spirituality
breathing exercises, 58–59, 180–81
Brehon law, 224
Brighid, 191–93

C

Cailleach Bheur, 38–39
caoineadh, 107
Carmichael, Alexander, 142–43
catharsis, 107, 108

Catholic Church, 214–15
Celi De', 149
cellular knowing, 109, 179–81
cellular memories, 59, 179
Celtic-Christian Church, 44
Celtic-Christian cosmology, 147, 153
Celtic-Christian tradition, xxv, 22, 27, 146, 150, 212, 213, 237, 250
Celtic-Christian vision, 152
Celtic Church, 96, 147, 213; ancient days of the early, 32
Celtic descendants and ancestry, 54–55
Celtic Mothers, 156. *See also* feminine (divine)
Celtic people, spiritual legacy of the, 44–47
Celtic roots/ancestry, 111; awakening of a sleeping lineage, 95–100
Celtic soul, 20, 53, 54, 151; longing of the, 50–53
Celtic spirit, xi, 19–22, 54, 56, 123
Celtic spiritual approach, 114
Celtic spiritual path, xxiv, xxxii
Celtic spiritual traditions, xxiv, 229–30
Celtic spirituality, xii, 19, 22, 32, 53, 56, 58, 113, 124, 175–77, 185
Celtic traditions, cultural soul elements in, 63–64
chi, 237
children of the mist, wandering soul of, 42–48
choice, 84
Christianity, 161, 213–16; modern, 148. *See also* Celtic-Christian tradition
Christmas, 200
Churchanity, 161
Clan Grandmothers, 164
Communion, Holy, 208–12
communion with the spirit of water, 39–42
consciousness, states of, 71, 101
crannogs, 193
creation: matrix of, 144; primal myth of, 131–32; process of, 134. *See also* Great Song
Crucifixion, 152
cultural soul loss and retrieval, 181–82, 198

D

dancing, 90. *See also* Sun Dance
"dark night of the soul," 68
De Waal, Esther, xxxii
death and dying, 56–57, 81–82, 84, 100, 202
dharma, 52
divination, 231, 235, 237–38
divinity, 176–77
"domination myth," 165
dreams, 70, 77
Druid religion, 53
Druidic Prayer Posture, 27
druidism, 149, 152, 250; and shamanism, 126
druid(s), 96, 146–47, 149, 213; female, 192; meanings of the word, 149
drum, big, 100–101, 107

E

earth: healing of the, 168; way of, 229–30

earth awareness, 115–19, 123–25
earthiness, embracing our, 178–79
Eckhart, Meister, 148
ecopsychology, 171–72, 250
education, 232
elements, shaping power of the, 36–40
Eliade, Mircea, 105
embodied spirituality, 175–79, 188, 212
"enemization," 165–67
energy, 237
Eoin, 244–45
eolas, 22
Eriugena, John Scotus, 176
Evans-Wentz, W. Y., 10
exile, 5–7

F

fasting: protest, 224–25. *See also* prayer-fast
fear, 71
feminine (divine), 155–57, 163–66, 173–74, 191–93; denigration of the, 156, 159–62. *See also* anima
filidh, 213
fire people, 36, 37
fires, 193–95, 198–200
First Nations people, 98–99
food, 190
Fox, Matthew, 148

G

Gaelic, 136
Galacia, 47
"glimpses of memory," 59
God, 127, 148
goddesses, 156. *See also* feminine (divine)
goose, spirit of the wild, 83
Great Mirror of Nature, 231–33; working with the, 240–42
Great Shaper of Life, 153, 231
Great Song (of Creation), 129, 212; Celtic-Christian vision of, 146–51; connecting with, 144–46; as gift from ancestral soul, 137–40; many dwelling places of, 140–43. *See also Oran Mór*
green Martyrdom, 32–33
Green World, xxv
grief, fully embodied, 107
Gurr, Nathan, 162

H

Hall, Calvin, 169
healing, 6–7
healing work of men, 162–66
heart, the way of the, 205
hearth, 189–90; as heartbeat of the home, 193–94; as holy stopping place, 201; keeping the, 190–92; living around the, 194–97; as otherworldly doorway, 199–201
hearth altar, 202–4
hearth way, the, 189–90, 205, 229
Henderson, David, 57–58
Highland Clearances, 44
Hill, Julia Butterfly, 121
hillwalking, 231, 233–35
hiraeth, 3
holiness, 114. *See also* sacred world

homeland, longing for the, 53–55
horses, 34
hospitality: extending, 227–28; faces of the spirit of, 208, 209; southern and Celtic style, 205–8
human being and human life, as spiritual cosmos, 182–83

I

ice people, 37, 42
imbas, 56, 76, 201
immrama stories, 71
in-between, the, xxxii, 12, 17, 22, 134, 136, 199
Indra's Net, 233
initiation(s), 56, 67, 72, 76–77, 91, 104–5
intimacy, xxii

J

Jay, 223–25
Jesus Christ, 147–50, 153; as druid, 150
John, Saint, 147, 150, 214
joy, 21
Jung, Carl Gustav, 168

K

keening, 107
Kevin of Glendalough, 33–34
kinship, sense of extended, 57–58, 60
Kohanov, Linda, 34
kything, 204

L

Lakota elders, 104. *See also* Sun Dance
landscape: as mirror, 231–33; moving through the, 233–34
Lawlor, Anthony, xxi
life, 113; choosing, 84–85, 88
listening, sacred, 153
Listening for the Heartbeat of God: A Celtic Spirituality (Newell), 150–51, 212, 214–16, 219
Logos, 147–48, 150
longing, 49–50, 67; attuning to one's, 58–59; befriending one's, 55–58; of the Celtic soul, 50–53; contemplating one's, 51–53; to grow the soul green again, 59–65; for the homeland and for spirit, 53–55
Loretta, 225–27
Luna, 121

M

MacEwens, xxiii, 60–61, 166–67, 192, 249
MacGregors, 43
MacLeans of Duart, 51
Mary, omen hunt with, 243–51
masculine/male archetypes, 160–61
masculinity, 169, 170; and male domination, 163–65
Maslow, Abraham, 56
mater, 163, 167
matter, created, 165–66
Matthews, Caitlin, 26, 191–92
McNeill, F. Marian, 39
medicine traditions, 106
meditation, xxix, 58–59
memory(ies): ancestral (*see* ancestral transmission); cellular, 59, 179; "glimpses" of, 59; of our many shapes, 125–28; past-life, 108

Methodist tradition, United, 208–11
microcosmic spirituality, 181
Mills, Frank, 132
Mirror. *See* Great Mirror of Nature
mist, 3–4; as guiding metaphor, 17–23; and the shimmering peace of things, 10–17; as trickster-teacher, 7–9
mist-filled path, xxx, xxxii–xxxiii, 53, 110, 183, 185, 212
Morgan, 124–25, 214
Mothering Powers (of Creation), 156, 167, 174, 193; within, 168–70; around us, 159; going out to meet the mother, 170–72; remembering the, 157–59
music. *See* Great Song; sound(s)
"My Father's God Beneath the Waves" (Gurr), 162

N

Nada Brahma, 143
natural world, 13, 123–24, 213. *See also* earth awareness; Great Mirror of Nature
near-death experience. *See* out-of-body wandering
need-fire, 198–99
needs, hierarchy of, 56
Newell, J. Phillip, 150–51, 212, 216
Nordby, Vernon, 169

O

oak tree, 61–62
O'Donohue, John, 4
"Old Tradition, The" (Whyte), 78–79
omen hunt, 243–51
oppression and oppressed peoples, 98–99
Oran Mór, 133, 138–40, 144; essence of, 147; vision of, 133–37. *See also* Great Song
out-of-body wandering, 81–83, 88, 92

P

pain, 103
past-life memories, 108
pater, 167, 169
Pater Conspiracy, 160–63
peace, xxiv
Pelagius, 124–25, 214
Pennick, Nigel Campbell, 18
people: of the ice, 37, 42; of the shapes, 32–36
pipe ceremony, 90
place-bonding, 250
poets, 61
prayer-fast, Celtic, 157, 170–73
praying, 142
primal Celtic tradition, 34, 116, 123, 239
primal origins, 174

R

Ravit, Mr., 221–23
religions, 63, 210
religious freedom, 98
"Return" (MacEowen), xxiii
reviresco, 61, 249–51
rhythm(s), 73
Roach, Steve, 27–28, 142, 144, 179–80
Roith, Fergus Mac, 184

Ross, Anne, 207
Rule of Tallaght, 27, 219

S

sacred orientations, 189
sacred shapes of life, 34
sacred world, xxxi–xxxii, 129, 230; entering, 7, 121–25; feeling of being accepted by, 11; living in, 114
Scottish Highland tradition, 50–52
seanachies, 61, 195–96
"seeing," 107
seership, 231, 238, 250
self-care, 129
senses, holy: reclaiming our, xxiii–xxx, 118
setting one's root, xxiii–xxviii
sexual assault and abuse, 164, 168
"shamanic dismemberment," 70–71, 76
shamanic state of consciousness (SSC), 12, 102
shamanism, 34, 45, 68, 85–86, 114–15, 203, 245; initiation into, 72, 76, 104–5. *See also* soul flight
Shambhala, 123
shape-shifting, 126–27
shapers of life, 35–36, 148
shapes: memory of our many, 125–28; sensing the holy, 117–20, 125
shee, 13
sheltering spirit, 191
silence, xxix, 141, 201
sin, 151–53
sitchain, 13
Sith, 13
sitting, 201
sleepwalking and sleepwalkers, xix, xxii, xxiv, xxix, xxxiii
slowness and slowing down, xxix
smooring, 198–99
Somé, Malidoma, 37, 54
soul, 116; different parts of, 25–26; evolution of, 53; as having mind of its own, 4–5; loosening the, 240; relationship and connection with, xxii; shape of, 23, 116–20; as tangible energy, 235–37. *See also specific topics*
soul energy, 237, 246
soul exile, 5–7
soul flight, 239, 244
soul friend, 172–73, 204
soul loss, 4–5, 7, 25, 31, 181–82, 198, 226, 243–44
soul maintenance, xxiv
Soul of Life, 18, 116, 122, 124
Soul of Place, 9, 118
Soul of the World, 7, 25, 119, 122, 176, 188, 209, 212, 224, 228
soul retrieval, 31–32, 181–82, 244
soul watching, 238
sound(s), 102, 111, 143. *See also* big drum; Great Song; rhythm(s); silence
Spirit of Life, 152
Spirit of Nature, 110
spirit world, 12–13, 76, 83, 106. *See also* out-of-body wandering
spiritual cosmos, 190
spiritual emergency, 70
spiritual frameworks, 187–89

spiritual hunger, 4
spiritual nourishment, 190
spiritual practice, 176
spontaneous vocation, 105
Stewart, R. J., 109–10
suicidality, 70
Sun Dance, 84, 90–95, 110, 111; drawing back the veils, 100–104; pain of, 103; preparing to dance, 90–95
Sutherland, Elizabeth, 44–45
Synod of Whitby, 214–15

T

Taghairm, 106
taibhs, 87
taibhsear, 200
tannasg, 200
Tao of Equus, The (Kohanov), 34–35
teallach, 199
Terton-Mama (MacEowen), 166–67
trance postures, 27
transformation, xx, 14
trauma, 25
trees, 10–11, 61–62, 115
tribal ties: longing for sense of, 60. *See also* kinship
troscad, 224–25
Trungpa Rinpoche, Chögyam, 123–24
twi-states, 199
Two Trees, Chief, 69–70, 80

V

Villoldo, Alberto, 106
vision quest, 92. *See also* prayer-fast
vision-seeking practice, 134–38
visioning eye, 82

W

waking up, xxiv
walk, imagining a, 236
Walking the Time Line of the Soul, 26–31
wandering soul of children of the mist, 42–48
warriorship, 163, 170
water, 37–39; communion with the spirit of, 39–42
water people, 37, 42–43
water's edge, 38
Whyte, David, 78–79
women: wise, 164, 191–92. *See also* animus; feminine
Word, the, 147–48

Y

yew tree, 10

About the Author

Frank MacEowen, M.A., is a Mississippi-born Scots-Irish American poet, teacher, and shamanic counselor. A practitioner of a form of Celtic nature mysticism rooted in the visionary traditions of his ancestors, his work has also been deeply influenced by experiences with indigenous shamans, studies in transpersonal process psychology, and ecopsychology. In 1996 he earned master of arts degree in transpersonal counseling psychology from Naropa University in Boulder, Colorado. *The Mist-Filled Path: Celtic Wisdom for Exiles, Wanderers, and Seekers* is his first book. He is currently working on his second book.

Frank MacEowen teaches workshops and retreats internationally, facilitates wilderness rites of passage work, and can be sponsored by writing to the address provided below or by visiting his website: www.celticwisdom.org or e-mailing: Celticwisdom@cs.com.

The author wishes to say that while he cannot personally respond directly to all postal correspondence, you are welcome to write to:

Highland Wisdom Society
Celtic Wisdom Programs
Frank MacEowen
Box 1631-A, Newton Street NW
Washington, DC 20010

New World Library is dedicated to
publishing books and cassettes that inspire
and challenge us to improve the quality
of our lives and our world.
Our books and cassettes are available
at bookstores everywhere.
For a complete catalog, contact:

New World Library
14 Pamaron Way
Novato, California 94949

Phone: (415) 884-2100
Fax: (415) 884-2199
Toll free: (800) 972-6657
Catalog requests: Ext. 50
Ordering: Ext. 52

E-mail: escort@nwlib.com
www.newworldlibrary.com